Blowing the Roof Off the Twenty-First Century

Blowing the Roof Off the Twenty-First Century

Media, Politics, and the Struggle for
Post-Capitalist Democracy

ROBERT W. MCCHESNEY

MONTHLY REVIEW PRESS

New York

Library of Congress Cataloging-in-Publication Data

McChesney, Robert Waterman, 1952–
Blowing the roof off the twenty-first century : media, politics, and the
struggle for post-capitalist democracy / Robert W. McChesney.
pages cm
ISBN 978-1-58367-478-9 (hardback)
1. United States—Economic conditions—21st century. 2. United
States—Politics and government—21st century. 3. Capitalism—United
States. 4. Democracy—United States. 5. Mass media—Political
aspects—United States. I. Title.
HC106.84.M397 2014
320.973—dc23
2014026733

Typeset in Adobe Garamond Pro

Monthly Review Press
146 West 29th Street, Suite 6W
New York, New York 10001

www.monthlyreview.org

5 4 3 2 1

Contents

Preface

HOWARD ZINN FAMOUSLY SAID that "you can't be neutral on a moving train." In the twenty-first century it seems like the train is approaching the speed of light. In this book I chronicle the forces that are depressing our politics, our economy, our culture, and our ecology, to the point where sober minds now contemplate the prospect of human extinction with equanimity. I explain why these problems are not insurmountable; they can be addressed and solved. Indeed, we have within our grasp the possibility of building the most extraordinary society humans have ever known, and could scarcely imagine. But to do so will require nothing short of revolutionary change, the likes of which have only rarely been seen in history.

We have to blow the roof off the twenty-first century.

This is a radical argument: I contend that the central barrier to progress is the capitalist political economy. The solution to this barrier is to establish a post-capitalist democracy. This is the great and defining struggle of our times.

This book consists of eleven essays and an interview. One essay was written in 2001, and the interview was conducted in 2007; the balance of the book was written since 2008, and four of the essays were written in the past year with precisely this book in mind.

During the past six years as these essays were written, I was working on several other related books. These addressed the state of journalism, *The Death and Life of American Journalism* (2010), with John Nichols; the Internet, *Digital Disconnect* (2013); the U.S. electoral system, *Dollarocracy* (2013), with John Nichols; and the current state of U.S. capitalism, *The Endless Crisis* (2012), with John

Bellamy Foster. In only a few instances do the essays herein touch directly on the material in those books. But the material in the other books provides the foundation upon which this research and analysis is based.

The book has four sections. Part one deals with the state of politics in the contemporary United States, and the efforts of progressives and the left to democratize the nation. It begins with an assessment of the Nader presidential campaign in 2000, and goes on to discuss the popular uprisings of 2011. The section also includes research on the corrupt and anti-democratic nature of U.S. elections and governance, and assesses why the Democratic Party, including the Obama administration, has become such an abject failure in advancing a popular agenda when in power. Part two expands upon this critique with research essays on the extraordinary militarization of the U.S. political economy, both globally and domestically—including the rise of the prison-industrial complex.

Part three addresses the rise of the contemporary media reform movement and the increasing importance of media in politics and society. Two of the chapters, 9 and 10, are autobiographical in nature because I have been a direct participant in the development of the media reform movement—as a public radio talk show host and through my scholarship which led to co-founding the organization Free Press in 2003. Chapter 10 also brings forward fresh research on one of my central research preoccupations: the collapse of the commercial model of journalism and how we might develop policies to establish the caliber of independent, uncensored, competitive public service journalism necessary for any known theory of self-government to succeed.

Part four brings all these themes together with chapters 11 and 12 written specifically for this book. I make the historical case that by the early 1960s many of the leading radical thinkers in Europe and North America grasped the central importance of media in understanding contemporary capitalism and politics. These theorists also began the unprecedented and necessary process of understanding how establishing a free, uncensored, decentralized, noncommercial media system was central to generating a plausible democratic socialist society. Theirs was a critique of really existing communist societies and was prominent in the New Left. When the political momentum of that era faded, and the long decades of neoliberalism became dominant, this tradition was mostly lost to history.

I argue in this final section that this very rich tradition is exactly where progressives, socialists and small-*d* democrats need to turn as we look for workable and attractive alternatives to the dead-end street for humanity presented by really existing capitalism. The heart and soul of a post-capitalist democracy must be vibrant, independent media.

Many of these essays originally appeared in *Monthly Review*; I indicate in the chapter's endnotes where the original version appeared. I thank all of the original publishers for their permission to run these pieces. Four of the essays were co-authored in their original versions, and were very much joint collaborations. Chapters 3 and 11 were co-authored with John Bellamy Foster. Chapter 6 was written with Foster and Hannah Holleman. Chapter 7 was written with Foster, Holleman, and R. Jamil Jonna. I thank John, Hannah, and Jamil for allowing me to reprint these essays in this book. The interview in chapter 8 was conducted by Megan Boler. To make all the essays in the book consistent, I have switched the pronoun voice to first-person singular for the co-authored pieces herein. But that in no way is meant to imply that these were not entirely collaborative efforts, for which John, Hannah, and Jamil often did the heaviest lifting.

I have made minor revisions and copyedits on all of the essays, and significant changes to a few. I have not attempted to update the essays from 2008 to 2011 to make them appear *au courant*. This is intentional; I want to demonstrate how the sands have shifted since the economic collapse of 2008. In some ways it seems as if we have experienced an entire generation in the past seven years.

The people at *Monthly Review* and Monthly Review Press have been supportive since I first broached the idea of the book. I wish to thank my editor, Michael Yates, in particular, and also Scott Borchert, Spencer Sunshine, John Mage, John Simon, and Martin Paddio. This book would not exist without John Bellamy "Duke" Foster's assistance and guidance. I can't believe how fortunate I was more than forty years ago to cross paths with him in Olympia, Washington. The book also benefits from long conversations over the years with Duke, Vivek Chibber, Johnny Nichols, and Inger Stole. Many of my arguments and much of my analysis crystallized by talking with them.

The manuscript received a top-to-bottom edit from Jeff Cohen and Matt Rothschild. How fortunate I am that two of my best friends, whose knowledge I respect and whose judgment I trust *in toto*, happen to be extraordinary editors. Erin Clermont did the final editing job, and gets credit for making the book legible. Once again, Elliot Linzer proved to be indexer extraordinaire. Thanks, too, go to Sigurd Allern, Victor Pickard, Mandy Troger, Ryan Wishart, Bill Domhoff, Josh Silver, Ben Scott, and Toby Miller for assistance with some of the material herein. I could get no work done without the assistance of Amy Holland. And finally, thanks to my Department of Communication and the University of Illinois at Urbana-Champaign for supporting my research over the years. It is great to have public research universities in the public interest. Let's work to see that they survive and prosper.

As always, my heart belongs to Lucy, Amy, and Inger.

This book is dedicated to Noam Chomsky and the late André Schiffrin, two friends and mentors. The quality of this book and all of my work increases to the extent it reflects the lessons and values they taught me.

CHAMPAIGN, ILLINOIS
MADISON, WISCONSIN
JUNE 2014

1

America, I Do Mind Dying

Please, mister foreman, slow down that assembly line
I don't mind working but I do mind dying.
—JOE L. CARTER, "Please, Mister Foreman," blues song, 1965

THESE ARE PERILOUS TIMES for capitalism, the reigning political economic system of the United States and the world. The economy is stagnating, and Mother Earth is gravely ill. In the second decade of the twenty-first century, we face widening economic inequality, plutocratic governance, endless militarism and mounting planetary ecological degradation.

Not many years ago, this would have sounded hyperbolic to many people. But today, it is not just radicals who are sounding alarm bells. Nobel Prize–winning economist and *New York Times* columnist Paul Krugman has been writing about secular stagnation in the past year in remarkably alarmist terms, arguing that the rich economies may be caught in decades of slow growth. No less an establishment figure than former World Bank Chief Economist and U.S. Treasury Secretary Lawrence Summers warned the International Monetary Fund in 2013 that the United States and the advanced economies may be facing a generation of stagnation.[1]

Moreover, some of our leading social and natural scientists have recently established the magnitude of the difficulties we face with cutting-edge research. There is now wide agreement on what the influential French economist Thomas Piketty has demonstrated, which is that growing economic inequality is built into the core logic of the capitalist system.[2] His research also suggests that a new oligarchy of inherited wealth has come to dominate society and the state, and the process is accelerated by stagnation. According to Krugman, writing on Piketty's discoveries, "We're going to look back nostalgically on the early 21st century when you could still at least have the pretense that the wealthy actually earned their wealth. And, you know, by the year 2030, it'll all be inherited." Indeed, "we are seeing not only great disparities in income and wealth, but we're seeing them get entrenched. We're seeing them become inequalities that will be transferred across generations. We are becoming very much the kind of society we imagine we're nothing like."[3]

In other acclaimed new empirical research, Martin Gilens and Benjamin Page examined 1,800 policy decisions made by the U.S. government between 1981 and 2002:

> The central point that emerges from our research is that economic elites and organized groups representing business interests have substantial independent impacts on U.S. government policy, while mass-based interest groups and average citizens have little or no independent influence. . . . Ordinary citizens might often be observed to "win" (that is, to get their preferred policy outcomes) even if they had no independent effect whatsoever on policy making, if elites (with whom they often agree) actually prevail.[4]

In short, when organized wealth wants one thing and the mass of the people wants another, money wins—*always*. "Democracy" has been reduced to powerless people rooting for their favored billionaire or corporate lobby to advance their values and interests, and hoping such a billionaire exists and that they get lucky. Doesn't that sound like the oligarchy that was explicitly rejected in this nation's founding in Philadelphia in 1776, and reaffirmed in Lincoln's speech at the bloodstained earth of Gettysburg some four score and seven years later?

Matters are, if anything, worse when it comes to our environment. The scientists on the United Nations Intergovernmental Panel on Climate Change released a report in 2014 that ought to terrify any sentient being. Its conclusion: continuing on the present economic path of "business as usual" will lead to certain catastrophe for human society.[5] The failure of governments to enact effective climate policies, due in large part to corporate lobbying, is pointing us toward the worst outcomes. In the United States, for example, no law on the environment has been passed by Congress without the Business Roundtable's approval since 1975. The Business Roundtable is a pro-business lobbying group composed of CEOs from the very largest corporations, including the handful of energy giants.[6] With growing inequality and unlimited billionaire spending on politics, the already grave present moment may be remembered fondly decades down the road, if anyone is around to remember it.

In the coming decades we are almost certainly going to see a society the likes of which has never existed and can scarcely be imagined. I argue in this book that if that new society is going to be one in which we want to live, it will require fundamental change in the political economy. Capitalism as we know it has got to go.

Although this is a radical idea, it is not necessarily a marginal one. Criticism of capitalism is no longer *verboten* in the United States, especially among young people, and there is good reason to believe this critical stance may grow by leaps and bounds. Capitalism today does not appear to offer youth much hope, and as a result, they are far more open to alternatives to it than their peers were a generation ago. In 2011 there were massive, almost spontaneous, demonstrations, beginning in Madison, Wisconsin, in February and then spreading in the fall to the various Occupy encampments nationwide. Such uprisings had not been seen in the United States for decades, maybe generations. A sleeping giant, it seemed, had been awakened and aroused, its power harnessed by young people. Since 2010, I have given around two hundred public talks across the United States on these themes, roughly half of which were on college campuses, and I couldn't help but notice the heightened awareness.

Yet, especially after 2011, the optimism generated by these movements had dissipated, and the most arresting sentiment I encountered as I traveled the nation was one of tremendous pessimism about the possibility of progressive social change. While I found support for my critique everywhere I went, in a manner I had never experienced before, I also found people had concluded that there were no alternatives to the status quo. Or, if there were alternatives, there was no way to bring them into being. The fix was in, and political activity could not yield positive results. It was hopeless, and only deluded fools would bother to think otherwise. The ironic lesson of the Wisconsin uprising and Occupy was not that there was a vast underground ocean of untapped and inchoate support for progressive and radical politics in the United States, but rather that we had been there and done that and it had failed. Game over.

One is reminded of the title of one of William Faulkner's novels, *As I Lay Dying*—a sad reality for an individual, but an unthinkable tragedy for an entire society or civilization.

By the fall of 2013, when I was on a 60-event speaking tour for *Dollarocracy* with my co-author John Nichols, the pessimism was so predictable and palpable that we altered our talks and became ersatz motivational speakers. We said that it was too early to harshly judge the impacts of the Madison uprising or Occupy. Effective social change requires more than showing up at a demonstration and holding a sign, as valuable as that may be. John discussed the extraordinary growth of grassroots activism on a number of progressive issues, including a campaign to amend the Constitution to get money out of politics—a beat he covers for *The Nation*. Because there was almost no mainstream news media coverage of these grassroots developments, people assumed they did not exist.

In my talks I emphasized that it was human nature to assume something entrenched at the moment will remain so into the future. People rarely accurately predict social change; it is almost always a surprise, so we have to keep our minds open to the possibility. No one saw the Madison uprising coming, or Occupy. Howard Zinn used to talk about how no one saw the civil rights movement coming, either. The immediacy of the present weighs like a 300-pound barbell across our chests as we attempt to look ahead. The shift from hopelessness to hope can be very sudden. Occupy showed us that. One can't judge from current sentiment.

I told the story about how one of my professors in graduate school was a white South African who had moved to the United States in the 1960s and was strongly supportive of the anti-apartheid movement. He had family in South Africa and followed political developments there voraciously. I went to say goodbye to him just before I moved to Madison in May 1988 and found him unusually glum. I asked him what was wrong. He said that the political situation in South Africa was the worst he had ever seen and the chances of abolishing apartheid were more remote than ever. He said that the only way blacks would get justice would be through extraordinary, almost unimaginable, violence that would make the country uninhabitable for anyone. He depressed me, too, because he knew more about South Africa than anyone I knew by a wide margin.

So what happened? Two years later, Nelson Mandela was released from prison. Four years after that, he was the first elected president of a post-apartheid democratic South Africa. And in those intervening six years, there was less violence than one might find in a New Jersey bar fight on a Saturday night. My friend, the most knowledgeable person I knew about South African politics, at the precise moment before this revolution occurred, had it exactly wrong—180 degrees wrong. (I learned subsequently that his pessimistic view was not uncommon at the time among anti-apartheid activists.)

From that I learned humility. And I also learned that the future is impossible to predict. There was only one Nostradamus. So we should not allow predictions about the likely course of future events to limit how we proceed with our lives. As Noam Chomsky put it, if you act like social change for the better is impossible, you guarantee it will be impossible. That is the choice we all have to make when we look into the mirror. Pessimism is self-fulfilling; it is no way to live.

Then what is a person to do in times like these, when the prospect for change seems dim, yet the conditions of society are unraveling and untenable? Our job is to understand the present and put it in historical perspective. It is to grasp the dynamics, the tensions, and the contradictions. It is to be prepared so that as crisis points emerge or explode onto the scene, as they inevitably do, people will be in a position to generate humane and sustainable solutions. We know the roof is going to get blown off the status quo. What we don't know is if it will be change for the better . . . or not. That will depend upon what we do now and in the coming years.

THIS IS WHY I decided to do this book. I wanted to respond to the sense that we are entering perilous times and provide a sense of how we might imagine and achieve a brighter future. I had written a handful of essays that addressed the politics of this period and provided a diagnosis of the crises of the U.S. political economy. I had also written related pieces on media politics and the burgeoning media reform movement, of which I am a part. These essays form the core of this book, and I have added several chapters written with this book in mind, to give the volume coherence and to formally make my case.

The basis for my argument is that the United States and the world experienced a sea change with the economic collapse of 2008. The crisis was not a fluke or an accident; it was the result of core problems built into the modern capitalist system that give it a pronounced tendency toward economic stagnation. The massive growth of the financial sector and the mountain of consumer debt that preceded the Great Recession did not create stagnation; these were, in fact, the antidote to stagnationist tendencies dating back to the 1970s. But the spur that financialization gave to capitalist growth produced a bloated debt structure that was unsustainable. In the book I wrote with John Bellamy Foster, *The Endless Crisis* (Monthly Review Press, 2012), we explained the stagnationist tendency in modern U.S. capitalism, and why mainstream policy prescriptions can offer no solution to it, except austerity, which brings only more stagnation, not to mention unnecessary misery and hardship for the vast majority of the population.

Stagnation aggravates all the great historic problems associated with capitalism. Economic inequality mushrooms, poverty increases, public services are slashed, there is tremendous downward pressure on wages. And at the same time, corporations and wealthy investors successfully demand ever greater concessions from governments and communities as the quid pro quo for their investment. Capital generally struggles to find profitable investment outlets, but today the problem is particularly acute. In 2014 there is by some accounts as much as $2 trillion in capital sitting on the sidelines while there are tens of millions of workers unemployed or only partially employed. It has been this way for years. By any objective measure, this is socially absurd.

The current pattern for capital is to zero in on public services like a heat-seeking missile and to take over those government operations and convert them into profit-centers for corporations. Many government activities have been, or are in the process of being, privatized or outsourced, from the military to surveillance to prisons to education. The evidence demonstrates these privatizations and outsourcings basically benefit the investors, who often reap monopoly profits, but degrade the quality and cost efficiency of the services otherwise. They are corrosive to effective democratic governance.[7] Likewise, government regulations to protect workers, consumers, and the environment have to be jettisoned to encourage the "job creators" to get off their butts and swing into action. These have proven to be palliative measures for ravenous investors, but a disaster for everyone else. To stay alive today, capitalism is eating our future.

My recent research has tracked dimensions of this broad crisis. In *The Death and Life of American Journalism* (Nation Books, 2010), John Nichols and I chronicled the historic tension between commercialism and democratic journalism. This is what led to the creation of professional journalism a century ago, a system that improved upon the blatant corruption and owner propaganda of what immediately preceded it but also had deep flaws. In the past decade, especially since 2008, the corporate sector has abandoned the hope of making a profit from doing journalism, and the news media are in freefall collapse. There is dramatically less reporting and coverage of politics and the affairs of state than a generation ago, and the situation is getting worse every year. This is unacceptable for an ostensibly self-governing society.

In my 2013 book *Digital Disconnect* (New Press), I examined how the Internet has been converted from a "militantly egalitarian" space, as Netscape founder Marc Andreessen put it, and an anti-commercial zone as recently as the early 1990s, to the center of capitalism that is extending the market into every aspect of our lives. The Internet, rather than being an engine of economic competition, has spawned the greatest monopolies ever known to capitalism in the course of less than two decades. This has seriously undermined its potential to be a force for democracy.

This point bears elaboration. In their 2014 book, *The Second Machine Age*, M.I.T. business professors Erik Brynjolffsson and Andrew McAfee describe the mind-boggling digital technologies that may be on the verge of revolutionizing manufacturing and overall economic productivity in a manner comparable or superior to the first great Industrial Revolution. This digital bounty, they suggest optimistically, provides the basis for eliminating poverty worldwide, cleaning up the environment, and generally taking civilization to staggeringly unimaginable heights. But as even these unvarnished champions of capitalism concede, the way capitalism works means that this almost certainly will not take place because there is no place in digital capitalism for the preponderance of the population to gainfully participate. Brynjolsson and McAfee conclude that strong policy measures are mandatory to aggressively counteract inequality.[8] Or, to put it in my language, the digital revolution will have the ironic effect of aggravating all the core problems of contemporary capitalism that are highlighted at the top of this chapter.

And what are the chances that the U.S. government will institute policies to radically decrease economic inequality and see that the economy works for all? In *Dollarocracy*, John Nichols and I provided a detailed look at the "money and media election complex" that has decimated the caliber of the American election system and has made the governing process evermore the domain of wealthy interests. In the book we present the developments as part of a broader campaign, begun in the 1970s, by corporate America to crush the democratic gains established from 1900 to 1970 and return control over the government to the wealthy, as in the Gilded Age.

These books—which addressed capitalism, communication, and democracy—do more than provide a diagnosis of a problem; they provide a battery of tangible proposals that, if enacted, would go a long way toward asserting the primacy of democratic values. Because journalism is a public good, the proposals center on the creation of independent, uncensored, nonprofit, and noncommercial news media, that would have sufficient public funding but whose content the government could not control. As for the Internet, the key is to eliminate corporate monopoly bottlenecks, eliminate commercial and government surveillance, and make access ubiquitous and free. With regard to elections, we proposed a number of measures to get money out of the game, democratize the governing process, and reassert the primacy of one-person, one-vote.

Implicit in all these books was the notion that there could only be successful change in any of these areas if there was a broad movement that created sufficient pressure for change in *all* of them. And such a movement would, by definition, be premised on the conviction that the current really existing capitalist system is deeply flawed, if not rotten to the core. That is the topic I address here, and in the rest of the book. It is time to start thinking about and talking about the need for a post-capitalist democracy.

WHAT DO I MEAN by post-capitalist democracy? I mean a society expressly committed to democratic practices first and foremost, and one that directly addresses the ways that really existing capitalism is inimical to democracy, human freedom, and ecological sustainability. I use the term "really existing capitalism" for a reason. I refer to the capitalism of massive corporations, commercial propaganda, political corruption, obscene inequality, poverty, stagnation, militarism, and endless greed. That the capitalism, the one people actually experience, is the main impediment to democracy in the United States today.

I am not therefore referring to the classroom fantasy of capitalism as a bunch of heroic little-guy entrepreneurs competing for the betterment of consumers, and creating jobs in the communities they inhabit. This is the "free market" system of public relations missives and politicians' blarney. It has about as much to do with the American economy and society today as the official rhetoric of "workers' democracy" did to Soviet communism in much of the twentieth century. I have no particular problem with small business. I started two successful concerns in my life, one a commercial rock music magazine and the other a nonprofit public interest group. In both cases the success of the organization was due in large part to me and my partners working our butts off, i.e. exploiting our own labor. If someone wants to start an enterprise, more power to you. In this sense, I am as much a product of Lincoln—who saw small business as an extension of labor, not a part of big business—as I am of Marx.[9]

That is one of the reasons, when I deal with immediate political struggles, I prefer the term *post-capitalist democracy* to the term *socialism*, though for me they point in essentially the same direction. I have considered myself a socialist since I was eighteen or nineteen years old, and I still do. The term has always signified to me the creation of genuine political democracy, its extension into the economic realm, and having the wealth created by society directed to social needs. To me a socialist outlook recognizes that a capitalist society can never be more than superficially democratic, and whatever democratic victories are won will always be in jeopardy. This is in the spirit of the person whose words inspired the American Revolution, Thomas Paine, as well as the great socialists of our more recent history: Eugene Debs, Upton Sinclair, Jack London, Helen Keller, W. E. B. Du Bois, Albert Einstein, and Martin Luther King Jr. It is post-capitalist, egalitarian, and democratic; it has never been more pertinent to the human condition than it is today.

But the term *socialism*, it needs to be said, means wildly different things to different people. To some it is the social-democratic welfare state of Scandinavia; to others, it is *any* form of government spending on matters aside from police work, prisons, and the military. For some, predominantly on the right, socialism of any kind leads inexorably to Soviet one-party dictatorships. To others, suspicious of grounding socialism in the state, it is primarily a society of democratic workers' cooperatives. Many on the left see it as a basic set of values and practices more than a single, coherent model.

In this sense, the term *socialism* begs as many questions as it answers, and carries a lot of baggage. We can spend so much time discussing arcane theoretical issues that we lose sight of the pressing immediate issues that drive us to ponder a post-capitalist political economy. Instead of addressing real problems and discussing real solutions, we float toward an abstract discussion in order to reach consensus on how to structure some futuristic world that doesn't have a chance of existing until we start doing the hard work of creating a more democratic society right here and now.

Hence my use of the term *post-capitalist democracy* in this book. The emphasis is on democracy, flowing from the recognition of democracy's incompatibility with capitalism in crucial areas. The term explains itself, I hope, and leads discussion in a more productive direction. The economics follow the politics and not vice versa. Framed this way, the discussion can be more inclusive, without any sort of political litmus test as the ante to admission. It is imperative that this discussion attract people of all stripes, and that we not use a term that permits a sizable part of the population to dismiss the debate out of hand. I know from personal experience in media reform activism that there are some important issues in which people on the right or center can find common ground with those on the left.[10] They believe the reforms will encourage the idyllic type of capitalism they prefer; I believe they will lead to a post-capitalist democracy, and possibly socialism. We can thrash that out down the road. In the meantime, where we have common interests, we have to exploit them if we are to have success.

In short, I propose post-capitalist democracy as a big tent to cover everyone who wants democracy and leaves out only those who put their blind faith in the wealthy, giant corporations, and the profit motive regardless of the evidence or social costs. There are a lot more people in group A than group B, fortunately.

The importance and value of being inclusive will become apparent, I hope, in the pages that follow. In addition to those on the left whose names appear throughout the book, I have learned from, and been influenced by, an eclectic group of writers. I demonstrate how the writings on journalism by Walter Lippmann, no leftist after a dalliance with socialism as a youth, provide keen insights into our current situation and turn the discussion toward radical solutions. Some readers may be surprised to see that I have found value when drafting policy proposals in aspects of the work of conservative "free market" economists like Herbert Simons and Milton Friedman. This tradition was especially fruitful when it stood outside of power and delivered intellectually consistent criticism. In the past fifty years, as it has become the official dogma of global capitalism, "free market" conservatism has accommodated itself to the powers-that-be. So it is that once formidable criticism of monopoly power, political corruption, and advertising, for example, has been marginalized or replaced with non sequiturs and apologetics.

Many of the writers who have influenced me are political liberals, Keynesian in economics, largely unsympathetic to socialism, and convinced that capitalism is the best possible system, and its problems can be reformed away so that it has a human face. I am deeply skeptical about that project, but in all honesty I cannot rule that possibility out. In the meantime, I think there is tremendous common ground between those on the left and liberals when the discussion turns to specific real world issues. The point is to identify those specific areas where the evidence is strong that capitalism is truly damaging to democratic values and governance, and struggle for radical changes there.

SO WHAT, PRECISELY, ARE some of the immediate areas to pursue to establish a post-capitalist democracy? For starters, end military profiteering. While many of the founders of this nation were certainly expansionists who envisioned the United States becoming a powerful country, they were simultaneously concerned with limiting the role of the military, which they regarded as a singularly anti-democratic force. The Constitution was written to "impede" warmaking, as George Mason put it, and there was considerable skepticism about the idea of a standing army. Through much of American history, the military was small, except for the occasional major war, and even much of the production of battleships and armaments was kept under public control. It was considered scandalous that a business might enrich itself through militarism. In the 1930s, U.S. Senator Gerald Nye of North Dakota famously denounced the munitions industry as "an unadulterated, unblushing racket."[11] As recently as the U.S. entry into the Second World War, President Franklin Roosevelt stated, to popular acclaim, "I don't want to see a single war millionaire created in the United States as a result of this world disaster."[12]

That seems so very, very long ago. Today military spending is hardwired into really existing capitalism, and in the past generation many of those elements of Pentagon spending that were once controlled by the military have been outsourced to corporate interests. The military/national security budget is a trillion-dollar grab bag of risk-free monopoly profits for a handful of gigantic corporations. These firms employ a lobbying armada in Washington filled with retired military officers and congressmen who promote ever-expanding militarism regardless of the social consequences. This is simply inimical to constitutional rule, and possibly poisonous for human survival. As much as possible, we need to take the profit out of warmaking and political surveillance; otherwise they will only grow. How to do that is where the discussion needs to go, and the sooner the better. Traditionally this has been a conservative issue as well as one for liberals and the left. It should be so again.

The same post-capitalist democracy reasoning applies to other public services (or public goods) that are in the process of being privatized and outsourced. Consider the stunning growth of the prison-industrial complex; here too we now have commercial interests with an immense stake in seeing that the United States remain the world leader in incarcerating the highest percentage of its citizenry of any nation, not just in the world today but in human history![13] Along similar lines, one of the defining issues of these times is the effort to privatize public education and turn the massive public school budgets over to corporate interests. Diane Ravitch has heroically demolished the baseless claims of the privatization movement and demonstrated the dire consequences for society if the plans proceed.[14]

Then there are those industries that are highly concentrated, closely associated with the government, and whose pursuit of profits leads to enormous "externalities" or costs that the firms can avoid but that society must either pay for or suffer unacceptable consequences. The handful of banks that dominate the economy are more dangerous than beneficial for society. We need to take the crucial function of allocating society's savings out of the hands of billionaire speculators who have tremendous incentive (and capacity) to rig the system. Or consider the small number of energy behemoths that have a decided stake in an industry that enhances global warming and the climate crisis. Can we really afford to let a few firms rake in tens of billions of dollars in profits annually while the planet roasts like a marshmallow over a summer campfire? And similarly, we have the parasitic health insurance industry, which is indefensible economically and does not even exist in most democratic nations, which have superior and more cost-effective health care systems.

Finally, this post-capitalist democracy logic applies in spades to journalism and communication. There are solutions to the vexing problems of Internet surveillance and the collapse of journalism, but they require confronting and eliminating corporate power and profit-making in specific industries. Sometimes it can be done through regulation, but generally it requires the conversion of the sector into public enterprise. The policy debate should then be about how to structure those public enterprises to maximize the benefits and minimize the dangers—and create institutions that are democratic and accountable.

As radical as the above ideas may seem, as completely outside the range of legitimate debate as they presently are, even if all of them were implemented this would still be a capitalist economy. Profit-making would drive most economic activity. One could even make an argument that markets would actually thrive in this environment. But it would be a different type of capitalism, and point the way toward a possible post-capitalist future—what I call socialism—if the people of the nation elected to move in that direction.

YOU CAN'T GET THERE from here, is the standard refrain. Hence my concern for the nitty-gritty of political strategy and tactics as well as programmatic issues. The task of social transformation is daunting, if only because much of the institutional power that the labor movement and the left used to have has been dismantled. When you compare the resources of progressives to the resources of the largest corporations and their allies, you feel like you are lining up for the Indianapolis 500 on a tricycle. But harder battles—ending slavery, anyone?—have been won by humanity.

Building a popular movement is the primary task. Using such a popular movement to generate effective institutions to challenge political power grows from that. The issues that logically draw people together are demands for the right to full-time employment at a living wage, something considered entirely appropriate in the mid-twentieth century in the United States but that subsequently was dispatched in mainstream discourse to the outer limits of kooky ideas. It is not a kooky idea; it is the most important demand to organize around. It requires that the state put people to work if need be, and it shifts power to the working class so that the threat of unemployment, debt, poverty, and destitution cannot loom over a person's head like a guillotine. From this increased power a cascade of core progressive demands flows, including the need for a truly accessible and democratic media system.

Many liberals who wish to reform and humanize capitalism are uncomfortable with seemingly radical movements, and often work to distance themselves from them, lest respectable people in power cast a withering eye at them. "Shhh," they say to people like me. "If we antagonize or scare those in power we will lose our seat at the table and not be able to win any reforms." Yet these same liberal reformers often are dismayed at how they are politically ineffectual. Therein lies a great irony, because to enact significant reforms requires a mass movement (or the credible prospect of a mass movement) that does indeed threaten the powerful. The influence of mild reformers rises greatly when people in power look out the window and see a million people demonstrating. If there is an iron law of politics, this is it.

People in power certainly know this. Nothing frightens them like popular uprisings they do not and cannot control. For that reason, cynicism and political apathy are generally encouraged in the United States. It is not a fluke that voter turnout in the United States is well below that of nearly every other nation in the world. In the 1970s, on the heels of the popular uprisings of that era, people in power spoke candidly (to each other) about the need to have young people and the dispossessed return to apathy. Much of their work since then has been to achieve that goal. When we tune out politics, when we abandon hope, we aren't being cool or hip or ironic or even realistic—we are being played.

This elite fear of genuine democracy should encourage all those dedicated to building a more humane and sustainable post-capitalist democracy. Those atop the system know we have the numbers on our side. They know the system is rigged for them, and they want to keep it that way. They know they cannot win a fair fight. Hence billionaires' energy goes to matters like wholesale voter suppression and flooding election campaigns with unlimited secretive spending. They must feed the machinery of pessimism and despair because they know they cannot defeat an aroused citizenry. That tells me that if we do effective organizing it will be like planting a seed in rich Iowa topsoil. Put this way, I like our chances. I like them a lot.

PART ONE

Putting the Politics Back
in Political Economy

2

After the Nader Campaign: The Future of U.S. Left Electoral Politics

THE UNLIKELY POST-ELECTION contest between Al Gore and George W. Bush, which ultimately led to the anointing of Bush as president by the Republican majority on the U.S. Supreme Court (despite the fact that Bush received fewer popular votes than Gore both in the United States as a whole and most likely in Florida, the state that gave Bush his Electoral College win), has tended to erase all other developments associated with the election. But all of this should not cause us to forget that the Ralph Nader Green Party campaign for the presidency was arguably the most extraordinary phenomenon in U.S. left politics in many years. On Election Day he drew nearly three million votes, representing about 3 percent of the vote. Even former vice president Henry Wallace did not fare as well in his third-party run for the presidency in 1948, the last progressive third-party presidential campaign of this nature and magnitude. Although exit polls show that Nader received few racial minority votes (a major weakness of his campaign), he nonetheless drew his strongest support from those without a college education, those with incomes less than $30,000 a year, and those without full-time employment. Until the intense scare campaign instigated by the Democrats in the final two weeks before the election, Nader was getting as much as 7 percent in some tracking polls.

Nader ran quite far to the left on issue after issue; this was no warmed-over version of mainstream liberal Democratic politics. The Green platform was an anti-neoliberal progressive platform that any socialist could support openly. At the same time, Nader enjoyed tremendous and enthusiastic crowds on the campaign trail, often appearing before paying crowds that ranged from ten to fifteen thousand with hardly any advance work. Were there no public opinion polls, one who merely watched the size and nature of crowd responses to the candidates on the campaign trail might have thought Nader the likely winner or at least a strong contender for victory. Moreover, these crowds were dominated by young people. Such a response would have been unthinkable one or two decades ago.

Nader was the best suited and arguably the only feasible candidate to make a progressive third-party run in 2000. He came of age in the 1960s when progressive political figures had some opportunity to gain exposure in the media culture; he has long been a household name. (As Nader notes, with the rightward shift of our political landscape and the hyper-commercialism of our media culture, serious progressive critics of the status quo have had far less opportunity to gain national exposure in the past two decades, unless they are political humorists like Michael Moore or people who become celebrities for other reasons and then discuss politics, like Susan Sarandon.) He is also highly regarded for a list of accomplishments in the public interest that is nothing short of stunning. Nader turned to electoral politics only when it became clear that the degree of corporate domination over both parties made the sort of public interest work he did nearly impossible to pursue with any hope of success. Nader is not a socialist, but he is a principled democrat who has the courage to call for sweeping reforms in the political economy when it is apparent that corporate domination and class inequality are undermining democracy. Nader spoke brilliantly in plain language to everyday Americans from a range of backgrounds about the need for sweeping structural reform, a lost art among many on the left.

The issue that was the foundation of the Nader campaign was his opposition to the World Trade Organization (WTO), North American Free Trade Agreement (NAFTA), and the entirety of the global pro-capitalist trade, investment, and regulatory system. Unlike nationalist opponents of the WTO like Pat Buchanan, Nader's opposition was on democratic grounds: these agencies were not subject to popular control in the United States or elsewhere and were therefore illegitimate. Moreover, Nader was and is one of the world's foremost experts on exactly how these institutions of global capitalism are generating disastrous results across the planet for workers, consumers, and the environment. Nader and the Greens also favored deep cuts in the U.S. military budget and apparatus and opposed U.S. material support for reactionary regimes and policies around the world. Nader, who drew 19 percent of the total Muslim vote (70 percent of which went to Bush), declared that there will be no peace in the Middle East "without justice for the Palestinians." In sum, Nader and the Greens offered a progressive and non-imperialist foreign policy that was decidedly outside the "bipartisan consensus" that is almost never debated in the U.S. electoral arena.

This is a point that merits consideration because the discussion of the Nader campaign, even on the left, has focused almost entirely on his critique of the domestic imbalance of power, giving very slight attention to the international aspects. The United States is the dominant imperial power in the world and this is the central unspoken truth of our times. In the global capitalist order, the U.S. state has a number of responsibilities: to keep the system functioning, to control the underlying populations, to safeguard the United States as the center of the international financial system, to maintain the United States (and specifically U.S. capitalists/corporations) in the top perch in the imperialist pecking order, and to prevent countries from breaking away from the system of global controls. For these reasons, in addition to domestic pressure from the military-industrial complex, the United States maintains, by a very wide margin, the world's largest military, though it has no rival whatsoever in any traditional sense. The wider foreign policy implications of Nader's campaign were almost never reported in the media, but they clearly represented a threat to the status quo.

Indeed, Nader the candidate never got the opportunity to communicate these or any other positions to the great mass of Americans because his campaign was absolutely butchered in the news media. Nader's coverage in the *New York Times* resembled, in some respects, the coverage Andrei Sakharov got from *Pravda* and *Izvestia* back in the 1970s. This should be no surprise, but it was sobering nonetheless. Without gobs of money to purchase TV advertising—the lingua franca of U.S. politics—or, better yet, without the sort of massive grassroots operation that could overcome the media blackout, many citizens never had any idea that Nader was running vigorously or what his positions were on the issues he was addressing. (If the winner of the election were determined by who spent the least for each of his votes or who received the least amount of news coverage per vote, Nader would have won in a landslide.) Most of the media attention Nader did receive was obsessed with how his candidacy would affect the fortunes of Democrat Al Gore. This was true even on the left and among progressives. Numerous leftists who supported Nader on the issues opposed his candidacy, often with startling bitterness, because it would take votes away from Gore, the "lesser of two evils"—which became a mantra to a greater extent than at any time since 1968. The 2000 race highlighted again how the U.S. electoral laws have a deeply conservative and undemocratic bias that increases dramatically the degree of difficulty for both third parties and progressives.

In my view, the Nader campaign was the electoral side of the mass organizing that produced the extraordinary demonstrations in Seattle in 1999 and in Washington, D.C., and at the two national political conventions in 2000. As with those demonstrations, there is no guarantee that this upsurge in activism will produce a sustained movement capable of fundamentally changing the existing order. But I believe the evidence suggests that there are new openings for popular left organizing in the United States, and that the chance to organize for progressive electoral candidates is better than at any time in memory. It is possible that a left electoral movement can, within a generation, become a dominant political force in the nation. It may not be an explicitly socialist movement that will invoke the icons of the left but it will be a progressive anticorporate movement by any measure. There is an important and necessary role for the socialist left in this movement. The implications of these developments go well beyond the United States, in view of the U.S. role as the dominant global capitalist power. If a viable pro-democracy, anti-imperialist movement can emerge here, it will improve the possibilities dramatically for socialists and progressives worldwide.

The Electoral Politics of the Left

It is an indication of how much times are changing that one can actually discuss the U.S. left and electoral politics without being purely hypothetical or dismissive. The last notable attempt at a left third-party presidential campaign was Henry Wallace's run in 1948. That Wallace was clobbered so badly was a signal that the left was under attack and entering a long period of decline. The notion of an electoral third party was soon abandoned. Many on the left, along with those generally sympathetic to it, opted to work through the Democratic Party in the second half of the century, to make it more progressive than it would have been otherwise. Communist Party USA–instigated groups, the Democratic Socialists of America, and the Rainbow Coalition have been but a few of the vehicles used by progressives in attempts to push the Democrats to the left. Other leftists downplayed electoral work, though they usually hoped the Democrats would win (to the extent that they cared). With little to show for these efforts, it was easy for some on the left to dismiss electoral politics as inherently corrupt and limited in value, if not a waste of valuable time and resources.

The left's suspicion of political strategies that emphasize electoral politics to the exclusion of everything else, or privilege electoral strategies over all else, is firmly grounded. It is an illusion to think that electoral work is the be-all and end-all of politics. Parliamentary systems are the result of intense mass struggle, among other things, and ruling classes will invariably dismiss the results and turn to extralegal measures if their interests are threatened in a fundamental manner. Indeed, as the 2000 election highlighted, capitalist political parties will abandon their commitment to fairness even in squabbles with each other, let alone a Green or socialist party. The moral of the story is that there is always a necessary place for non-electoral—in Europe called "extra-parliamentary"—left political work.

Viable left electoral politics has always found its basis in well-developed non-electoral political organizations and activism. With non-electoral popular movements in place, the electoral campaigns have a foundation to build upon, and answer to. If this link is broken and the electoral campaign achieves success yet loses touch with popular movements, bad things tend to happen. Likewise, if a progressive candidate gets caught up in the personalization of politics and loses the necessary sense of humility and political principle, worse things tend to happen. This justifies skepticism toward, but not outright dismissal of, electoral politics. Relatively well-conducted electoral movements like the Nader campaign or, going back in history, the Eugene Debs Socialist Party campaigns early in the century, can help build non-electoral movements, and vice versa. Although Debs never got more than 6 percent of the vote as a presidential candidate, his campaigns were instrumental in galvanizing socialist and union organizing. And in our current closed political culture, a presidential campaign is one of the very few places where meaningful political issues can be raised at a national level and political education take place. Even with all the obstacles in its way, the Nader campaign probably exposed more Americans to progressive positions on political issues than anything else has for quite some time. The campaign was an important and necessary step to take the straitjacket off U.S. political debate. But electoral campaigns without corresponding non-electoral movements end up being mostly of the protest variety and of limited value.

Moreover, electoral politics does not mean simply working on presidential campaigns. It might be judged strategically sound, for example, for those on the left to emphasize referenda and other races over making another presidential run in coming years. That will depend upon circumstances that develop over time. In recent years, there has been a debate among U.S. progressives who do electoral work over whether it is better to emphasize local races or national races. The argument for the former goes that local races are more winnable and less expensive and can therefore give left parties a chance to be effective and attract new supporters. The argument for the latter, as I state above, is that in a depoliticized society like the United States, it is only in presidential races that people (and the news media) will pay much attention to political ideas; it is an opportunity to be used for political education. An electoral strategy geared to the genuine transformation of society would ideally pursue both local and national races, as well as link with non-electoral popular movements. In Brazil, for example, the Workers' Party is using its control of local offices to democratize decision making and bring poor people and workers into the process that determines budgets. Some of the success of the local Workers' Party candidates is attributable to the publicity for the party generated by the dramatic presidential runs of Lula over the past twelve years. Eventually Lula, or another Workers' Party candidate, may win the presidency of Brazil and, if she or he does, that person likely will find an aroused and involved mass base, both in the electoral and non-electoral arenas. It is as intriguing a recipe as I have seen for using electoral politics to assist in establishing democratic socialism.

The rise of several popular movements in the United States in recent years laid the foundation for Nader's relatively successful run. To Nader's credit, he made clear the importance of non-electoral activism in any progressive electoral movement. Likewise, Nader and the Greens always argued that the 2000 campaign was part of building a long-term majoritarian movement to overturn corporate domination of politics and the economy. These points seemingly were lost on (or dismissed by) some of the left critics of Nader, who argued that it was incomprehensible to "throw away" a vote for a lost cause like Nader and therefore assist in electing the greater of the two evils. In 1992, such a claim might have carried some weight, when Nader ran as a symbolic "protest" candidate in the New Hampshire primary, or in 1996, when he did not campaign although he was on many ballots as a candidate for president. But in 2000, with rising movements against sweatshops, military imperialism, corporate globalization, capital punishment, the prison-industrial complex, economic and racial inequality, and environmental devastation, among others, it would have been absurd to tell activists to bury the hatchet and work for Gore, who upon election would become their direct opponent in most battles on these issues. Indeed, exit polls showed that a large share of Nader's voters would not even have voted if Nader had not been on the ballot.

In addition to rising popular movements, and related to them, is another factor that explains the surge of interest in left third-party electoral activity: the thoroughgoing deterioration of the U.S. electoral system over the past three decades. In discussing this deterioration of citizen participation in and influence over the electoral process, I am by no means arguing that there was a "golden age" of electoral politics in the United States to which we should return. Even at its best, electoral politics in the United States in the past century has been fairly gruesome, with the wealthy holding far too much power and the poor and working class significantly depoliticized (and in some cases, such as the Jim Crow South, disenfranchised).

Far from there ever being a "golden age" of democracy in the United States, in the broadest sense the marriage of political democracy and class society has always been a contradiction. From the heyday of Athens through the founding of the United States, the major battle on the part of the ruling classes in quasi-democratic societies across the world has always been to limit the franchise, so that the propertyless majority could not dominate the wealthy few. The masses, of course, struggled to extend the franchise, and truly great democratic milestones are marked by those victories. Capitalism subtly but importantly reduced the immediate threat of political democracy by removing direct control over crucial economic matters from the political sphere to the sphere of investors seeking maximum profit. But the threat of popular rule remained and, once universal adult suffrage became the norm during the twentieth century, it posed a distinct challenge to the ruling class and to the survival of capitalism.

Brute force in this context was ineffective, except in times of severe crisis. Rather, as C. B. Macpherson has written, the best way to reconcile inegalitarian economics with egalitarian politics was to foster depoliticization by the masses. Sometimes, as sociologists Frances Fox Piven and Richard Cloward note, this has taken the form of extraordinary measures to limit the ability of working-class and poor Americans to exercise their legal right to vote. (This is still evident in the African American precincts in Florida where, through a number of dubious measures, tens of thousands of African Americans who tried to go to the polls in November 2000 did not have their votes counted.) More often, it means ideological warfare by business, through various forms of public relations, to limit the capacity of working-class and oppressed people to act in their own interests. The goal, as historian Alex Carey put it, is "to take the risk out of democracy."

The net result is that in the United States around half the adult population never votes and only a bit more than one-third of the adult population votes in non-presidential years. Whether a person is likely to vote is directly related to class: the more wealth and income a person has, the more likely that person is to vote. The higher the voter turnout, the greater the likelihood of a serious left presence in the electoral system. So it is that the greatest left victories in electoral politics have generally come in environments where 80 to 95 percent of the adult population votes.

Consider the class dimensions of voting in the United States, based on exit polls following the November 2000 election. Those Americans making less than $50,000 per year, nearly 80 percent of the adult population, accounted for only 47 percent of the voters. To put it another way, the top fifth or, to be generous, the top quarter of highest-income Americans, accounted for more than half the votes cast. Moreover, the class bias has become more pronounced in the past twenty-five years, as an inordinate number of working-class and middle-class Americans have stopped voting, or have never begun to vote.

Those proponents of capital *über alles*, like economist Milton Friedman, are explicit in their contempt for notions of political democracy. This point must never be forgotten in the barrage of propaganda that equates markets with democracy, all to enhance the power of the rich at the expense of everyone else. In Friedman's dream world, people put all their energy into commercial affairs and the point of government is to protect private property. Voter disinterest, apathy, and cynicism are highly desirable, especially among those eligible voters who might have insufficient appreciation for the joys of class society and capitalist living. An informed and active public sphere, argues this line of reasoning, can only produce negative effects because it might lead to government policies that interfere with profit maximization.

The situation is not hopeless for the left, though the playing field is tilted. Working-class parties can make headway, especially if backed by powerful non-electoral movements, most notably trade unions. So it has been in Scandinavia, where left parties have managed to generate social policies quite beneficial to the working class although sharply opposed by nearly the entirety of the ruling class. In recent years these victories have been cut back, as they have been under sustained attack by business. The United States has never come anywhere near the degree of left influence in electoral politics as Scandinavia. A key difference was that the ostensible "progressive" political party in the United States—the Democratic Party—was always a party with strong ties to Wall Street and corporate interests and, until the 1970s, embraced by the most vicious racists and segregationists in the nation. The high-water mark for progressive electoral politics in the past century was the New Deal in the late 1930s, fueled by a massive upsurge from below and, in particular, the rise of militant trade unionism. From the standpoint of U.S. history, some quite radical reforms were passed, most notably the Works Progress Administration (WPA) under which the unemployed were given jobs fitting their abilities, working at socially useful tasks—entirely independent of the market. But even in FDR's administration many far-reaching measures that business found unacceptable were blocked or had their original purposes subverted. The left was soon met by a crushing ruling-class response that culminated in the Red Scare of the postwar years.

Then, in the 1960s and early 1970s, as a result of massive popular protests, a range of unusually progressive domestic policies was adopted, even by such notorious figures as President Richard Nixon. The business community reacted with alarm to its decline in prestige and influence during this period. As the global neoliberal group the Trilateral Commission noted in the mid-1970s, the United States (indeed the world) was awash in a "crisis of democracy," created by the fact that traditionally apathetic poor people, young people, women, and people of color were getting too involved in the political process. They did not use the term "crisis of democracy" with any sense of irony.

In response to this "crisis of democracy," the stage was set for our current predicament. The concern of the right in the 1970s was that, in the prevailing culture, capitalist business as usual, militarism, and "being tough on crime" were regarded as negative factors and there was far too much sympathy for the interests of workers, women, ethnic minorities, poor people, and the environment, along with approval for aggressive government policies to serve these interests. The political right mounted a well-funded, full-throttle ideological assault on labor unions, social welfare policies, and "liberalism." This assault took many forms, including lavish monies spent by right-wing foundations and business groups to push the media debate to the right and make it more pro-business, which was assisted by the deregulation of media ownership.

Today the range of political commentary in the news media extends from the far right to the neoliberal "center," and in a medium like commercial radio there is hardly anything but the right. What passes for political journalism effectively bounces between the walls of legitimate debate that are set by the elites of the two main parties. It is easily manipulated by the powerful and highly resistant to, and contemptuous of, issues and positions that fall outside the narrow mainstream. The assault also has pushed university teaching and research to the right. The use of sophisticated propaganda techniques and fire-tested buzzwords like *markets, entrepreneurs, competition, deregulation, growth,* and *choice* abound. As has been well documented, the campaign has been remarkably successful. In short, the political right ideologically promoted an environment conducive to the adaptation of ferociously anti-labor, pro-business neoliberal policies in the United States and worldwide—policies that had been anathema to the vast majority of citizens for generations.

Democrats and Republicans Go Right

A critical development in the rightward turn of the U.S. electoral culture has been the demise of progressive forces having any meaningful influence in the higher reaches of the Democratic Party. Business has always been important in the Democratic Party, and the campaign to increase corporate influence grew after progressive George McGovern won the nomination in 1972 and wrote the most anti-corporate platform since Franklin Delano Roosevelt's 1936 campaign. But the main institutional development in this regard was the rise and operation of the business-funded Democratic Leadership Council (DLC) under Bill Clinton and Al Gore, among others, starting in 1985. The explicit purpose of the DLC was to make the Democrats almost as pro-business and pro-military as the Republicans. It was the DLC that pushed the Democrats to adopt neoliberal policies like industry deregulation, budget balancing at all costs, privatization of public services, lower business taxes, and support for global corporate trade deals like the General Agreement on Tariffs and Trade (GATT) and NAFTA. For its traditional constituencies of women, minorities, environmentalists, and labor it offered a far smaller meal of lukewarm support for civil rights, affirmative action, abortion rights, and the oft-repeated argument of "Hey, we are nowhere near as bad as the Republicans." But genuine progressive policies like single-payer health insurance, equalization of school spending, demilitarization of the political economy, quality public transportation, increasing the ability of workers to form trade unions, reducing economic inequality, rehabilitation rather than retribution for those convicted of crimes, opposition to drug prohibition, and guaranteed employment at a living wage—most of which had a viable basis of support within Democratic circles in the 1970s—were fully purged from the party platforms with the DLC's inspiration and guidance.

The transformation of the Democrats was fully accomplished over eight years. A turning point came when Clinton selected Gore as his vice presidential candidate in 1992. Prior to that date, conservative or centrist Democrats like Lyndon Johnson and Jimmy Carter had "balanced" the ticket with liberals like Hubert Humphrey and Walter Mondale. With Clinton's selection of Gore, it was a formal recognition that the liberal wing of the party was losing serious clout. Any short list of the major legislative accomplishments of the Clinton-Gore administration would include passage of a draconian crime law, the approval of NAFTA and GATT, and the creation of the WTO, the Telecommunications Act of 1996, the tearing down of banking regulations like Glass-Steagall, the elimination of federal welfare guarantees to poor children and single mothers, and maintenance and expansion of military spending. These are all issues traditionally championed by the right wing of the Republican Party. There are hardly any progressive measures to be found on the Clinton-Gore report card and not one major issue where they squared off against the needs of the wealthy and put all their influence on the line to go to bat for their voting base.

Moreover, reports by administration insiders like former labor secretary Robert Reich indicate that in cabinet debates over nearly all of these issues, it was Vice President Al Gore who generally pushed for the most conservative, pro-business position. The dominance of the "New Democrats" within the party emerged in full force in 2000, when they cornered the entire market on presidential aspirants, for a number of reasons but notably because the exorbitant cost of campaigning scared off all but those who could comfortably nuzzle up to the money trough. Hence, the "liberal" primary challenger to Al Gore was Bill Bradley, another DLC poster child, described approvingly by one conservative as second only to Robert Rubin as "Wall Street's favorite Democrat." His liberalism was based, apparently, on a more sincere and higher grade of rhetoric for the dispossessed. Then, as the icing on the "New Democrat" cake, when Gore won the nomination, he selected Joseph Lieberman, the current DLC chair, as his running mate. Gore, arguably the most conservative Democratic nominee since 1924, managed to locate one of the only Democratic senators whose record was even more cravenly pro-business than his own. The Republican *Wall Street Journal* was left fumbling, as it had to acknowledge that Lieberman was as devoted to the interests of the capitalist class as nearly any other member of Congress, party notwithstanding.

Another part of the DLC agenda—one that received considerably greater discussion in the news media—was the need for the Democrats to appeal to more socially conservative voters "turned off" by what was perceived as the Democrats' allegiance to the interests of women, gays and lesbians, poor people, marijuana smokers, and ethnic minorities. This was especially important because all the Clinton-Gore-Lieberman rhetoric about the evils of Republicans could not keep an increasing percentage of poor and working-class voters from dropping out of the electoral process in the 1990s, for quite rational reasons. Attracting socially conservative white males (who used to be called "Reagan Democrats") to the Democrats was to be accomplished by being super tough on crime and drug use, and supporting capital punishment and militarism. The notion that a more fruitful way to generate new votes would be to appeal to the nonvoting 50 percent of the population—disproportionately poor and working class—with a platform that delivered the goods rather than piles of rhetoric was never even countenanced, as that went directly against the pro-business orientation of the DLC, the interests of the party's corporate benefactors, and the imagination of the brain-dead punditocracy in the news media.

A real progressive platform might also have appealed to many working-class social conservatives, who are rarely given a reason to vote other than their attitude toward issues like guns, school prayer, and the death penalty. Indeed, Republicans—who seem to have a firmer grasp of how to win or steal elections than many Democrats— live in fear of such a "populist" strategy on the part of Democrats. This led to constant preemptive attacks on the Democrats for initiating "class warfare" at the slightest sign that Democrats were appealing to the economic interests of the working class. The DLC Democrats fall all over themselves to repudiate the Republican charges, for fear of scaring off their wealthy and corporate benefactors, not to mention their own actual political views. Today the lack of class consciousness among Democratic leaders is palpable, and a clear majority of the party's candidates and officials have backed off from any marked differentiation of politics on economic lines.

The effort by the Democrats to move "rightward" for votes was a thoroughgoing flop in the 2000 presidential election. The "New Democrat" record notwithstanding, the Republicans paint the Democrats as the party of tax-and-spend maniacs and social liberals. "We were hurt," said DLC president Al From, exhibiting the tortured logic that insists the Democrats head ever more rightward, "because we were viewed in this election as being too liberal and too much in favor of big government." The truth is that nearly every state that Al Gore won in 2000 could have been won, arguably, by someone like Senator Paul Wellstone from the party's most liberal wing, assuming they had anywhere near the campaign war chest Gore commanded. (And, by this reasoning, had a Wellstone pressed economic issues on class lines in a manner that would have scared the pants off the DLC, the Democrats might have made much larger inroads with the white working class and even non-voters.) The appeal to social conservative white males did not even net Gore historically Democratic states like West Virginia, Bill Clinton's Arkansas, or Gore's own home state of Tennessee; if conservative credibility is one's criterion for voting, people logically will tend to go to what is perceived as the genuine (Republican) article. President Harry Truman said it this way in addressing a convention of liberal Democrats in 1952: "If it's a choice between a genuine Republican, and a Republican in Democratic clothing, the people will choose the genuine article every time."

So it is one of the great ironies of our times that Democrats like Gore and Lieberman can win elections only by getting enormous support from what remains of the traditional progressive coalition of African Americans, Latinos, labor, feminists, and environmentalists. (Early in the fall, Americans witnessed the ludicrous spectacle of Gore seeking to attract voters by proclaiming his commitment to populism and protecting the little people from corporate bullies, even as Lieberman told the *Wall Street Journal* that business should pay no attention to Gore, because it was meaningless rhetoric to get voters, not a discussion of actual policies that might be implemented.) African Americans alone provided some 20 percent of all of Gore's votes in 2000. Yet in return, these voters get crumbs, while the DLC's big money backers get the keys to the country.

It was only a matter of time until there was a revolt in the ranks, like the one represented in 2000 by the Nader campaign. The Democrats' absolute reliance on progressive voters, along with the party's absolute refusal to offer progressive policies, might explain the hysterical tone as well as the unprincipled and generally groundless nature of the attacks on Nader and his presidential campaign by Democrats and liberal leaders in 2000. A candid and honest debate over the Clinton-Gore record and the likely contours of a Gore-Lieberman administration was the last thing liberal Gore apologists wanted. Instead, the refrain heard over and over was, "Regardless of what you think of Gore, he is vastly superior to the Republicans." (Curiously, the Republicans, hardly an upstanding bunch in any calculation, appeared far more charitable toward Ross Perot, who did serious damage to their presidential chances in 1992. Likewise, they pretty much laid off attacking Pat Buchanan in 2000, even though evidence suggests he may have done damage to Bush in the Electoral College.)

This "lesser-of-two-evils" mantra is predicated on the sheer evil of the Republican Party, and this leads to a less noted but quite significant development in U.S. politics over the past forty years: the consolidation of the Republican Party as a hard-right, militantly neoliberal party. For much of this century, and well into the 1960s, the Republican Party included a liberal wing, featuring many prominent figures with political records well to the left of Clinton, Gore, and Lieberman. When Lieberman first won his Senate seat in 1988, he did so by running from the right against one of the last of the Senate Republican liberals, Lowell Weicker. Lieberman red-baited Weicker on foreign policy and had the support of William F. Buckley and the right-wing Cuban terrorist crowd.

In the past, the Republicans also had a moderate or centrist wing, typified by someone like Dwight Eisenhower. This offered progressive constituencies a modicum of competition for their votes in some instances. As late as 1960, for example, around one-third of African

Americans voted for Nixon rather than Kennedy for president. But the hard-right takeover of the party, beginning with Barry Goldwater and culminating in Reagan, left conservatives like Bob Dole and George Bush as the "moderates" and the liberals like John Lindsay, Earl Warren, John Anderson, and Pete McCloskey nowhere to be found. And what is called "conservatism" today has none of the principled commitment to individual liberty, small-scale institutions, and the rule of law, or a skepticism toward market excess and imperialism, that was seen occasionally in earlier versions. This is a conservatism that is dedicated purely to serving the needs of the wealthy under any and all circumstances and to seizing power by any means necessary. It is this new Republican Party with its bare-knuckle, know-nothing "conservatism" that opened the door for the DLC strategy to push the Democrats to the right. Now the Democrats could march into Wall Street's open arms with little fear of losing progressive voters to the Republicans.

The bankruptcy of the U.S. electoral system is not merely that it is well under the thumb of the rich and powerful and has a range of debate more suitable to a quasi-dictatorship than to a self-governing people. It is also that the electoral and governing systems have became grotesquely corrupt. It is one of capitalism's contradictions that it ostensibly works best when there is a culture dominated by the rule of law and a governing system typified by transparency, integrity, and civic virtue. Indeed, mainstream pundits and academics often argue that it is the lack of these attributes in the "crony capitalism" of eastern Europe, Latin America, and Asia that prevents sustained economic growth. Yet capitalism, with its incessant pressure to reward personal greed and penalize altruism, invariably eats away at any public service values and institutions if they stand in the way of profit. That is why whenever neoliberal policies gain the upper hand in a nation, they almost invariably lead to a tidal wave of corruption. So it has been with electoral political culture in the United States—as symbolized by the Clinton administration's renting out of the Lincoln Bedroom in the White House to big donors.

Corporate domination of the electoral process in the United States is locked in by a campaign system that requires enormous sums of money for candidates to have almost any chance of being victorious. The cost of the 2000 federal election campaigns was well over $3 billion, up some 40 percent from 1996, which was up 40 percent again from 1992. Much of this money goes to pay for manipulative and insulting TV advertisements.

Unless candidates can afford TV advertising, they lose their place in the tireless roundups presented by the news media, and they cannot answer TV ads that attack them by their opponents, which has proven to be mandatory for winning races. Most of this money comes from powerful and wealthy corporations and individuals. Ninety percent of the money that comes from individual campaign contributions, for example, comes from the wealthiest 1 percent of Americans.

Senator Russell Feingold (D-Wisconsin) has accurately described the electoral system as one of "legalized bribery and legalized extortion." Corporations need to make hefty campaign contributions to guarantee a slice of the action when Washington doles out the goodies. Hence, scores of major corporations gave at least $100,000 to both political parties in 2000. Rupert Murdoch's News Corporation was a classic example of how two-party politics works nowadays. His Fox News Channel served as little more than a propaganda dispenser for the Bush campaign in 2000; at the same time Murdoch was funneling hundreds of thousands of dollars to the Democrats and candidate Gore. That way, whichever party wins, Murdoch wins. And so it is for the wealthy and corporate America. The "room for maneuver" against the interests of capital in mainstream U.S. political culture—never very pronounced—has all but disappeared. And in the "screw you, I'm out for number one" culture that comes with the rule of money, the entire governing process has become a stinking cesspool of corruption. The bamboo prison of class rule has become an iron cage.

But the situation is anything but locked in for all time or even for very long at all. This is a political moment with notable openings for progressive organizing, electoral and otherwise. There are several reasons for this. In the broadest sense, although depoliticization is a rational immediate response to the status quo, it is untenable over the long haul. People are social beings and politics goes a long way toward shaping the quality of our lives. Social problems require social solutions, and all the public relations and spinmeisters in the world cannot eliminate that truth. This is especially true in a world with enormous social inequality, and where the civic religion is the bankrupt notion that "you are what you own." In the United States, 1 percent of the population now has more wealth than the bottom 90 percent. As Canadian singer Bruce Cockburn explains, "The trouble with normal is it always gets worse." The corruption of the U.S. political system assures that conditions will only get worse for most Americans. When the dispossessed and disaffected believe that political activity can improve their lives, they get politically active and change the world. Hence, as noted above, there has been the emergence of a new wave of social activism in the past few years. But there are openings for progressive politics that go far beyond that.

A crucial difference today from, say, forty years ago, is that support for and enthusiasm toward the political status quo is paper thin. Only 48 percent of adult Americans voted for Gore and Bush in the 2000 election. Of those, one-half said they did not really care for the candidate they voted for; they were voting against the other candidate. So that leaves 12 percent that actually supported each candidate, and I suspect a significant percentage of those voters were people who vote habitually for the Democrat or the Republican, regardless of the candidate.

And it goes well beyond the personalities of specific politicians. The neoliberal thrust of Reagan Republicans has lost whatever steam it had among voters; George W. Bush and many Republicans actually ran for office in 2000 on the claim that they would use the government to improve Social Security, health care, and education. It is notable, too, that the Republicans have concluded that openly attacking gays, lesbians, and feminists and making more coded attacks on immigrants and African Americans are also counterproductive to the goal of winning elections. I have already explained the failure of the DLC approach to attract popular support, such that Gore was forced to run as a pseudo-populist as the election neared to find enough votes to win. What is striking, and what has been confirmed in research by political scientist Joel Rogers and others for many years now, is that the voting electorate seems open to more progressive policies than either party is willing or able to offer. And this does not even take into consideration the one hundred million Americans who do not vote, who are disproportionately poor, working class, young, and people of color. It is here that the foundation of progressive electoral politics lies.

New Openings and New Uncertainties

In short, the opening for progressives to engage in electoral work in the coming years is clearly wider than it has been for some time. This new opening is emerging not as an alternative to non-electoral organizing, but as a complement to a vibrant mass movement arising outside of the electoral sphere. Nevertheless, there are severe obstacles in the way, which may undermine left electoral activity. In particular, reactionary electoral laws that make it extremely difficult to launch a viable third party, as well as a campaign system that requires enormous amounts of money to reach potential voters (and counteract scurrilous charges by well-heeled opponents) have a deadening political effect. U.S. Representative Tom DeLay (R-Texas) candidly and approvingly admits that by having the wealthy bankroll the electoral system it virtually guarantees that the "free market" will never face a significant political challenge. Without these laws and this campaign finance system—say the United States had a system of proportional representation and publicly funded campaigns for all parties—the actual support for the Republicans and Democrats would plummet. My own guess is that the two parties would soon receive the same percentage of the vote—around 30 to 40 percent—that the old communist parties have gotten in parts of eastern Europe after elections were opened to multiple parties. But their duopoly and the protection of their wealthy benefactors are dependent upon this system, so they are loath to change it.

Still, the debacle in Florida has pointed toward the need for electoral reforms—ranging all the way from publicly financing elections, making Election Day a paid holiday, allowing convicted felons who have done their time the right to vote, and registering voters on Election Day, to even more radical arguments for proportional representation, instant runoff voting, and other steps that would eliminate the case for lesser-of-two-evils voting.

Simply succumbing to the lesser-of-two-evils logic means that progressives should never challenge Democrats in general elections, even if they are as heinous as Gore and Lieberman, because they will only take votes away from the Democrat and assist in electing the greater of two evils, the Republican. This was an argument made not only by people who hate the left, like Thomas Friedman of the *New York Times* and many mainstream Democratic hacks (all determined to see Al Gore regarded as the left wing of legitimate thought). It was also made by former radicals who still flash their left credentials to earn holier-than-thou points in academia despite that they are increasingly willing to accept the status quo as the best of all possible worlds, the be-damned-glad-to-have-Gore-instead-of-a-Republican crowd. Were that the extent of the criticism, it could be easily dismissed.

But the lesser-of-two-evils critique was also made by serious leftists who understand how terrible Gore and the Democrats are and who believe we can and must blow open the range of legitimate debate but argue that the third-party option simply cannot work. In their view, the only option is to work within the Democratic Party, using a left caucus to advance progressive candidates and policies—much like the DLC moved the party to the right. Their argument is that it will be easier to take over the Democrats, or at least gain a dominant position in the party, than it would be to launch a new party that has any hope of contending for power in a system rigged by the two major parties. After all, a significant portion of the current voting base already is relatively progressive, certainly well to the left of the DLC. Indeed, the argument goes, if third-party efforts only succeed in putting Republicans in office, they will open up deadly splits on the left and between left organizers and progressive constituencies.

These are serious concerns not to be dismissed categorically. But it bears repeating that the Democratic Party has been restructured in such a manner over the past two decades as to make the possibility of a McGovern-type insurgency campaign, not to mention something to the left of that, far less plausible. The Democratic Party, at its commanding heights, is now so linked with the needs of business and the military and has so completely cast off its New Deal past that the routine litmus test of support for the party's candidates means endorsing an increasing number of truly dreadful candidates, like Gore and Lieberman. Any progressive approach for working within the Democratic Party that has to water down its critique of the DLC one iota, or that pays its dues by serving as an attack dog on the third-party left, as seemingly was the case in 2000, almost by definition undermines the very goal it professes: to make the left more powerful in the United States.

There is no doubt that the fundamental electoral challenge for the coming generation on the left is the establishment of a viable working-class–based, anti-neoliberal political party that will be strong enough and large enough to contend for power. Barring a change in electoral laws, it is arguable that this party will succeed only if it is one of the existing two main parties or a new force that has displaced one of them. This means the Democratic Party cannot simply be dismissed. Moreover, many traditional Democratic voters are going to have to be part of any progressive electoral movement, as well as some progressive Democratic elected officials. If those relationships explode, the entire progressive electoral project will be set back, perhaps irreparably. But because of the inherent difficulty in taking over the Democratic Party and the party's severe limitations at present, the prospect of developing a viable third party will continue to be raised. The situation calls for caution rather than bombast, organization rather than polemics. In the near term, at least, it may be wise to work both sides of the street, continue building the movement at the grassroots level, and see how events unfold.

3

A New New Deal under Obama?

WITH U.S. CAPITALISM mired in an economic crisis of a severity that increasingly brings to mind the Great Depression of the 1930s, it should come as no surprise that there are widespread calls for a "new New Deal."[1] Already the Obama administration has been pointing to a vast economic stimulus program of up to $850 billion over two years aimed at lifting the nation out of the deep economic slump.[2]

The possibility of a new New Deal is to be welcomed by all of those on the left, promising some relief to a hard-pressed working population. Nevertheless, it raises important questions. What are the real prospects for a new New Deal in the United States today? Is this the answer to the current economic crisis? What should be the stance of the left? A full analysis of all the issues would require a large volume. I shall confine myself here to a few points that will help to illuminate the challenges ahead.

The New Deal was not initially an attempt to stimulate the economy and generate recovery through government spending, an idea that was scarcely present in the early 1930s. Rather it consisted of *ad hoc* salvage or bailout measures, principally aimed at helping business, coupled with work relief programs. The lion's share of New Deal expenditures at the outset were devoted to salvage operations. As Harvard economist Alvin Hansen, Keynes's leading early follower in the United States, explained in 1941 in his *Fiscal Policy and Business Cycles:*

For the most part, the federal government [in the New Deal era] engaged in a salvaging program and not in a program of positive expansion. The salvaging program took the form of refinancing urban and rural debt, rebuilding the weakened capital structure of the banks, and supporting railroads at or near bankruptcy. . . . The Reconstruction Finance Corporation, the Home Owners' Loan Corporation, and the Farm Credit Administration poured $18 billion into these salvaging operations. The federal government stepped into the breach and supported the hard-pressed state and local governments—again a salvage operation. . . .

That a salvaging program of this magnitude was necessary was, of course, due to the unprecedented depth of the Depression reached by early 1933. . . . Under such circumstances the economy dries up like a sponge. Vast governmental expenditures, designed to float the "sponge" to a high level of prosperity, are instead absorbed by the sponge itself. The expenditures seemingly run to waste. This is the salvaging operation. Only when the economy has become thoroughly liquid can further funds float it to higher income levels. A deep depression requires vast salvaging expenditures before a vigorous expansionist process can develop.[3]

Federal spending on public works, which has become almost synonymous with the New Deal in popular culture, expanded nearly every year from 1929 to 1938 (see Figure 3.1). Yet total government spending on public works did not regain its 1929 level until 1936, due to drops in state and local public works spending that undercut the federal increases. At first, state and local governments had responded to the deep slump by increasing their public works outlays. However, within a couple of years their resources were largely exhausted and spending on public works dropped below that of 1929. By 1936, state and local public works expenditures were less than half their 1929 level. Hence, for most of the Depression decade "the federal government," as Hansen observed, "only helped to hold back the receding tide." Despite the fact that federal outlays in this area had increased by almost 500 percent, total government public works expenditures rose only 12 percent over the period, not enough to offer much of a stimulus to the overall economy.

FIGURE 3.1: Outlays for Public Works (millions of dollars) 1929–38

Year	Federal Public Works and Aid to Local Units	State and Local Public Works	Total Government Public Works
1929	357	2,952	3,309
1930	445	3,288	3,733
1931	540	2,884	3,424
1932	590	1,949	2,539
1933	785	1,133	1,918
1934	1,266	1,208	2,474
1935	1,433	1,125	2,548
1936	2,180	1,316	3,496
1937	1,938	1,391	3,329
1938	2,099	1,612	3,711

Source: Alvin H. Hanson, *Fiscal Policy and Business Cycles* (New York: W. W. Norton, 1941), 86.

It was only later on in the Depression decade, in what historians have called the "second New Deal," culminating in Roosevelt's landslide 1936 election victory, that the emphasis shifted decisively from salvage operations to work relief programs and other measures that directly benefited the working class. This was the era of the Works Progress Administration, headed by Harry Hopkins, along with other progressive programs and measures, such as unemployment insurance, Social Security, and the Wagner Act (giving the *de jure* right to organize). These advances were made possible by the great "revolt from below" of organized labor in the 1930s.[4] The WPA spent $11 billion and employed 8.5 million people. It paid for the building of roads, highways, and bridges. But it did much more than that. The federal school lunch program got its start with WPA dollars. Indeed, what distinguished the WPA from other work programs was that it employed people to do the things that were needed in all areas of society, working at jobs they were already equipped to do. The WPA financed over 225,000 concerts. It paid artists to paint murals and actors to do stage productions.[5]

None of this conformed to the later precepts of Keynesian economics. As late as 1937, Roosevelt's New Deal administration had still not given up the goal of balancing the federal budget—a core aim of Secretary of Treasury Henry Morgenthau Jr.—even in the midst of the Great Depression. It thus clamped down on federal spending, with expenditures being reduced in the budgets for fiscal years 1937 and 1938. Meanwhile the new Social Security program, passed in 1935, began taxing workers in fiscal year 1936 based on regressive payroll taxes, with no payouts for old age insurance supposed to occur until 1941, thereby generating a massive deflationary effect.[6]

These and other contradictions came to a head in the recession of 1937–38, during which the recovery that had been taking place since 1933 suddenly came to a halt prior to a full recovery, with unemployment jumping from 14 to 19 percent. It was only in response to deepening economic stagnation that the Roosevelt administration was at last induced to move decisively away from its attempt to balance the federal budget, turning to the strategy promoted by Federal Reserve board chairman Marriner Eccles to utilize strong government spending and deficit financing to lift the economy. These actions corresponded to the publication of *An Economic Program for American Democracy*, signed by Richard V. Gilbert, George H. Hildebrand Jr., Arthur W. Stuart, Maxine Y. Sweezy, Paul M. Sweezy, Lorie Tarshis, and John D. Wilson—a group of young Harvard and Tufts economists representing the Keynesian revolution. This work was a Washington, D.C., bestseller and immediately became the intellectual defense *after the fact* for the New Deal expansionary policies of 1938–39.[7] Nevertheless, the stimulus measures adopted at this stage were too meager to counter the conditions of depression that prevailed at the time. What rescued the capitalist economy was the Second World War. "The Great Depression of the thirties," John Kenneth Galbraith wrote, "never came to an end. It merely disappeared in the great mobilization of the forties."[8]

But this raises further questions. As Paul Baran and Paul Sweezy asked in *Monopoly Capital* in 1966: "Why was such an increase [in government spending] not forthcoming during the whole depressed decade? Why did the New Deal fail to attain what the war proved to be within easy reach? The answer to these questions," they contended, "is that, *given the power structure of United States monopoly capitalism*, the increase of civilian [government] spending had about reached its outer limits by 1939. The forces opposing further expansion were too strong to be overcome." [their emphasis]

Baran and Sweezy's thesis that civilian government spending had "about reached its outer limits" by the end of the New Deal was directed primarily at total non-defense government purchases as a percentage of GDP. This constitutes almost the entire direct contribution of government to the welfare of the population, encompassing public education, roads and highways, health, sanitation, water and electric services, commerce, conservation, recreation, police and fire protection, courts, prisons, legislators, the executive branch, etc. By 1939, Baran and Sweezy contended, these critical elements of government taken together had reached their maximum share of GDP, given the power structure of U.S. monopoly capitalism.[9]

Remarkably, Baran and Sweezy's civilian government ceiling thesis has been borne out in the more than forty years since it was

FIGURE 3.2: Non-Defense Government (Federal, State, and Local) Consumption and Gross Investment as a Percentage of GDP, 1929–2007

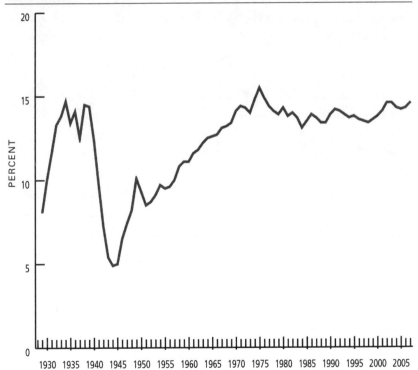

Sources: Bureau of Economic Analysis, National Income and Products Accounts, Table 1.1.5. Gross Domestic Product, and Table 3.9.5. Government Consumption Expenditures and Gross Investment.

formulated (see Figure 3.2). Civilian government consumption and investment purchases as a percentage of GDP rose to 14.5 percent of GDP in 1938 (14.4 percent in 1939), fell during the 1940s due to the great expansion of military spending during the Second World War, and then regained lost ground in the 1950s, 1960s, and early '70s. Civilian government spending on consumption and investment reached its highest point of 15.5 percent of national income in 1975 (dropping in 1976 to its second highest level of 14.9 percent), and then stabilized at around 14 percent from the late 1970s to the present. In 2007 non-defense government consumption and investment purchases constituted 14.6 percent of GDP, *almost exactly the same level as in 1938–39*!

The reasons for this are straightforward. Beyond some minimal level, real estate interests oppose public housing; private health care interests and medical professionals oppose public health care; insurance companies oppose public insurance programs; private education interests oppose public education; and so on. The big exceptions to this are highways and prisons within civilian government spending, together with military spending. "The point can be elucidated," Baran and Sweezy wrote,

> by considering two budget items simultaneously, say housing and health. Very few people nowadays are opposed to a modest public housing program, and of course everyone is in favor of at least enough spending on health to control epidemic diseases. But beyond a certain point, opposition begins to build up in each case, at first from real estate interests to housing and from the medical profession to public programs of medical care. But real estate interests presumably have no special reasons to oppose medical care, and doctors no special reasons to oppose housing. Still, once they have each gone into opposition to further increases in their own spheres, they may soon find it to their joint interest to combine forces in opposing both more housing and more public health. The opposition to each individual item thus builds up faster when two items are under consideration, and fastest of all for across-the-board increases in the whole budget. We might say figuratively that if one item is being considered, opposition grows in proportion to the amount of the

FIGURE 3.3: Selected Components of Government Spending as a Percentage of GDP, G-7 Countries plus Sweden, 2007

	Government Spending as Percent of GDP[a]	Government Final Consumption as Percent of GDP[b]	Social Security Transfers as Percent of GDP	Military Spending as Percent of GDP (2006)
Sweden	52.6	25.9	15.3	1.5
France	52.4	23.1	17.4	2.4
Italy	48.5	19.8	17.3	1.8
UK	44.6	21.6	12.8	2.6
Germany	43.9	18.0	17.3	1.3
Canada	39.3	19.3	9.9	1.2
United States	36.6	16.0	12.1	4.0
Japan	36.0	17.7	11.4	1.0

a) OECD data for Canada, Japan, and the United States is from 2006.

b) Final Consumption figures include military consumption expenditures.

Source: (columns 1–3) Organisation for Economic Co-Operation and Development, *OECD in Figures* (OECD: Paris, 2008), 57–58; (column 4) Stockholm international Peace Research Institute, SIPRI Military Expenditure Database, http://www.sipri.com.

increase; while if all items are being considered, opposition grows in proportion to the square of the increase.[10]

The fact that the ceiling to government expenditures in the U.S. system is a political rather than an economic barrier is demonstrated by the very different levels of government spending as a share of GDP in advanced capitalist countries. Figure 3.3 provides comparative data for the G-7 countries plus Sweden for 2007. Total government spending (column 1) includes both (a) direct government purchases, which add directly to total aggregate demand, and (b) expenditures which reallocate income and capital within the economy, such as interest payments, social insurance transfer payments, farm subsidies, and investment subsidies.[11] Final consumption expenditures of government (column 2) make up the largest component of the government purchases portion of column 1, and include consumption for military purposes. Social Security transfers (column 3) encompass the totality of social insurance schemes covering the community as a whole, the major component of social welfare spending. Military expenditure data (column 4) are taken from the *Military Expenditure*

Database of the Stockholm International Peace Research Institute (data are for 2006). (Note: Columns 2, 3, and 4 do *not* add up to column 1, but rather show selected components of the latter. Some of the other components of total government spending not included are capital formation, interest payments, and other transfer payments.)

Examining these figures, it is clear that the United States has the lowest government final consumption (which includes military consumption) as a percentage of GDP, and is near the bottom in government spending and Social Security transfer payments as a percentage of GDP. The United States also expends a greater share of its national income on the military. U.S. government consumption expenditures, minus military consumption, came to only 11.8 percent of GDP in 2007. It is obvious, then, that there is ample room for the United States to expand its civilian government spending and social insurance transfers. The ceiling on such expenditures as a share of national income is a reflection of the power structure of U.S. society, including the relative weak organization of labor and the relative strength of big capital. The United States, despite its formally democratic character, is firmly in the hands of a moneyed oligarchy, probably the most powerful ruling class in history.

All of this is inseparable from the U.S. role as an empire and the effects that this has on its domestic power structure. Acknowledged (Office of Management and Budget) U.S. military expenditures in 2007 were $553 billion (4 percent of GDP), while actual U.S. military expenditures were $1 trillion (7.3 percent of GDP). Federal non-defense consumption and investment purchases in 2007 were, according to the Bureau of Economic Analysis, less than half federal defense consumption and investment purchases.[12]

My argument therefore is simple. Given that a political ceiling on U.S. civilian government purchases as a percentage of GDP has persisted for more than seven decades, it is unlikely that this will change without a massive, indeed a social-transformative struggle, despite what is purported to be a relatively progressive administration and the worst economic crisis since the Great Depression. Even the greatest environmental crisis in the history of civilization, threatening life throughout the planet, is unlikely to result in a sufficiently massive response by government without the U.S. system first being turned upside down. The forces holding down civilian government spending are too strong to be affected by anything but a major upsurge in society.

Of course, the history of U.S. capitalism since the Second World War might suggest that the most likely recourse of those in charge in these dire circumstances would be to attempt to stimulate the economy through an extraordinary increase in military spending. That the incoming Obama administration has already announced plans to maintain the current war budget and expand the war in Afghanistan only fuels this concern.[13] For this reason it is imperative for the left to redouble its efforts to oppose militarism and demand that resources be put to civilian use.

At the same time, the notion that military spending can provide an effective economic stimulus under present circumstances is dubious, even to sectors of the ruling class. For starters, U.S. military spending is already at active-war levels and accounts for half (or more) of global military spending. One would arguably have to return to ancient Rome to find a comparable situation of military dominance. This is not 1939–41, when U.S. military spending had to be built up virtually from scratch. To double or triple military spending at this point would mean that the United States would be spending two or three times as much as the rest of the world on war and war preparation (assuming that other nations maintained their current levels of military spending). This would be politically difficult both globally, with the other major powers the United States needs to work with already alarmed by U.S. unilateralism, and domestically, where even the lapdog U.S. news media would have difficulty explaining the rationale for diverting more of the economy to militarism as the quality of life crumbles.

Perhaps most important, the notion that increased military spending would effectively stimulate the balance of the economy has been repudiated by economists, even within the mainstream, who note that marginal increases in "defense" expenditures have far less of a positive employment impact than most civilian government spending, given the technology-intensive nature of modern military spending and the fact that a very large share of the purchases take place abroad.

Hence, the main impact of a doubling of U.S. military spending would be to increase greatly the likelihood of bigger and wider wars, and the destruction of human civilization. As C. Wright Mills wrote, "The immediate cause of World War III is the military preparation of it."[14] Even members of the ruling class may balk in the face of the threat of a rising recourse to war and war preparation in an age of nuclear proliferation.

If I am right on this, and I hope I am, then increases in government spending in response to this crisis will be mainly a question of expanding civilian expenditures. Such spending will, initially, be dedicated primarily to salvage or bailout operations. These salvage efforts, so crucial to capital, will be legitimated by smaller public works programs directed at the underlying population. Government spending increases as a whole will be conceived as temporary, pump-priming measures rather than permanent increases in the level of government. Although federal spending increases are likely to loom large in budgetary terms, they are unlikely to come anywhere near compensating for the declines in consumption, investment, and state and local government spending. With the economy as a whole drying up like a sponge, a great deal of government spending designed to float the sponge to higher levels of income will likely be absorbed, as in the 1930s, by the sponge itself, leaving little visible effect. Consequently, recovery will be held down, and the economy, already deeply mired in problems of stagnation and financial de-leverage, will continue to be weak.[15]

A return to the kind of social programs associated with the *real* or second New Deal can be expected to come, if at all, only later, after the initial salvage effort. Moreover, this is unlikely to materialize to any considerable extent apart from a revolt from below on the scale at least of the mid-1930s. Labor must rise again from its ashes. Only a very radical shift in U.S. politics resulting from a major groundswell from below will be able to budge the ceiling on civilian government spending significantly.

Under these circumstances, it is the specific responsibility of the left to urge not only the militant organization of the underlying population, but also the kinds of change, going against the logic of the system and relying on an expansion of government, that will contribute substantially to bettering the conditions of those at the bottom. In terms of demands this should include, for starters, that: (1) government assume the responsibility for providing useful work at a livable wage to all who need it, utilizing existing skills; (2) unemployment compensation be extended beyond its present inadequate limits; (3) those in danger of losing their homes be granted government assistance; (4) a crash housing program be initiated on behalf of those who are homeless or wretchedly housed (including mortgage relief and support to renters); (5) a truly progressive tax system, incorporating a wealth tax, be established; (6) food stamps and food programs for the poor be expanded along with other welfare provisions and easier access; (7) national health insurance (a single-payer system) be provided for the entire population; (8) pension funds be guaranteed by government; (9) Social Security be augmented and regressive payroll taxes eliminated; (10) restrictive laws on unionization be removed; (11) the federal minimum wage be raised; (12) a thirty-hour working week be introduced; (13) a nationwide program of mass transit be promoted; (14) publicly owned and controlled communications systems be greatly enlarged and extended throughout the nation; (15) public education funding be enormously elevated; and (16) environmental protection be vastly increased, in line with the ecological revolution now necessary to keep the planet habitable by humans and countless other species.[16]

Of course, given the existing power structure of U.S. society and the seven-decades-long ceiling on civilian government purchases as a percentage of GDP, all of this may appear to be pie in the sky. And my message is that it is, unless the power structure of U.S. society can be altered. Only a reform movement so radical that it would appear revolutionary within the context of the existing U.S. economic and social order, fundamentally reducing the field of operation of the capitalist market, holds any chance of substantially improving the conditions of most people in society. Needless to say, for such a struggle to succeed people will have to have a sense of real things to struggle for that will materially affect their lives. We must begin to organize a revolt against the ruling class–imposed ceiling on civilian government spending and social welfare in U.S. society.

4

The Wisconsin Uprising

AS ONE WHO WAS in Madison in the winter and early spring of 2011, and who participated in the historic protests against Governor Scott Walker's attack on unions, I can assure you there was most definitely something special happening, and everyone present knew it. For much of my adult life the actual prospects for social change seemed slender, and political work was too often distasteful, with petty bickering and mindless egotism playing an outsized role— hence the common description of left-wing politics as a "circular firing squad." I was there in the 1970s when being political went from being in a community of friends, of comrades sharing values and experiences, to being pointless drudgery, a form of penance. No wonder so many people jumped ship.

The Wisconsin protests point toward several observations. First, they reaffirmed what many Americans had forgotten or never knew: that when people come together in solidarity directed toward social justice they are capable of great sacrifice and unrivaled joy. When there is a sense of solidarity, of hope, of dynamism, everything changes. The feeling this engenders, this bonding, is like breathing fresh air for the first time. I had experienced this in a handful of political campaigns in my life, but absolutely nothing came close to what was happening in the streets of Madison. It reminded me why the right to assemble is a core democratic liberty—inscribed in the

First Amendment to the U.S. Constitution—and probably the one liberty those in power fear the most.[1]

Second, the Wisconsin revolt confirmed that the United States in the second decade of the twenty-first century is not a reactionary country. The participants, by and large, were the sort of folks the corporate media tell us inhabit Tea Party events. But the Tea Party and its billionaire benefactors could barely get a thousand people to show up at one of their Wisconsin demonstrations—even though they flew in the Koch Brothers' favorite union-hating worker, Joe the Plumber, to hype the gate. Compare this to the tens and ultimately hundreds of thousands of Wisconsinites who came out to the protests. The demands and signs were overwhelmingly progressive and far to the left of what most political and labor leaders would countenance. I did not see a scintilla of immigrant-bashing or racism. The signs and chants reflecting progressive positions on unions, taxation, social services, and military spending would never be found in the corporate news media. The cynical claim that the American people are a bunch of shop-till-you-drop airheads incapable of critical thought was purged from my system. It made me remember that people are far more complex and beautiful.

When the events in Madison began, they seemed the natural and proper course, both to me and to the other participants. No one felt like what we were doing was a flight of fancy, or something people in other states could never do. Yet it also seemed as if we were on an island, and that once the matter receded, there was the threat that we would get sucked back into the depoliticized neoliberal hell of the past generation. It was a fear that haunted everyone there. How do we see that this is not a blip on the screen, but the beginning of something bigger, with national dimensions? Something that connected to the great uprisings across the planet, in Egypt and Tunisia and Greece and Spain? How do we avoid falling into the seeming black hole of American ignorance, what Gore Vidal termed the United States of Amnesia?

Then Occupy Wall Street began in September and the Occupy movement spread like wildfire across the nation. That put all those concerns to rest. Wisconsin was no longer an isolated skirmish. It was the first chapter in the current phase of popular and democratic

struggles that will define this nation going forward. Now we will
have to work to see that it is a long book with a happy ending.

Third, the Wisconsin revolt provided yet another case study in
how atrocious and anti-democratic the corporate news media system
is. I include public radio and television under the umbrella of "corporate," as they follow the same conventions. The second day of
the demonstrations, when maybe five or ten thousand people sur-
rounded the capitol on a weekday, provided a case study. Several local
TV crews were huddled around a group of maybe five or six people.
I wondered who on earth demanded all this attention. I soon got
the answer: a few Republicans brought out pro-Walker signs for a
counterprotest. They received coverage almost commensurate to the
coverage of the demonstration itself. Lazy analysts and apologists
write this off to professional journalism's obsession with presenting
"both sides," but nothing is further from the truth. Take five labor
activists with a sign to the next Tea Party or Republican Party event
and see how many TV crews come over to get your side of the story.
Do not hold your breath.

Political players who do not correspond to the range of legitimate
debate (that is, the range countenanced by capital) simply disappear
from the official record. Most working journalists have internalized
this value so they are oblivious to it. That is why nearly any gathering
of the pro-corporate Tea Party gets ample attention, yet when 15,000
progressives meet as they did in 2010 at the U.S. Social Forum in
Detroit, the event received a near-total blackout in the mainstream
news media. Had the head of the FBI ordered the news media not to
cover the U.S. Social Forum under threat of death, it could not have
been more effective.

So it was in Wisconsin. MSNBC did the best coverage on the
corporate front, but it was the exception that proved the rule. Most
devastating was a hack piece on the front page of the *New York
Times* purporting to demonstrate how private-sector union workers supported the Republican attack on public-sector unions. The
piece was played up by Scott Walker and the Republican Party as
clear evidence that their campaign had broad support from workers and even the liberal media. The story was a fraud, however. The
alleged union worker the story was based upon had never been in
a union. Indeed, the true story, unknown in mainstream news, was

the spectacular, almost unimaginable, solidarity of all Wisconsin workers with the protests.

Crappy media coverage matters—it did incalculable damage. People around the nation, even those sympathetic to the protests, were confused by the coverage. And as soon as possible the coverage stopped and Wisconsin fell down the memory hole. Political journalism effectively forgot the protests ever took place and returned to its conventional wisdom.

The lesson of the Wisconsin revolt for media is clear: good coverage matters, which is why the work of independent media like *Democracy Now!*, The Real News Network, *The Nation*, *The Progressive*, Workers Independent News (WIN), the Center for Media and Democracy, and Madison's WORT-FM radio made an enormous difference. Locally, it helped activists compensate for the predictably lame coverage of the anti-labor morning newspaper, the *Wisconsin State Journal*. It points to why structural media reform must be a mandatory part of any democratic reform platform going forward.

Fourth, the political crisis in the United States today is not merely that corporations and billionaires own the government and have turned elections into a sick joke, or that the news media accept this state of affairs as a given, and woe be it for a journalist to question the status quo without appearing ideological and "unprofessional." The crisis is that public opinion is no further to the right on major issues than it was in the 1970s, and in some cases is moving to the left.[2] But the political system has moved sharply to the far right over the past thirty-five years, such that the range of legitimate debate in Washington and in state capitals is the range countenanced by capital, and the system has very little to say to the majority of the people in the nation. The gap between the concerns of the masses and the solutions countenanced by the corporate-run political system are wider than at any point in generations. It is the defining political story of our times.

This is why the Republicans are presently obsessed with limiting the franchise as much as possible; they need to maintain the astonishing (and almost never discussed) class bias in U.S. voting, whereby the top-income groups vote at around a 75 percent rate of the adult population and the lowest-income groups vote at around a 25 percent rate, and there is a straight line from rich to poor that connects all income groups. Republicans know full well that they cannot possibly win a fair election in which the turnout rate is the same for all classes, or even win an election with a turnout of 60 percent or more of Americans over the age of eighteen. At 65 or 70 percent, the United States moves decidedly to the left. If nothing else, this should provide a tremendous measure of optimism for progressives. *We have the numbers on our side!* Now we need a party to represent our interests.

Fifth, the Wisconsin revolt brought home the political dilemma that labor and progressives have faced for decades: whether to work through the Democratic Party and attempt to get some support for progressive policies by making it possible for Democrats to win elections or throw support to a third party that is explicitly on the left and avoid the pitfalls of the two-party system. Both routes have well-known pitfalls. The Democratic Party has delivered next to nothing to labor for decades, except the knowledge that Democrats are not Republicans. Labor and progressives have been triangulated, because the Democrats know they can serve the corporate community and Wall Street and keep labor support because labor has nowhere else to go. The Democrats are now more closely attached to Wall Street and corporations than ever, or at least since before the New Deal. The third-party option seems a clunker, at least in the near term where everyone lives, because its immediate effect would be to give Republicans even more power. This is due to the way the two parties have written electoral laws to effectively give themselves a duopoly.

Both options, it is now obvious, are dead-end streets, and the Wisconsin revolt only crystallized the point. AFL-CIO president Richard Trumka, on the heels of the Madison protests, stated that labor would scale back its support for Democrats in 2012. "For too long, we've been left after Election Day holding a canceled check, waving it about—'Remember us? Remember us? Remember us?'— asking someone to pay a little attention to us," he recalled in an interview, sharing, among other things, his frustration with the failure of the Obama administration and Democrats in Congress to pass the Employee Free Choice Act and other needed labor law reforms. "Well, I don't know about you, but I've had a snootful of that shit!"[3]

But what to do? An emerging consensus connecting activists across labor and the entire progressive community is that labor and progressives need to develop an independent body, unattached to the Democrats, which will only support candidates who are on board with a progressive platform. It will run primary challenges, work with people not associated with the Democrats, and make electoral reform a mandatory part of its work, such that the two-party duopoly bankrolled by billionaires will be quashed. Every bit as important, the emphasis will be on year-round organizing—education, outreach, and general hell-raising—with electoral work getting a smaller percentage of the resources. Little or no money will go to idiotic TV political ads. The discussions are amorphous at this point, but the logic is pointing in this direction, and not a moment too soon. There is considerable risk, but what other option is there?

Along these lines, a fairly coherent platform of progressive policies is emerging, including issues like universal single-payer health care, sharp cuts in the military, guaranteed employment at a living wage, green jobs and conversion to a green economy, massive infrastructure spending, trade unions for all workers who wish them, expansion of public education, free higher education, and expansion of Social Security. We are very close to the point at which there will have to be a demand for the nationalization of the big banks. It is, effectively, a left-Keynesian, social democratic platform that unites liberals, progressives, and socialists. The plan would be to cut down corporate power while working in a capitalist system. For some in the coalition, the reforms will stand to make capitalism work more efficiently and productively and in a more humane manner, a supercharged New Deal, if you will. For some, the social democracies of Scandinavia provide a model of what can be squeezed out of a capitalist system with sufficient political organizing.

This leads to my final point: although left-liberals and socialists will join forces to battle effectively for a progressive platform, we have to understand that the political crisis of our times is at its core an economic crisis. Political activists, like generals, routinely fight the last war, and the notion of battling for progressive reforms within capitalism has become *de rigueur* on the left. There is little doubt that progressives have exacted significant reforms within a capitalist system, and it has seemed throughout the neoliberal era that capitalism, for better or for worse, is here to stay.

But we need to be prepared for the possibility that this is not your grandfather's capitalism, and the sorts of reforms that high-growth rates made possible are unlikely going forward. Even the rosiest forecasts for U.S. capitalism for the next decade or two see the growth rate as little better than the first decade of the twenty-first century and that was the worst decade since the 1930s. Most forecasts are more pessimistic and that puts United States and global capitalism in the most precarious position it has been in for a very long time, or perhaps ever. And that is before we factor in the escalating costs of the environmental crisis. The downward pressure on wages is staggering. The attacks on necessary social services are unprecedented. To keep itself alive, capitalism is eating our future. We are moving in leaps and bounds back to the age of Dickens, except that was a time when the world had a future and now capitalism allows us only a past. While we work with reformers of all stripes in the here and now, we have to acknowledge that capitalism itself may prove to be a barrier to any meaningful reform. We may be at or approaching that point in history, with all that this suggests.

It should not surprise us. Marx, of course, zeroed in on capitalism's contradictions and understood that at some point in time—the sooner the better in his view—capitalism's disadvantages would far outnumber its advantages, and the system would be replaced. But it was not only Marx or socialists who understood that capitalism as a system had a necessary historical expiration date attached to it. John Stuart Mill and John Maynard Keynes—classical liberals of the first order, and staunch proponents of capitalism in their times—both anticipated that eventually capitalism would run its course and need to be replaced by a different economic system, one better suited to the needs of humanity. In such a world it would be necessary, as Keynes said, to break with the alienated moral code, in which "fair is foul and foul is fair," that governs the present society of greed and exploitation, dedicated above all to the accumulation of capital.[4] If that moment is at last before us, it is imperative we put our minds to work on what comes next as we organize to get there.

There was a scene in the classic American television sitcom *Cheers* in which the bar's resident intellectual, Frasier Crane, grew frustrated with the dismal intellectual timbre of the bar's conversations and leapt atop the bar to rectify the situation. Crane began reading aloud from Dickens's *A Tale of Two Cities*: "It was the best of times, it was the worst of times, it was the age of wisdom, it was the age of foolishness." Unimpressed with Crane's offering of high culture, Cliff Clavin barked, "That guy sure knows how to cover his butt."

One feels like Dickens when assessing these times, and that makes one susceptible to criticism like that of Clavin. Across the progressive community there has been an understandable sense of dismay. "In forty years I've not seen a gloomier political landscape," wrote Alexander Cockburn.[5] Mike Davis noted that "the United States is showing incipient symptoms of being a failed state."[6] On its own this can feed a demoralization that engenders a self-fulfilling pessimism about the prospects for social change.

But these commentators wrote those words in the brief interregnum between Wisconsin and the Occupy movement, when the future still had mostly dark hues. We can see now, for the first time in decades, a truly radical potential to U.S. society today. If this country does have a future, it began on those frozen snowy days on the streets of Madison in February 2011, and it spread across Wisconsin, and across the nation, to the point where hundreds of thousands, and then millions, of previously quiet Americans rose up and said, "Enough already. This is our country."

5

This Isn't What Democracy Looks Like

THE MOST STRIKING LESSON from contemporary U.S. election campaigns is how vast and growing the distance is between the rhetoric and pronouncements of the politicians and pundits and the deepening, immense, and largely ignored problems that afflict the people of the United States. The trillion dollars spent annually on militarism and war is off-limits to public review and debate.[1] Likewise the corporate control of the economy, and the government itself, gets barely a nod. Stagnation, the class structure, growing poverty, and collapsing social services are mostly a given, except for the usual meaningless drivel candidates say to get votes. The billions spent (often by billionaires) on dubious and manipulative advertisements—rivaled for idiocy only by much of "news" media campaign coverage—serve primarily to insult the intelligence of sentient beings. Mainstream politics seems increasingly irrelevant to the real problems the nation faces, or, perhaps more accurately, mainstream politics is a major contributing factor to the real problems the nation faces.

The degeneration of U.S. politics is a long-term process. It can be explained and it can be reversed. Indeed, the core problem was understood at the very beginning of democracy in Athens some 2,500 years ago. "Democracy is when the indigent, and not the men of property, are the rulers," Aristotle observed in his *Politics*. "If liberty and equality are chiefly to be found in democracy, they will be best attained when all persons share alike in government to the utmost."[2]

For that reason, capitalism and democracy have always had a difficult relationship. The former generates severe inequality and the latter is predicated upon political equality. Political equality is undermined by economic inequality; in situations of extreme economic inequality it is effectively impossible. The main contradiction of capitalist democracy (making it for the most part an oxymoron) lies in the limited role played by what was classically called the *demos,* or the poorer classes, as compared to the well-to-do. Capitalist democracy therefore becomes more democratic to the extent that it is less capitalist (dominated by wealth) and to the extent to which popular forces—those without substantial property—are able to organize successfully to win great victories, like the right to unionize, progressive taxation, health care, universal education, old-age pensions, and environmental and consumer protections. In the past four decades such organized popular forces in the United States—never especially strong compared to most other capitalist democracies—have been decimated, with disastrous consequences. The United States has long been considered a "weak democracy"; by the second decade of the new century, that is truly an exaggeration. Today, the United States is better understood as what John Nichols and I term a "Dollarocracy"— the rule of money rather than the rule of the people—a specifically U.S. form of plutocracy. Those with the most dollars get the most votes and own the board.

Dollarocracy is now so dominant, so pervasive, that it is accepted as simply the landscape people inhabit, much like the way that the Rocky Mountains provide an unavoidable barrier if one wishes to travel from the Great Plains to the Pacific Ocean. By now, Americans—and certainly the punditocracy and what remains of the news media—are mostly inured to the corruption of our politics that results from having the politicians doing the bidding of large corporations and billionaires with little resistance. The notion of "you get what you pay for" applies in spades to the spoils of government, and the tens of billions spent by corporations and the wealthy on lobbying, public relations, and campaign donations translates into hundreds of billions, eventually trillions, in dollars' worth of revenues. It is a large part of our overall economy.[3]

Lawrence Lessig's 2011 *Republic, Lost* chronicles how much Congress has changed as a result of the influx of corporate lobbying dollars. A generation ago Mississippi senator John Stennis thought it would be inappropriate to accept donations from firms that were affected by the work of the committee he chaired; today that is a huge incentive for getting a committee chair. A significant portion of the work of being a member of Congress is about fundraising, and that is the main measurement of success on Capitol Hill. That and setting oneself up for a lucrative high six- or seven-figure annual income as a K Street lobbyist once one's stint in Congress is done. In the 1970s 3 percent of retiring members became lobbyists; by 2012 the figure is in the 50 percent range.[4] As Lessig makes clear, the corruption in Congress and across the government today is only rarely of the traditional bribery variety. It is instead a far more structural dependence upon corporate money built into the DNA of the political system—traditional payoffs are not necessary.

The major political fights in Congress today are most likely when large corporate lobbies square off against each other for the spoils of government, and a large part of the congressional workload today, aside from fundraising, is mediating these conflicts so everyone gets a piece of the action. But when one corporate lobby has an overriding influence in a policy, or its main adversary is the public interest, fuhgetaboutit. Big pharmaceutical companies make hundreds of billions through getting free access to publicly funded research as well as shaping patent laws and regulations that allow them to charge consumers through the teeth?[5] *No problem.* Cable and telephone firms get government licenses and quasi-monopolies basically to privatize the Internet and fleece consumers?[6] *That's the American Way.* Health insurance companies convert health reform into a program to expand their markets while maintaining their stranglehold over the flawed system with its insane cost structure? *Hey, free markets are the name of the game.* Oil and energy companies get tens of billions in annual government subsidies while derailing all significant measures to address the climate crisis?[7] *It's morning in America!*

Nowhere is the systemic corruption more apparent and deadly than in the manner in which the largest banks have effectively taken over the federal government. "Deregulating" the financial sector has been the signature policy move of Dollarocracy since the 1980s, and has been embraced by Republican and Democratic administrations alike. Much of the "deregulation" was about letting financial institutions enter formerly restricted areas, greatly enhancing both profits and risk, and therefore allowing a merger wave that would have been illegal under the banking regulation that prevailed since the New Deal. In 1995 the six largest bank holding companies (JPMorgan Chase, Bank of America, Citigroup, Wells Fargo, Goldman Sachs, and Morgan Stanley—some of which had somewhat different names at that time) had assets equal to 17 percent of U.S. GDP. By the end of 2006, this had risen to 55 percent, and by 2010 to 64 percent.[8] Too big to fail, indeed.

Former IMF economist Simon Johnson shined a light on what he termed "the quiet coup" in a devastating 2009 piece in *The Atlantic*. Johnson wrote of "the easy access of leading financiers to the highest U.S. government officials, and the interweaving of the two career tracks." The financial sector went from getting 16 percent of corporate profits in the 1970s to over 40 percent of corporate profits by the new century, and executive compensation shot through the roof.[9] Big banks pushed for deregulations that allowed them to speculate recklessly. They often bent and sometimes broke laws. And then, after they collapsed the global economy, they received hundreds of billions (and access to trillions) in bailouts, while not a single executive went to prison.[10] In 2009 alone the financial sector had seventy former members of Congress lobbying on its behalf.[11] As Senator Richard Durbin famously put it, Congress voted a blank check to the reviled big banks, "And the banks—hard to believe in a time when we're facing a banking crisis that many of the banks created—are still the most powerful lobby on Capitol Hill. And they frankly own the place."[12]

Nor was the executive branch any different. As Glenn Greenwald documents, the Obama administration simply elected not to prosecute bankers even when the evidence of illegal activity was clear; financial CEOs and billionaires have become effectively above the law.[13]

We could add in numerous other industries that receive similarly immense privileges. What is striking in almost every case is that these are industries where the giant firms are sometimes, perhaps frequently, disliked by much of the population. Even the vaunted Tea Party received part of its initial propulsion—before the Koch Brothers got out their checkbook and career Dollarcrat Republicans grabbed the steering wheel—from widespread antipathy for how the government was serving Wall Street over Main Street. "The Tea Parties are right about the unholy alliance between business and government that is polluting the country," David Brooks wrote in 2011, although by then it had assumed a strictly rhetorical stature, at least the closer one got to Washington, DC, or to Republicans in power.[14]

Dollarocracy and Inequality

An important sign of Dollarocracy's triumph may have been provided in the recent research of political scientists Larry Bartels, Martin Gilens, Jacob S. Hacker, and Paul Pierson. They demonstrate in independent studies and analyses that the interests and opinions of the great bulk of Americans have virtually no effect over the decisions made by Congress or executive agencies today, at least when they run up against the interests of either a powerful corporate lobby or wealthy people as a class. When the opinions of the poor diverge from those of the well-off, the opinions of the poor cease to have any influence. Although there is a high likelihood that politicians will adopt the positions of their very wealthiest constituents, the research shows politicians will generally take the *opposite* position of that favored by the poorest third of their constituents.[15]

The other side of the coin in Dollarocracy is that those basic and essential government functions that do not necessarily have a major corporate industry lobbying for them get the short end of the stick. Public education and libraries are under constant attack, as their existence runs counter to the values of Dollarocracy.[16] Social Security and Medicare, likewise, are in the crosshairs. Noted economist Joseph Stiglitz explains: "The more divided a society becomes in terms of wealth, the more reluctant the wealthy become to spend money on common needs. The rich don't need to rely on government for parks or education or medical care or personal security—they can buy all these things for themselves. In the process, they become more distant from ordinary people, losing whatever empathy they may once have had."[17]

The physical infrastructure of the nation—roads, transit, bridges, electrical and water systems—has become increasingly dilapidated and is pathetic by comparison to other advanced nations, whereas fifty years ago the United States was the envy of the world. Of course, this is penny wise and pound foolish for the champions of Dollarocracy—they seemingly would benefit in the long run by having an educated workforce and a world-class infrastructure—but the point of the system is to get while the gettin' is good, and let some other chump worry about (and pay for) these abstract matters. A flustered E. J. Dionne observed that "the American ruling class is failing us—and itself." He claimed, in language unimaginable a few years ago, "America needs a better ruling class."[18]

This leads to the evidence that best demonstrates the successful counterrevolution more than anything else: the dramatic shift in wealth and income away from the bottom 99 percent of Americans to the wealthiest 1 percent of Americans over the past three plus decades. More than anything else, Dollarocracy is all about shifting resources to the wealthiest Americans, and the simplest assessment of whether it has succeeded is to look at the data. Graphs 5.0 and 5.1 provide some graphic demonstration of the trend. The degree to which the United States' income distribution has skewed over the past thirty-five years in an inegalitarian manner, primarily to the wealthiest 1 percent— and within that group, skewed toward the top one-tenth or even top one-one-hundredth of 1 percent—is historically unprecedented and so dramatic it is almost impossible to wrap one's mind around it. It is like trying to calculate the distance from Earth to a distant galaxy in centimeters using roman numerals. Nearly all the gains in real income over the past generation have gone to the very richest Americans. If the United States had maintained the same income distribution it had in the 1960s or 1970s in the 2010s, the bottom 90 percent of the population, and especially the bottom 60 percent, would be dramatically better off today. Instead, the United States is approaching levels of inequality found in the third world, leaving the other advanced economies with which it was comparable thirty-five years ago fading in its rear-view mirror.[19]

Figure 5.1 shows the percentage of income accounted for by the top 1 percent of the U.S. population since the First World War. By the beginning of the twenty-first century the income share of the top 1 percent had once again reached the level attained in the late 1920s, just prior to the stock market crash that led to the Great

Depression. And just as in 1929, this once again led to a financial crash and depression (referred to by Paul Krugman as the "Lesser Depression").[20] Only this time the 1 percent seem to be much more successful at retaining their income share in spite of the crisis. As Timothy Noah wrote for *The New Republic* in an article titled "The One Percent Bounce Back" in March 2012, "The top one percent's income share peaked in 2007, fell the following two years, and then began growing again in 2010. As of 2010 the one percent's income share remained below the 2007 peak. But give it time."[21]

Stiglitz states that establishment economics has provided no credible evidence to justify anything remotely close to America's staggering inequality.[22] The punditocracy and the politicians tell us increasing inequality is a function of a new global economy that rewards skilled workers and the necessary consequence of an innovating and dynamic economy. Hacker and Pierson, in their extraordinary 2010 book *Winner-Take-All Politics*, systematically demolish this rationale for growing inequality. They establish that the skewing of American incomes was due primarily to major policy changes, especially pro-billionaire revisions in the tax code, changes in trade policies and business regulations, and the weakening of organized labor.[23] (Thomas Piketty's magisterial *Capital in the Twenty-First Century*, published in 2014 by Harvard University Press, concluded after examining empirical data from twenty nations going back two centuries that capitalism has a strong tendency to *increase* economic inequality built right into its inner logic.)

Regarding taxation, in 1961, families with annual incomes of at least $1 million paid on average 43.1 percent of their income in federal income taxes; in 2011 the percentage fell to 23.1 percent. Corporations paid on average 47.4 percent of their profits in federal taxes in 1961; in 2011 the percentage fell to 11.1 percent.[24] Warren Buffett, one of the three or four wealthiest persons in the world, made headlines in 2011 when he called attention to the absurd situation that he was paying a lower income tax rate than his employees or many American middle-class workers. "Legislators in Washington," Buffett wrote, "feel compelled to protect" mega-rich people like himself "as if we were spotted owls or some other endangered species."[25]

Dollarocracy has been hostile to the interests of organized labor at every turn and has been able to successfully game the system so it

FIGURE 5.1: Income Share of Top 1 Percent, United States, 1917–2010

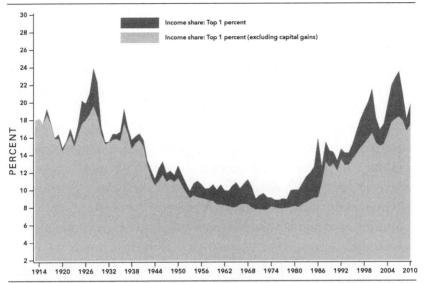

Source: Facundo Alvaredo, Anthony B. Atkinson, Thomas Piketty, and Emmanuel Saez, "The World Top Incomes Database," http://g-mond.parisschoolofeconomics.eu/topincomes.

has been all but impossible to launch successful private-sector unions since the 1970s, even when evidence suggests workers would very much like union representation. (Public-sector unions have survived and grown because governments cannot engage in the same union-busting activities as corporations.) This has enhanced inequality directly, as a 2011 study in the *American Sociological Review* demonstrated, because unions are a significant factor in raising the wages not only for union workers, but for all workers in the labor market. Unions also tend to promote more egalitarian wages among workers.[26] The loss of private sector unions has enhanced inequality indirectly, too, because unions are the one organized institution that has the resources and strength to be a political adversary to corporations and the wealthy. When unions are out of the picture, Dollarocracy has a much easier task getting and keeping political power, and that means an acceleration of policies promoting inequality.

A mountain of research has arisen in the past decade on the consequences of growing inequality for the health of U.S. society, or any nation, for that matter. It is not just the economic damage that inequality creates; nor is it just that inequality undermines the possibility for political democracy. Richard Wilkinson and Kate Pickett's *The Spirit Level* has earned justifiable acclaim for its careful documentation of how increasing inequality—far more than simply the actual amount of wealth/poverty in the society—damages almost every measure of well-being, from life expectancy and mental health and violence to human happiness. This is largely true for the very rich, the beneficiaries of Dollarocracy, as well as the poor. People and cultures thrive in more egalitarian societies.[27]

These policy changes were hardly inevitable, nor were they desirous; they reflected the naked, brute power of corporations and the wealthy over the political process. In other advanced economies where the political balance of power remained closer to the postwar standards, such dramatic changes were not enacted, and those countries have fared, as a rule, better than the United States. They are certainly less unequal, though they have their problems. In the United States, these policy changes were championed at all times by the Republicans, but the Democrats have generally been willing accomplices. Oftentimes it was the Democratic Party leadership that made possible the more egregious concessions to corporations and the wealthy, like trade deals, financial deregulation, and reduced income tax rates for billionaire hedge-fund managers.

In making this argument I do not mean to romanticize U.S. politics of the 1960s or 1970s. This was an extraordinarily turbulent period, and a remarkably large portion of Americans thought social inequality, militarism, racism, and poverty, even political corruption, were so severe at the time that they required radical solutions. The 1972 Democratic presidential candidate George McGovern argued passionately that "at no time have we witnessed official corruption as wide or as deep as the mess in Washington right now."[28] While some of the economic and social problems of those days seem almost quaint by today's Dollarocracy and depression standards, the important point is simply that the political culture at the time was better equipped to deal with popular dissent; it even contributed to a progressive like McGovern getting the Democratic Party nomination, the last time someone not in bed with the moneyed interests was able to do so. It was still very much an uphill battle, to which the demonstrations and riots of the period attest, but organized people were more serious players in U.S. politics than they have been subsequently.

A more concrete sense of the change in the political culture is found in the career of consumer advocate Ralph Nader. In the 1960s and early 1970s Nader and his activist organizations of "Nader's Raiders" were able to win a stunning series of legislative and regulatory victories for consumer rights, open governance, and environmental regulation. The accomplishments of this revitalized consumer movement are scores of laws and regulations, including the creation of the Environmental Protection Agency and the Occupational Safety and Health Administration, the passage of the Freedom of Information Act, and the seminal 1966 National Traffic and Motor Vehicle Safety Act. Not for nothing is it said that Ralph Nader has saved more lives than any other American except Dr. Jonas Salk. During this period, Nader was arguably the most popular living American. He stood for honest and effective government and against corrupt crony monopolistic capitalism. He encouraged a generation of young people to take an optimistic view that organized political activity was capable of positive outcomes, and that public service was an honorable life's work.

Nader was Public Enemy No. 1 to the champions of Dollarocracy, because their primary objective was to eliminate the notion of the government as a progressive force on behalf of an informed and organized citizenry. (A secondary objective was to eliminate the notion among the young of public service as a worthy career goal.) In the 1970s the corporate community organized to limit or terminate Nader's influence and, by extension, the myriad of activist groups that he, along with the women's, student, and civil rights movements, had inspired to influence public policy by grassroots organizing.[29] By the Carter administration, the corporate campaign began to bear fruit and by the 1980s Nader and his ilk were cast into the wilderness, as there is no place for his work under Dollarocracy. He then turned to the next stage of his career, as a prophetic voice against corruption and corporate power and periodically as a presidential protest candidate.

The Economics of Dollarocracy

No more important example of the dominance of Dollarocracy exists than the changing debates over economic policy. During the postwar decades U.S. economic policymaking was steadfastly committed to capitalism and corporate profitability, but the prevailing vision at that time, now sometimes called "the golden age" of U.S. capitalism, was one where the foundation of a successful economy was a relatively prosperous working class or middle class. The idea was that as worker productivity increased, labor compensation would as well so workers would get a portion of the gains in output. Workers would then use their increased income to purchase more products from businesses, hence boosting the economy forward. The government would play a central role in assuring a smooth economy without deep recessions, and keeping the economy out of depression like the one that enveloped the capitalist world in the 1930s.

Of course this vision of a full-employment capitalism and of a "social contract" between capital and labor was never extended to the workforce as a whole. It was only conceivable in the very favorable historical conditions of the post–Second World War years. And it was dependent even then on racial segregation, expanding empire, and Cold War militarism. The only times that the United States reached anything like full employment in the immediate postwar decades were during the Korean and Vietnam wars.

Still, in the postwar years, full employment was a stated core goal of federal policymakers, and as recently as 1978 Congress passed the Humphrey-Hawkins Act, which required the federal government to create jobs for workers if the private sector was incapable of providing for full employment. In this climate, even Republicans like Richard Nixon gave limited consideration to a guaranteed annual income for all adult Americans as a way to effectively eliminate poverty once and for all. Though not known for his veracity, Nixon famously stated, "We are all Keynesians now," to describe this activist role in economic policies. Indeed, during his presidency civilian government spending as a percentage of GDP reached record heights, never surpassed before or since.[30]

The corporate right seemingly tolerated this approach in times of high growth—or possibly found it politically untouchable—but as the economy stagnated in the 1970s, it came to regard this "Keynesian" approach, with its emphasis on high wages and full employment, as an intolerable barrier to corporations' immediate and future profitability. When the pie is growing, capital can get a bigger slice and allow labor to have a somewhat bigger slice as well. When the pie is not growing, the only way capital can increase its slice is by diminishing labor's slice. In this zero-sum world the government would continue to play a central role, but the policies would be geared toward lowering costs for corporations, including wages, and maximizing the post-tax profits. Deregulating finance, expanding private and consumer debt, and shipping manufacturing jobs to low-wage areas became the favored policies.[31] Dollarocracy has been obsessed with changing the terms of the political discussion about the economy and how best to encourage economic growth, and to a large extent it has succeeded.

In the second decade of the twenty-first century, the postwar era seems like some sort of bizarre parallel universe where gravity works backwards. The range of legitimate policy debate about the economy is now dominated by the corporate right and has been returned to the era of Herbert Hoover and Treasury secretary Andrew Mellon, if not the age of the robber barons. The prevailing ideas serve corporations and the 1 percent as never before:

- Budget deficits are the main problem of the economy and their elimination is a necessary precondition for growth, especially if the deficit can be attributed to social programs that benefit the bulk of the population.
- Budget deficits, however, are not a problem—are not to be raised as an issue—where tax cuts on the corporate "job creators," increases in military spending, or bailouts of banks and giant corporations are concerned.
- The tax rates on the wealthy and regulations on business that existed in the 1950s to 1970s undermine investment and economic growth.
- Business creates jobs and government basically interferes with the private sector as it attempts to create jobs.
- Real jobs are those connected to a profit-making venture, even if it is something as dubious as a gambling casino or a porn shop.
- Fake jobs are those jobs connected to government spending, even if it is for something of immense social value, like mass transit, education, or health care.

- Labor unions, rather than bolstering incomes and thereby creating a more prosperous population able to purchase goods, drive up costs and choke off profitable investment; they get in the way of the "job creators."
- Monopolistic mergers and enormous corporations are no particular danger to the economy; indeed, they generally make the economy more efficient and competitive.
- Inflation is a more serious threat to the economy than unemployment.
- Unemployment is not necessarily all that bad, as it keeps wages down, makes workers "hungrier," and makes the United States more competitive.
- Extensive poverty, growing inequality, and tens of millions unemployed or underemployed are regrettable—but the only way to address them is to give even more breaks to business.
- The environment is not an economic issue, and efforts to address ecological calamity should not put additional expenses on corporations or interfere with profit making.

Astute observers will see that this liturgy was the dominant thinking up to the Great Depression. Such views were discredited and roundly repudiated during the Depression and the more prosperous postwar era. The traditional capitalist austerity view in the face of economic crisis, as John Maynard Keynes definitively demonstrated in his *General Theory of Employment, Interest, and Money*, offered little real hope of escaping economic stagnation. Today, because such supply-side capitalist views are generally accepted as the starting point for economic policymaking by both political parties, there is likewise little hope to escape the economic stagnation in which the system is now mired. A deepening tendency toward stagnation is, in fact, endemic to the entire phase of monopoly-finance capital.[32] In this context all workers, and the impoverished and the unemployed in particular, carry the brunt of austerity, having little economic power and scarcely more political leverage.[33]

Figure 5.2 starkly illustrates the trend. Since the 1970s increases in real GDP have been detached from real median family income—a further manifestation of the dramatic gains made by the Dollarocracy. The increased income created in the economy has gone almost

FIGURE 5.2: Index of Growth in Real GDP Per Capita and Real Median Household Income, 1960–2010

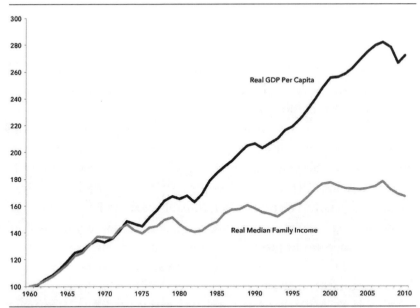

Sources: "Median family income, 1947–2010 (constant 2011 dollars)," Economic Policy Institute, Open Data, http://stateofworkingamerica.org/data; "GDP per capita (constant 2000 dollars)," World Bank National Accounts Data and OECD National Accounts Data Files, http://databank.worldbank.org.

entirely to the wealthy, not to the workers. This is even more startling when one considers that these were decades when women entered the labor force in large numbers, increasing the number of workers, and hours worked, per household.[34] As a result, higher consumer spending on the part of the larger part of the population became more dependent on debt, so that households could maintain their standard of living. People increasingly were driven to utilize the equity in their houses like credit cards, which contributed to a vast speculative bubble in the economy—until the bubble burst in the 2007–2009 Great Financial Crisis.[35] With consumption once again contracting, markets were saturated, and business, faced with vast amounts of idle productive capacity, saw even less reason to invest. As a result, U.S. corporations in 2012 are sitting on around $1.7 trillion in cash and have no plans to invest it because there is no market demand for additional products.

The first decade of the new century was the worst since the Great Depression—a true lost decade that lived off speculation and debt until the markets crashed. And the current decade, left to the policies of Dollarocracy, will almost certainly be worse in terms of growth than the last one. Not only has the economic pie been sliced to give ever larger portions to the top 1 percent, but it has also stopped growing so there are fewer resources for everyone else or for socially necessary projects. Working-class living standards are plummeting.

There may be no policy solutions to all of the growth problems endemic to contemporary corporate capitalism—it may well be that consideration of a new economy is in order. But, in the short term, some policies could stimulate greater employment and more sustainable economic development than the United States has enjoyed in recent decades.[36] These policies—like strict antitrust law enforcement, progressive taxation, strict controls over credit and financial markets, single-payer health insurance, vibrant labor unions, and massive public works projects—bump up against corporate interests and the ethos of Dollarocracy, even when some of the policies would benefit capitalists themselves.

This is an issue that has perplexed many left-liberal reformers. How can the capitalists be so shortsighted as to oppose the use of government to build infrastructure, create jobs, and end stagnation when the historical record appears to demonstrate that democratic governments have it within their power to make capitalism operate far more efficiently and effectively? Can't these business interests look at the historical track record and see that ultimately capitalism was far more stable in the higher-wage, higher-growth, relatively full-employment economies following the New Deal, and in the social democratic nations of northern Europe? Why do they obsessively cling to the antiquated economic theories that were discredited in the 1930s and 1940s, which have led present-day capitalism to crisis, stagnation, and decline? Some of the more independent, free-thinking liberal economists like Paul Krugman are almost apoplectic as they chronicle the absurdity and tragedy of this apparent paradox.

In his 2012 book *End This Depression Now!* Krugman supplies an answer to this riddle. He cites a classic 1943 essay by Michal Kalecki, the great Polish economist who independently of Keynes developed the crucial breakthroughs in the theory of employment in the 1930s associated with the Keynesian revolution.[37] Kalecki argued that if the public realizes the government has the resources to establish full employment, it would undermine the notion that the central duty of the government is to instill business confidence so that it will invest in creating jobs. If the population widely understood that government policies could guarantee full employment, Kalecki observed, a "powerful indirect control over government policy" enjoyed by business would end, a prospect discomfiting to business.[38] "This sounded a bit extreme to me the first time I read it," Krugman writes, "but it now seems all too plausible."[39] A successful state generating full employment might logically lead people to question why capitalists have so much economic power and what purpose they provide that could not be better provided by more democratic means. In short, the wealthy and corporations would prefer a depressed and stagnant economy to a growing one led by state policies, if those in any way jeopardized their control over the government and their dominant position in society.

Of course, there are other possible answers to the above riddle as well. Monopoly-finance capital at the beginning of the twenty-first century is quite a different animal from the "golden age" monopoly capitalism of the post–Second World War years. Today we are faced with a far more financialized and globalized system. Financial power has gained in relation to industrial power and is increasingly in the driver's seat, economically and politically.[40] Neoliberalism is not simply an aberration or a misstep but represents the political counterpart of this more financialized system. Capitalism today is arguably more interested in protecting its financial assets and capital gains (and its monopoly power) than in the risky enterprise of investment in new productive capacity. Much of production (and employment) is globalized, relying on cheap labor in the global South, or what is termed global labor arbitrage.[41] In this transformed environment the old Keynesian, nation-state-based "solutions" are less viable than ever.

The fact remains that Dollarocracy, to put it mildly, has a much greater comfort zone with stagnation and austerity than the general population.

Dollarocracy, then, is more than wealthy and powerful corporate lobbies dictating policies and getting lucrative subsidies, favorable regulations, collapsing unions, and low tax rates. It represents the triumph of neoliberalism and the transformation of the political domain into a domain of dollars, making the notorious corruption of the Gilded Age seem tame by comparison. Dollarocracy raids the Treasury. It strips the government for parts, sometimes called the "outsourcing" of public services, and handing these off to corporations, which increasingly manage our prisons, conduct key military functions, and even direct (while privatizing and degrading) our schools. These private firms then generate guaranteed healthy profits by tapping into public monies, and in some cases by degrading public services so as to promote private "alternatives" funded with public money. The evidence today suggests that while outsourcing is becoming a corporate cash cow, there are few if any benefits for taxpayers and citizens and many problems, not the least of which is a lack of accountability.[42] The government's own bipartisan study of military outsourcing in Iraq and Afghanistan, for example, revealed that of the $180 billion in outsourced contracts it examined, at least $30 billion was stolen, lost, or wasted.[43] Not surprisingly, one of the areas in which the Dollarcrats have cut the federal budget to the bone is overseeing and enforcing these contracts.[44] It is basically open season for graft and all kinds of chicanery.

We find it difficult to avoid Lessig's conclusion that the first and immediate effect of the corrupt political regime in Washington is "bad governance."[45] Thomas Frank argues that this is not ironic; it is precisely the point of Dollarocracy. What better way, he argues, to make the case for government being inherently evil than to run government in a grotesquely incompetent and corrupt manner when in power?[46]

The Consequences of Dollarocracy

Dollarocracy exacerbates three threats to the survival of the Republic: the environmental crisis, the military expansion, and the erosion of civil liberties.

The first of these, the environmental crisis, has received just a smidgen of the attention it requires. The ongoing economic activities in the United States are taking us ever closer to the climate cliff and away from the dramatic shift in policies that climatologists and other scientists say are necessary for human existence to remain even remotely close to what has been the case for the past 10,000 years. To some extent this is simply a consequence of a market economy, where the environment is an "externality" and will always be given short shrift by economic actors who have competitive pressures upon them to maximize profit regardless of the consequences.

But the environmental problem is greatly magnified under Dollarocracy, because as corporate interests effectively dominate government, they undermine the capacity of the democratic state to address market failure on behalf of the general public.[47] Indeed, facing up to the ecological calamity seems so impossible for Dollarocracy that it has abandoned even feigning interest; in recent years there has been a pronounced effort, bankrolled in part by energy corporations, to deny that environmental crises even exist. Dollarocracy does not give the impression of having much of a "long-term view." The only quote of Keynes that its proponents seem to have remembered is his quip, "In the long run, we are all dead."[48]

Second, the United States accounts for around half of the world's military spending (counting only its acknowledged military expenditures), although it represents less than 5 percent of the world's population.[49] The United States has a massive nuclear arsenal and enough weapons to kill every living creature many times over. It has some one thousand overseas military bases and installations, extending over much of the globe, and is engaged in a chain of wars and military buildups in Asia (as well as in other areas of the global South)—so that there is never any peace, much like Oceania's war with Eurasia in *Nineteen Eighty-Four*.[50] Few Americans have any idea why the nation is at war or how one war leads to another, or indeed about the nature of U.S. empire. War and empire are complex matters, but the one factor that is certain is that corporations are making a killing on the trillion-dollar war and war-preparation budget and on the exploitation of much of the globe that this makes possible. And they provide an exceptionally powerful lobby to see that the imperial war complex remains sacrosanct. The peace forces on the other side are equipped with excellent arguments and a proverbial peashooter. The balance of power has shifted dramatically to the forces of militarism; wars that once would be protested and ended after a few years now can go on permanently, even with precious little popular support. For U.S. capital, military spending serves as a sponge to absorb excess productive capacity and to support employment. It increases profit margins and overall profits, and keeps the world open for multinational corporations.

Dollarocracy may allow for some cuts in military spending—after all, who are we in an arms race with when our military spending rivals that of the rest of the world put together?—but even at its outer limits, these cuts will only be marginal. As Andrew Bacevich states, "Within Washington, the voices carrying weight in any national security 'debate' all share a predisposition for sustaining very high levels of military spending for reasons having increasingly little to do with the well-being of the country."[51] The likelihood is just as good that militarism will increase, as it is one of Dollarocracy's favorite forms of economic pump-priming. (Debt is the other.)[52]

Third, as inequality grows and corruption deepens, our civil liberties are on softer ground. Militarism also expedites this process, with its emphasis on secrecy and hierarchy. Under Dollarocracy the foundation of our freedoms is slipping. This is seen most directly in the Patriot Act and other national security measures that compromise our constitutional liberties, and give the state extraordinary ability to police the citizenry on flimsy grounds. As Daniel Ellsberg has commented, "All the crimes Richard Nixon committed against me are now legal."[53]

Under Dollarocracy the threat to civil liberties is enhanced because of the sharp increase in government outsourcing of military activities, prison management, and surveillance to corporations like Halliburton and Xe (formerly Blackwater) that are even less accountable than the government. But it is also seen in the broader corporate invasion of privacy, typified by marketing and the Internet, where there is enormous money to be made monitoring and collecting information on people all their waking hours. The cozy relationship between the government and our largest corporations makes this process easier rather than more difficult, as we saw when Edward Snowden revealed that the National Security Agency is monitoring our phone and Internet communications. On top of these invasions of our privacy, corporations themselves, along with law enforcement, have engaged in spying on those who lawfully oppose Dollarocracy, including Occupy activists and anti-Keystone XL pipeline campaigners.

We are witnessing the collapse of the "rule of law," the *essential* democratic value that everyone is treated equally before the law. It has never been the case that the rich and poor, powerful and power-less, have received evenhanded treatment before the law. Even when they do receive formally equal treatment it simply exacerbates the real inequality of their positions. As Anatole France said, "The law, in its majestic equality, forbids the rich as well as the poor to sleep under bridges, to beg in the streets, and to steal bread." But under Dollarocracy the rules themselves have become more and more one-sided, enshrining double standards that explicitly favor the rich and those serving their interests. Those "too big to fail" receive bailouts, and everyone else pays the penalty. Government officials face no consequences for illegal wars or torture or violations of interna-tional law. Powerful bankers and telecom company executives face no prosecution for lawbreaking. Yet poor people are being rounded up, prosecuted, and incarcerated in record numbers, for crimes that pale in comparison. As Glenn Greenwald forcefully documents, the legitimacy of the entire system hangs in the balance.[54]

If there is any sort of iron law, it is that civil liberties cannot sur-vive in a sharply economically unequal society. One need not look at a Pinochet-style police state to get the answer; in fact, for our pur-poses it is better to look at pseudodemocracies like Mexico or Egypt for much of the late twentieth century. In those societies the wealthy and elites tended to have a reasonable amount of freedom, but that freedom diminished as one went down the social pecking order and as the political ideas became more threatening to those in power. As Dollarocracy continues to widen the class divide, and generate ever more poverty, this looks more and more to be the U.S. future as well.

The present state of freedom for the poorest 25 percent of Americans is a far cry from that experienced by the wealthiest 10 percent. One major factor has been the war on drugs, which has been the major domestic policy initiative over the past three decades. This war has been directed overwhelmingly at poor communities, especially people of color, and has led to an extraordinary increase in prisons and prisoners, often for mere possession of illegal recreational drugs. Prison and police spending has increased markedly compared to spending on education by government over the past three decades. It is Dollarocracy's favorite civilian government program, the domes-tic version of military spending.[55] In 1980, for example, 10 percent of California's budget went to higher education and 3 percent to prisons; in 2010, almost 11 percent went to prisons and only 7.5 percent to higher education.[56] As Michelle Alexander documents, the drug war has shredded constitutional protections and consigned a significant percentage of poor and working-class African American males to permanent status as felons, which means a formal loss of the right to vote and protection from employment and housing discrimination. She makes a compelling case that this system is so extensive it constitutes a "new Jim Crow."[57]

In sum, Dollarocracy is an excellent system for those with plenty of dollars but not very good for everyone else. And eventually the problems that it creates or accentuates—and makes much more difficult to address—result in an unsatisfactory world for everyone.

Politics and Depoliticization

Some two decades ago a number of our smartest observers, people like Kevin Phillips and William Greider, saw that the problems of our emerging Dollarocracy were mounting. They both anticipated or advocated the equivalent of another New Deal, to bend the stick back toward democracy.[58] Lester Thurow noted in the early 1990s that economic inequality had already grown in the United States at a greater pace than any other nation in history during peacetime. Many expected a popular revolt, like that periodically seen in the streets of Paris or Athens. Yet nothing close to reform was in the offing, and the problems have only grown worse, much worse. Why this has been the case has been one of the important issues of our times. Why it should remain so under Dollarocracy, as problems grow ever more severe, is even more puzzling.

A response emerged, finally, and thankfully, in the great public popular outbursts of 2011. But simply to point to these welcome demonstrations begs the question of why it has taken so long for such protest to emerge—and why they seem to ebb more than flow.

"Depoliticization" is the term to describe this phenomenon; it means making political activity unattractive and unproductive for the bulk of the citizenry. This is, to varying degrees, an important and underappreciated issue for all democratic societies in which there are pronounced economic inequalities. It moved to the fore when all the great battles over suffrage were won and there was universal adult suffrage. Scholars have pointed out that some, perhaps much, of the impetus for the creation of the field of "public relations" a century ago was to lessen popular understanding of, and opposition to, corporate power, and to discourage informed popular participation in politics. The idea was to "take the risk out of democracy" in a society where the majority of potential voters may not be sympathetic to the idea that government's job was first and foremost to serve the needs of big business and the wealthy few.[59] An omnipresent commercial culture that emphasizes consumption over civic values, along with a lack of organized political power, goes a long way toward greasing the wheels for depoliticization. Twentieth-century voter turnout among eligible adults in the United States has been low compared to much of the rest of the world and its own nineteenth-century standard. It has been a generally depoliticized society, even before Dollarocracy.

The value of depoliticization is well understood to rulers, who tend to prefer a population that voluntarily disengages rather then one that needs to be suppressed violently to get it to cooperate. The actions of General Augusto Pinochet, the convicted serial human rights abuser, torturer, mass murderer, and dictator who (with U.S. support) overthrew Chile's elected socialist government in 1973, speak louder than words. Five years into his dictatorship Pinochet could see that Chile would have to return eventually to some semblance of constitutional civilian rule, as mass demonstrations were growing, and even for a psychopath like Pinochet, there were effective limits to the use of violence. He commissioned the top political scientist in Chile who supported his dictatorship to draft a new constitution for a democratic Chile. What Pinochet wanted to prevent was a return to pre-1973 Chile, in which voter turnout rates were in the 90 percent neighborhood and the citizens were routinely regarded as among the most engaged and civic-minded in the world.

How to solve the problem of having a democracy in form but not in substance? Pinochet sent the political scientist to the United States to learn how to devise a democracy American-style, one where relatively few people care much about politics, if only because no matter which party wins nothing much ever changes. The structure of the economy is effectively off-limits for political debate. Pinochet's constitution was enacted and Chile returned to civilian government under it in 1990. By 2011, Chile was rocked with the largest student demonstrations in its history, with one demand being the replacement of Pinochet's constitution with one democratically drafted and approved, a constitution more concerned with creating the basis for participatory self-government than protecting property.

Under Dollarocracy the promotion of depoliticization moves front and center. The uprisings of the 1960s sent tremors through elite circles. The elite group the Trilateral Commission published its report *The Crisis of Democracy* in 1975 in response to this threat of too much democracy by the wrong people. It concluded that "the effective operation of a democratic political system usually requires some measure of apathy and noninvolvement on the part of some individuals and groups."[60] Dollarocracy depends and thrives upon depoliticization. If one looks closely one will see that the dollarcrats don't campaign to get everyone to vote as a civic duty. Quite the contrary. Beneath it all is a candid recognition that the policies of Dollarocracy are fundamentally elitist and unpopular with the majority of the people. Paul Weyrich, founder of the Heritage Foundation and one of the great organizers of the corporate right since the 1970s, put it bluntly in a 1980 speech to conservative activists: "I don't want everybody to vote. . . . Our leverage in the elections quite candidly goes up as the voting populace goes down."[61]

The United States of the past generation is a classic example of a depoliticized society: most people know little or nothing about politics and are estranged from it except at a superficial level. Young people are constantly reminded it is not "cool" to be political, and the point of life is to take care of number one. The evidence suggests that most people, especially working-class and poor people, have no influence over politicians and policy, so to the extent people understand their real status they will lose incentive to participate. Regardless of which party wins it seems like nothing ever changes that much, at least for the better; elections are often fought over symbolic issues only loosely related to actual policies or actual political values. It is a game played by and for elites. But it is a spectator event for others, who are seen by the elites as objects to be manipulated.

Lessig recently described an example of the cynicism of politicians toward voters. He tells of being at a 2011 event with White

House senior political adviser David Axelrod and Beltway celebrity journalist Joe Klein. Lessig, a former colleague and longtime supporter of Obama's, had assembled a sizable number of 2008 campaign speeches, in which Obama professed his commitment to taking money and corruption out of politics when he got to the White House. It was a major theme of his campaign by any reckoning. Lessig explained to Axelrod and Klein that the young people he worked with who were all strong Obama supporters and organizers in 2008 had become incredibly disillusioned when they saw how, as soon as Obama got into power, it was business-as-usual for lobbying, pro-corporate policies, and endemic systemic corruption. It became clear nothing was going to be proposed, let alone enacted. Axelrod and Klein each responded with bewilderment, saying they found it hard to believe anyone would take the rhetoric in campaign speeches seriously.[62]

It is worth noting at this point that the electoral system itself goes a long way toward contributing to political disengagement. The two parties have rigged the system—in a manner having little to do with the U.S. Constitution—so that it is virtually impossible to launch a credible third party. One is reminded of the late great George Carlin's famous line that Americans love choice and have plenty of it . . . — except where it actually matters, such as with telephone companies or political parties. In politics the duopoly acts, as economic theory explains, much more like a classical monopoly than a competitive marketplace.

The two parties also gerrymander—i.e., draw district boundaries—so that as many congressional and legislative districts as possible are divvied up between themselves, and only a minority are competitive, except in rare landslide years. As a rule, a good 85 percent of House members are in what have been gerrymandered to be "safe seats," and they rarely face a tough reelection battle, despite the strong generic unpopularity of Congress.[63] Often the only state or federal contests a voter faces that are remotely in play are statewide races where gerrymandering is impossible. At that point one butts up against the matter of how much money it takes to run a credible campaign.

Is it any wonder people have become demoralized and depoliticized? Figure 5.3 demonstrates the low level of voting among adults

FIGURE 5.3: Voter Turnout* in U.S. Elections, 1960–2010

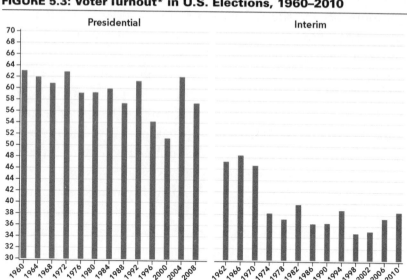

*Voter turnout is here defined as the percentage of the voting-age population that voted.

Source: Voter Turnout Website, International Institute for Democracy and Electoral Assistance (International IDEA), accessed September 20, 2011, http://idea.int/vt.

in the United States and how it has evolved over the past forty years. Elections in presidential election years get the greatest turnout of voting-age citizens, though since the early 1970s it has seldom broken 60 percent. Most other elections are lucky to get 40 percent turnout, which means one can get elected governor of Virginia (in an odd-year election race) or mayor of Chicago or countless other state and local offices with the votes of fewer than one in six voting-age adults. So much for majority rule. That being said, what may be most striking is not how few Americans vote compared to other democracies, but rather how many actually do vote in view of the factors undermining the legitimacy of the process.

The best predictor for whether or not a person votes is their income. Figure 5.4 compares the relative number of voters in the lowest and highest income quintiles. On average during the past four presidential elections, despite increasing low-income voter turnout, for every ten voters from the lowest income quintile there are sixteen voters in the highest income quintile. Voter participation increases step-by-step with income. Dollarocracy is based on a system where those with more dollars have more reason to vote. John Kenneth

FIGURE 5.4: Ratio of Number of Voters in the Top Quintile to Bottom Quintile in Presidential Elections

Year	Ratio of Top to Bottom Quintiles
1996	1.7
2000	1.6
2004	1.5
2008	1.5
Average	**1.6**

Sources: U.S. Census Bureau, Current Population Survey, "Voting and Registration Supplement," 1996, 2000, 2004, and 2008, DataFerret Microdata http://dataferrett.census.gov; Robert Sahr, "Inflation Conversion Factors," Oregon State University, 2011, http://oregonstate.edu.

Note: Cases with survey responses other than "yes" or "no" in the survey were dropped. Household income amounts for each year were converted into constant 2008 dollars to generate quintiles for each year. Over the entire 1996–2008 period the average household income was $102,052 or more for the top quintile, and $24,912 or less for the bottom quintile.

Galbraith noted two decades ago that the pro-corporate policies of the U.S. government did not reflect the desires of a majority of Americans, merely a majority of those who voted.[64]

Cases with survey responses other than "yes" or "no" in the survey were dropped. Household income amounts for each year were converted into constant 2008 dollars to generate quintiles for each year. Over the entire 1996–2008 period the average household income was $102,052 or more for the top quintile, and $24,912 or less for the bottom quintile.

The popular support for Dollarocracy in the United States—demonstrated since the Reagan era through elections—has always been overrated. As far back as the 1970s, research by scholars like Walter Dean Burnham lent credence to the notion that if Americans voted across income levels at the same rate as most northern European nations, the nation would be electing governments with far greater sympathy to social democratic policies.[65] Research demonstrated that Americans have not moved to the right on a battery of core political issues since the 1970s; indeed, they may have become more progressive.[66]

Research into voting and income, shown in Figure 5.5, suggests that if Americans at all income levels voted at an 80 percent turnout rate—typical in the nineteenth-century United States and some other democracies today—and if they voted in the same proportion

FIGURE 5.5: Hypothetical Number of Additional Votes* Assuming an Eighty Percent Turnout Rate for All Income Groups

Election Year	Democrat	Republican	Net Additional Votes to Democrats
1996	14,726,860	10,511,157	4,215,703
2000	14,838,948	12,712,427	2,126,521
2004	12,943,479	11,003,389	1,940,090
2008	13,827,797	9,633,106	4,194,690

* Vote totals do not equal the total popular vote because those not reporting income were left out of the calculations, and because they were computed based on U.S. Census data, not actual voting tallies.[67]

Sources and Notes: See endnote 67.

for parties as the other members of their income group do at present, the Democrats would have won landslide victories so large as to represent a critical realignment of party politics in three of the last four presidential elections, and would have been in shooting distance of winning in 2004. With voting equalized across class lines, Democrats would likely have dominant, possibly veto-proof, majorities in Congress.

Of course, this is all hypothetical and a thought game; if 80 percent of all Americans voted, the current parties as they are known and understood likely would be considerably different from what they are today, or they would not exist. To attract such a wide working-class vote would require a transformed Democratic Party, more like what it was in the 1930s during the New Deal, and therefore would mean a considerable break with the Dollarocracy.

A striking indication of the conversion of the Democrats into Dollarocracy's junior partner came in 1984, when Walter Mondale was the party's presidential nominee. By conventional standards, the chances of defeating President Reagan—then benefitting from an economic recovery—were all but hopeless. Early in the campaign, Mondale's aides prepared a 250-page internal report that concluded that "the only way Mondale can win is by pitching his appeal to the white working class and minorities, not the middle class." Mike Ford, Mondale's field director, argued that a Mondale victory "is nearly impossible with the current electorate. . . . We must consider dramatic and perhaps high-risk strategies." Ford specifically recommended an intense voter registration drive to get six million new black, Hispanic, and union voters. For the effort to succeed, it would be imperative to offer the new voters a compelling populist political interest in actually voting. Democratic Party leaders rejected this proposal, and opted to use available funds for get-out-the-vote campaigns among the existing electorate.[68] One can only speculate why the Democrats elected to ignore this approach in 1984, and thereafter, but the instinct to appeal to business and its resources looms large.

Nothing has changed for the Democrats in the subsequent years. As two leading political scientists put it in 2002, "Today neither party makes much effort to mobilize the tens of millions of poorer and less well educated Americans who are not currently part of the electorate."[69]

My argument is not that all politicians from both parties adhere to these postulates like some sort of blood oath. My point is that these austerity principles have become the default position of economic debates within the mainstream because they reflect the values and interests of very powerful interests, of Dollarocracy. It is true that some politicians, especially backbencher Democrats who truly find aspects of Dollarocracy's economics offensive, or those needing to scrounge votes in a tight election, will make bold but hollow public pronouncements contrary to this received economic wisdom. In recent years, on the whole the Democrats, when push comes to shove, have rarely challenged these presuppositions in any meaningful manner.

A majority of voters are opposed to the current plutocratic system. This poses a major problem for Dollarocracy. The notion that conservative, corporate interests and their fundamentalist allies in the religious right could win free and fair elections, a common belief back in the Reagan era, has been quietly abandoned. So now the dollarcrats bring a massive influx of cash into campaigns effectively to buy elections; for every voter the TV ads might influence there are innumerable people who will be so grossed out as to become apolitical. That is perhaps almost as good from the Dollarcratic standpoint. But neither buying elections nor driving away voters turned off by an inane political culture was deemed sufficient.

Just as essential was destroying the basis of a potential opposition, and particularly the supply of money to those forces that might oppose Dollarocracy. Much of the impetus for eliminating public-sector unions—private sector unionization has already collapsed over the past three decades—is that these have traditionally been the only non-corporate groups that rank in the list of top ten campaign funders, and all the other groups on the list give largely to Dollarcratic politicians. Those most interested in maintaining the Dollarcratic political and economic structure (Republicans but also most Democratic Party high rollers) will do everything in their power to maintain the draconian restrictions on ex-prisoners being able to vote, as well as maintain the drug war that removes countless poor people, especially African American men, from the voting rolls every year. This is now more than a question of a given election, but rather a necessity in keeping democracy from functioning—a necessity for the ruling class/power elite.

This has now been extended into a more general strategy aimed at suppressing the vote among constituencies most hostile to Dollarocracy, hence shrinking the number of actual voters to make the range of outcomes skew heavily toward candidates doing the bidding of corporate interests. Most striking, in fourteen states where they held control of both branches of the legislature and the governorship, the Republicans passed strict voter identification rules and a number of related measures with the very thinly disguised purpose of simply keeping poor, minority, and young voters away from the polls, and making voting such a pain in the ass that likely anti-Dollarocracy voters will simply blow it off. The notion that there is a serious problem with "voter fraud" justifying these extreme measures has been systematically and meticulously discredited by Lorraine Minnite.[70] "Study after study," E. J. Dionne writes, "has shown that fraud by voters is not a major problem—and is less of a problem than how hard many states make it for people to vote in the first place. Some of the new laws, such as those limiting the number of days for early voting, have little plausible connection to battling fraud."[71] A comprehensive review of the 2011 voter law changes by the Brennan Center for Justice at the NYU Law School concluded that they "could make it significantly harder for more than 5 million eligible voters to cast ballots in 2012."[72] One civil rights advocate terms these changes "the most serious setback to voting rights in this country in a century."[73]

None of this should surprise us. Capitalist democracy has always been more about capitalism than democracy. The trappings of democracy have served as a formidable tool for ensuring stability in a society dominated by those with substantial property. But the heyday of the union of property, legitimacy, and stability in the name of "democracy" is now in the past. The carefully cultivated belief that we live in a society governed by the *demos* (the popular classes) is patently absurd in the face of the reality of Dollarocracy. The task before us, then, is to shine so bright a light on the gross abrogation of democracy in the contemporary United States as to give rise to a social revolt aimed at the creation of a genuinely democratic and egalitarian order: what I term a post-capitalist democracy.

PART TWO

Money Doesn't Talk,
It Swears

6

The U.S. Imperial Triangle
and Military Spending

THE UNITED STATES IS unique today among major states in the degree of its reliance on military spending and its determination to stand astride the world, militarily as well as economically. No other country in the post–Second World War world has been so globally destructive or inflicted so many war fatalities. Since 2001, acknowledged U.S. national defense spending has increased by almost 60 percent in real dollar terms to a level in 2007 of $553 billion. This is higher than at any point since the Second World War (though lower than previous decades as a percentage of GDP). Based on such official figures, the United States is reported by the Stockholm International Peace Research Institute (SIPRI) as accounting for 45 percent of world military expenditures. Yet, so gargantuan and labyrinthine are U.S. military expenditures that their true magnitude reached $1 trillion in 2007.[1]

Externally, these are necessary expenditures of world empire. Internally, they represent, as Michal Kalecki was the first to suggest, an imperial triangle of state-financed military production, media propaganda, and real/imagined economic-employment effects that has become a deeply entrenched and self-perpetuating feature of the U.S. social order.[2]

Many analysts today view the present growth of U.S. militarism and imperialism as largely divorced from the earlier Cold War history of the United States, which was commonly seen as a response to the threat represented by the Soviet Union. Placed against this backdrop the current turn to war and war preparation appears to numerous commentators to lack a distinct target, despite concerns about global terrorism, and to be mainly the product of irrational hubris on the part of U.S. leaders. Even as insightful a left historian as Eric Hobsbawm has recently adopted this general perspective. Thus in his 2008 book *On Empire* Hobsbawm writes:

> Frankly, I can't make sense of what has happened in the United States since 9/11 that enabled a group of political crazies to realize long-held plans for an unaccompanied solo performance of world supremacy. . . . Today a radical right-wing regime seeks to mobilize "true Americans" against some evil outside force and against a world that does not recognize the uniqueness, the superiority, the manifest destiny of America. . . . In effect, the most obvious danger of war today arises from the global ambitions of an uncontrollable and apparently irrational government in Washington. . . . To give America the best chance of learning to return from megalomania to rational foreign policy is the most immediate and urgent task of international politics.[3]

Such a view, which sees the United States as under the influence of a new irrationalism introduced by George W. Bush and a cabal of neoconservative "political crazies," and consequently calls for a return from "megalomania to rational foreign policy," downplays the larger historical and structural forces at work that connect the Cold War and post–Cold War imperial eras. In contrast, a more realistic perspective, I believe, can be obtained by looking at the origins of the U.S. "military ascendancy" (as C. Wright Mills termed it) in the early Cold War years and the centrality this has assumed in the constitution of the U.S. empire and economy up to the present.[4]

The Permanent War Economy and Military Keynesianism

In January 1944 Charles E. Wilson, president of General Electric and executive vice chairman of the War Production Board, delivered a speech to the Army Ordnance Association advocating a permanent war economy. According to the plan Wilson proposed on that occasion, every major corporation should have a "liaison" representative with the military, who would be given a commission as a colonel in the Reserve. This would form the basis of a program, to be initiated by the president as commander-in-chief in cooperation with the War and Navy departments, designed to bind corporations and the military together into a single unified armed forces–industrial complex. "What is more natural and logical," he asked, "than that we should henceforth mount our national policy upon the solid fact of an industrial capacity for war, and a research capacity for war that is already 'in being'? It seems to me anything less is foolhardy." Wilson went on to indicate that in this plan the part to be played by Congress was restricted to voting for the needed funds. Further, it was essential that industry be allowed to play its central role in this new warfare state without being hindered politically "or thrown to the fanatical isolationist fringe [and] tagged with a 'merchants-of-death' label."

In calling even before the Second World War had come to a close for a "continuing program of industrial preparedness" for war, Charles E. Wilson (sometimes referred to as "General Electric Wilson" to distinguish him from "General Motors Wilson"—Charles Erwin Wilson, president of General Motors and Eisenhower's secretary of defense) was articulating a view that was to characterize the U.S. oligarchy as a whole during the years immediately following the Second World War. In earlier eras it had been assumed that there was an economic "guns and butter" trade-off, and that military spending had to occur at the expense of other sectors of the economy. However, one of the lessons of the economic expansion in Nazi Germany, followed by the experience of the United States itself in arming for the Second World War, was that big increases in military spending could act as huge stimulants to the economy. In just six years under the influence of the Second World War, the U.S. economy expanded by 70 percent, finally recovering from the Great Depression. The early Cold War era thus saw the emergence of what later came to be known as "military Keynesianism": the view that by promoting effective demand and supporting monopoly profits military spending could help place a floor under U.S. capitalism.[5]

John Maynard Keynes, in his landmark *General Theory of Employment, Interest and Money*, published in 1936, in the midst of the Depression, argued that the answer to economic stagnation was to promote effective demand through government spending. The bastardized Keynesianism that came to be known as "military Keynesianism" was the view that this was best effected with the least negative consequences for big business by focusing on military spending. As Joan Robinson, one of Keynes's younger colleagues, critically explained in her iconoclastic lecture, "The Second Crisis of Economic Theory," before the American Economic Association on December 27, 1971:

> The most convenient thing for a government to spend on is armaments. The military-industrial complex [thus] took charge. I do not think it plausible to suppose that the Cold War and several hot wars were invented just to solve the employment problem. But certainly they have had that effect. The system had the support not only of the corporations who make profits under it and the workers who got jobs, but also of the economists who advocated government loan-expenditure as a prophylactic against stagnation. Whatever were the deeper forces leading to the hypertrophy of military power *after* the world war was over, certainly they could not have had such free play if the doctrine of sound finance had still been respected. It was the so-called Keynesians who persuaded successive Presidents that there is no harm in a budget deficit and left the military-industrial complex to take advantage of it. So it has come about that Keynes' pleasant daydream was turned into a nightmare of terror.[6]

The first to theorize this tendency toward military Keynesianism under monopoly capitalism was the Polish economist Michal Kalecki (most famous, as Robinson pointed out in the above-mentioned lecture, for having discovered the essentials of Keynes's *General Theory* before Keynes himself). In a 1943 essay on "The Political Aspects of Full Employment" and in subsequent essays, Kalecki argued that monopoly capital had a deep aversion to increased civilian government spending due to its intrusion on the commodity market and the sphere of private profit, but that this did not apply in the same way to military spending, which was seen by the vested interests as adding to, rather than crowding out, profits. If absorption of the massive economic surplus of large corporate capital through increased government spending was the key to accumulation in post–Second World War U.S. capitalism, this was dependent principally on military expenditures, or what Kalecki in 1956 labeled "the armament-imperialist complex." This resulted in a "high degree of utilization" of productive capacity and "counteracted the disrupting influence of the increase in the relative share of accumulation of big business in the national product."[7]

For Kalecki this new military-supported regime of accumulation that came to characterize U.S. monopoly capital by the mid-1950s established a strong political-economic foundation for its own rule "based on the following [imperial] triangle":

1. Imperialism contributes to a relatively high level of employment through expenditures on armaments and ancillary purposes and through the maintenance of a large body of armed forces and government employees.
2. The mass communications media, working under the auspices of the ruling class, emits propaganda aimed at securing the support of the population for this armament-imperialist setup.
3. The high level of employment and the standard of living increased considerably as compared with before the war (as a result of the rise in the productivity of labor), and this facilitated the absorption of this propaganda to the broad masses of the population.

Mass communication occupied a central place in this imperial triangle. An essential part of Kalecki's argument was that "the mass communication media, such as the daily press, radio, and television in the United States, are largely under the control of the ruling class." As none other than Charles E. (General Electric) Wilson, then defense mobilization director, put it in a speech to the American Newspaper Publishers Association on April 26, 1951, the job of the media was to bring "public opinion, *as marshaled by the press*" to the support of the permanent war effort (italics added).[8]

The result by the mid-1950s was a fairly stable militarized economy, in which intertwined imperial, political-economic, and communication factors all served to reinforce the new military-imperial order.

Kalecki observed that U.S. trade unions were "part and parcel of the armament-imperialist setup. Workers in the United States are not duller and trade union leaders are not more reactionary 'by nature' than in other capitalist countries. Rather, the political situation in the United States is simply, in accordance with the precepts of historical materialism, the unavoidable consequence of economic developments and of characteristics of the superstructure of monopoly capitalism in its advanced stage." All of this pointed to what Harry Magdoff was to call the essential "one-ness of national security and business interests" that came to characterize the U.S. political economy and empire.[9]

Many of Kalecki's ideas were developed further by Paul Baran and Paul Sweezy in 1966 in *Monopoly Capital*. Baran and Sweezy argued there were at least five political-economic-imperial ends propelling the U.S. oligarchy in the 1950s and '60s toward the creation of a massive military establishment: (1) defending U.S. global hegemony and the empire of capital against external threats in the form of a wave of revolutions erupting throughout the world, simplistically viewed in terms of a monolithic Communist threat centered in the Soviet Union; (2) creating an internationally "secure" platform for U.S. corporations to expand and monopolize economic opportunities abroad; (3) forming a government-sponsored research and development sector that would be dominated by big business; (4) generating a more complacent population at home, made less recalcitrant under the nationalistic influence of perpetual war and war preparation; and (5) soaking up the nation's vast surplus productive capacity, thus helping to stave off economic stagnation, through the promotion of high-profit, low-risk (to business) military spending. The combined result of such political-economic-imperial factors was the creation of the largest, most deeply entrenched and persistent "peacetime" war machine that the world had ever seen.[10]

Like Kalecki, Baran and Sweezy argued that the U.S. oligarchy kept a "tight rein on civilian [government] spending," which, they suggested, "had about reached its outer limits" as a percentage of national income "by 1939," but was nonetheless "open-handed with the military." Government pump-priming operations therefore occurred largely through spending on wars and war preparations in the service of empire. The Pentagon naturally made sure that bases and armaments industries were spread around the United States and that numerous corporations profited from military spending, thus maximizing congressional support due to the effects on states and districts.[11]

For members of the U.S. oligarchy and their hangers-on, the virtuous circle of mutually reinforcing military spending and economic growth represented by military Keynesianism was something to be celebrated rather than held up to criticism. Harvard economist Sumner Slichter explained to a banker's convention in October 1949 that as long as Cold War spending persisted, a severe economic depression was "difficult to conceive." The Cold War "increases the demand for goods, helps sustain a high level of employment, accelerates technological progress and thus helps the country to raise its standard of living. . . . So we may thank the Russians for helping make capitalism in the United States work better than ever."

Similarly, *U.S. News and World Report* told its readers on May 14, 1950 (a month before the outbreak of the Korean War):

> Government planners figure they have found the magic formula for almost endless good times. They are now beginning to wonder if there may not be something to perpetual motion after all. *Cold war* is the catalyst. Cold war is an automatic pump primer. Turn a spigot, and the public clamors for more arms spending. Turn another, the clamor ceases. Truman confidence, cockiness, is based on this "Truman formula." *Truman era of good times*, President is told, can run much beyond 1952. Cold war demands, if fully exploited, are almost limitless.

In the same vein, *U.S. News and World Report* was to declare in 1954: "What H-bomb means to business. A long period . . . of big orders. In the years ahead, the effects of the new bomb will keep on increasing. As one appraiser puts it: 'The H-bomb has blown Depression-thinking out the window.'" (In 1959 David Lawrence, editor of *U.S. News and World Report*, indicated that he viewed with equanimity the suggestion that the United States "might conceivably strike first in what has become known as 'preemptive' rather than 'preventive' war.")

Henry Luce, the media mogul at the head of the *Time-Life* empire, who coined the term "the American Century," observed in

November 1957 in *Fortune* that the United States "can stand the load of any defense effort required to hold the power of Soviet Russia in check. It cannot, however, indefinitely stand the erosion of creeping socialism and the ceaseless extension of government activities into additional economic fields" beyond the military. This was directly in line with Kalecki's and Baran and Sweezy's contention that the system was tight-fisted where civilian spending was concerned and open-handed with the military.

Remarking on the success of military Keynesianism in promoting economic prosperity, the influential Harvard economist Seymour Harris wrote in the *New York Times Magazine* in 1959: "If we treat the years from 1941 to the present as a whole, we find again that a period of record prosperity coincided with a period of heavy military outlay. . . . About one dollar out of seven went for war and preparation for war, and this expenditure was undoubtedly a stimulus to the economy."[12]

A military Keynesian view was close to the heart of the major U.S. planning document of the Cold War. It was called NSC-68, and it was issued in April 1950 shortly before the Korean War by the U.S. National Security Council and signed by President Truman in September 1950 (but not declassified until 1975). Drafted by Paul Nitze, then head of the policy review group in the State Department, NSC-68 intended to construct a rollback strategy against the Soviet Union. It called for a vast increase in military spending above its already high levels and considered the possibility that "in an emergency the United States could devote upward of 50 percent of its gross national product" to the military effort as in the Second World War. "From the point of view of the economy as a whole," NSC-68 declared,

> the program [of military expansion] might not result in a real decrease in the standard of living, for the economic effects of the program might be to increase the gross national product by more than the amount being absorbed for additional military and foreign assistance purposes. One of the most significant lessons of our World War II experience was that the American economy, when it operates at a level approaching full efficiency [full capacity], can provide enormous resources for purposes other than civilian

consumption while simultaneously providing a high standard of living. After allowing for price changes, personal consumption expenditures rose by almost one-fifth between 1939 and 1944, even though the economy had in the meantime increased the amount of resources going into Government use by $60–$65 billion (in 1939 prices).[13]

U.S. militarism was therefore motivated first and foremost by a global geopolitical struggle, but was at the same time seen as essentially costless (even beneficial) to the U.S. economy, which could have more guns and more butter too. It was thus viewed as a win-win solution for the U.S. empire and economy.

By the time that President Eisenhower (who played a role in this military expansion) raised concerns about what he dubbed the "military-industrial complex" in his farewell address of January 17, 1961, it was already so firmly established as to constitute the permanent war economy envisioned by Charles E. Wilson. As Eisenhower's secretary of defense, Charles Erwin Wilson—best known for having created a major flap by saying that "what is good for General Motors is good for the country"—observed in 1957, the military setup was then so built into the economy as to make it virtually irreversible. "So many Americans," he noted, "are getting a vested interest in it: Properties, business, jobs, employment, votes, opportunities for promotion and advancement, bigger salaries for scientists and all that. . . . If you try to change suddenly you get into trouble. . . . If you shut the whole business off now, you will have the state of California in trouble because such a big percentage of the aircraft industry is in California."[14]

Hence, the concern that Eisenhower voiced in his farewell address about a "permanent armaments industry of vast proportions" and that "we annually spend on military security alone more than the net income of all United States corporations"[15] was a belated recognition of what had already become an established fact. The need for the gargantuan military-industrial complex that the United States developed in these years was not so much for purposes of economic expansion directly (though military Keynesianism pointed to its stimulating effects) but due to the reality, as Baran and Sweezy emphasized, that the capitalist world order and U.S. hegemony could only be maintained "a while longer," in the face of rising insurgencies throughout the world, through "increasingly direct and massive intervention by American armed forces."[16] This entire built-in military system could not be relinquished without relinquishing empire. And so from the early Cold War years to today, the United States has flexed its military power—either directly, resulting in millions of deaths (counting those who died in the Korean War, the Vietnam War, the Gulf War, the Kosovo war, the Afghanistan and Iraq wars, as well as dozens of lesser conflicts), or indirectly, as a means to intimidate.[17]

The most important left analysts of these developments in the 1950s and '60s, Kalecki, Baran, Sweezy, and Magdoff, insisted— going against the dominant U.S. Cold War ideology—that the cause of U.S. military spending was capitalist empire, rather than the need to contain the Soviet threat. The benefits of military spending to monopoly capital, moreover, guaranteed its continuation, barring a major social upheaval. The decade and a half since the fall of the Soviet Union has confirmed the accuracy of this assessment. The euphoria of the "peace dividend" following the end of the Cold War evaporated almost immediately in the face of new imperial requirements. This was a moment of truth for U.S. capitalism, demonstrating how deeply entrenched were its military-imperial interests. By the end of the 1990s U.S. military spending, which had been falling, was on its way up again.

Today, in what has been called a "unipolar world," U.S. military spending for purposes of empire is rapidly expanding—to the point that it rivals the entire rest of the world put together. When it is recognized that most of the other top ten military-spending nations are U.S. allies or junior partners, it makes the U.S. military ascendancy even more imposing. Only the reality of global empire (and the effects of this on the internal body politic) can explain such an overwhelming destructive power. As *Atlantic* correspondent Robert Kaplan proudly proclaimed in 2005: "By the turn of the twenty-first century the United States military had already appropriated the entire earth, and was ready to flood the most obscure areas of it with troops at a moment's notice."[18]

The Labyrinth of U.S. Military Spending

The most direct way of measuring the extent of the U.S. commitment to the military-imperialist complex over the post–Second World War period is through an examination of U.S. military spending itself. This is not, however, easily accomplished. Military expenditure is a labyrinth presenting numerous dead ends. What is treated by almost all analysts as a reliable data source for such expenditures is the Office of Management and Budget (OMB) *Historical Tables*, generated along with the federal budget. In the *Historical Tables for Fiscal Year 2009*, Department of Defense spending (OMB Table 3.2, line 051) is listed as $529.8 billion for 2007. Adding in atomic energy defense activities and defense-related activities brings total national defense (line 050) to $552.6 billion. This number can be considered acknowledged military spending, since it is what is usually reported as U.S. national defense spending and used (with only small differences) by NATO and SIPRI.[19]

However, there is another, fuller accounting of U.S. national defense spending included in the U.S. National Income and Product Accounts (NIPA), a source that constitutes the final word on the totals for the U.S. economy as a whole (see Figure 6.1). The National Income and Product Accounts give $662 billion as the total for national defense spending for 2007, or *over $100 billion more* than the OMB figures. Much of the difference is explained by the fact that the NIPA numbers for national defense, as opposed to the U.S. budget figures, take account of the following: government consumption of fixed capital, cash payments to amortize the underfunded liability for military and civilian retirement benefits (which in the budget accounting are included elsewhere as "intergovernmental transactions"), and expenditures recorded on a delivery (accrual) rather than cash basis (as in the budget).[21]

The NIPA figures thus capture far more accurately than the OMB data the economic resources directed to the military, emphasizing "full-cost budgeting." As economist and peace researcher Jurgen Brauer observes: "For the United States, the NIPA numbers are the most comprehensive and conceptually complete national defense outlays data we have, since they are expressly based on economists' national income accounting framework rather than on politicians' need to review and pass budget requests."[22]

FIGURE 6.1: Military Spending, 2007 (in billions of dollars)

A. Acknowledged		B. Actual	
National Defense (OMB)	552.6	National Defense (NIPA)	662.2
		Space (50%)	9.1
		Grants to foreign governments (80%)[a]	29.0
		Veterans benefits	40.0
		Military medical payments[b]	12.1
		Interest attributed to military[c]	250.1
Total	**552.6**	**Total**	**1,002.5**
Percent of GDP	4.0	Percent of GDP	7.3

a) Grants to foreign governments are conservatively considered here to be 80 percent military. For instance, under the International Affairs portion of the budget $8 billion was spent in 2007 on International Security Assistance, $16 billion on International Development and Humanity Assistance, most of which were imperial expenditures.
b) Includes one-third of "Other" government social benefits category (National Income and Product Accounts, Table 3.12), defined by BEA as consisting "largely of payments to nonprofit institutions, aid to students, and payments for medical services for retired military personnel and their dependents at nonmilitary facilities."
c) Assumes 80 percent of net interest payments attributable to military. This is less than other estimates by major analysts. Robert Higgs of the Independent Institute attributes 91.2 percent of the national debt to the military. See James Cypher, in his most recent estimate, uses a figure of 81 percent. See James M. Cypher, "From Military Keynesianism to Global-Neoliberal Militarism," *Monthly Review*, 59, no. 2 (June 2007): 47, 54.

Sources: National Income and Product Accounts; Office of Management and Budget, Budget for Fiscal Year 2009, Historical Tables, Tables 3.1, 3.2.20.[20]

Adopting the NIPA figures for national defense spending, however, only partly solves the problem of developing an accurate assessment of U.S. military spending. It still remains to add to this the military spending concealed in other economic categories and not captured by total NIPA national defense spending. Drawing on other lines in the National Income and Product Accounts, it is necessary to add to the NIPA national defense figures all or part of: economic grants to foreign governments, space, medical payments to military retirees and dependents at non-military facilities, veterans' benefits, and the net interest payments on the national debt attributable to military spending.

All of the above items are recognized in NATO and SIPRI definitions of military spending, except veterans' benefits and net interest payments, which are excluded as "legacy costs." Yet, since legacy costs are an important part of military expenditures (and some other legacy costs are included in the basic data) I incorporate veterans' benefits and the net interest payments attributable to past wars and military expansions here, in line with estimates of military spending provided by other analysts. This makes more sense, as I am concerned with the social, economic, and imperial legacy of the rise of a U.S. military establishment over more than half a century.[23]

My figures (Figure 6.1) show that actual U.S. military spending in 2007 came to $1 trillion. This contrasts with SIPRI's clearly understated estimate (in relation to countries other than the United States as well) for all the world's nations in 2007 of $1.3 trillion.[24]

The above estimate of total U.S. military spending in 2007 is in the same ballpark as those that have been derived by some other critics of U.S. military spending—through the alternative arduous process of adding up the many different components of military spending hidden in the budget. Chalmers Johnson, author of the anti-empire trilogy *Blowback*: *The Sorrows of Empire* and *Nemesis*, has contended that when all military spending elements of the U.S. 2008 fiscal year budget are added up the total comes to "at least $1.1 trillion."[25]

My method above has also been used to develop estimates of actual military spending levels as a percentage of GDP for the post–Second World War era as a whole.[26] According to these figures, total military spending as a share of GDP in 2007 was 7.3 percent, the highest level since 1997. In contrast, acknowledged national defense spending as presented by the Office of Management and Budget misleadingly shows military spending as a percentage of GDP at 4 percent in 2007 (Figure 6.1).

It is crucial to track military spending as a proportion of total federal government expenditures. In doing so, I follow the accepted practice of excluding Social Security, Medicare, and other transfer payments from my measure of federal expenditures, since transfer payments are self-financing, hence do not draw on the income-tax based general fund or contribute to the national debt. Actual military spending as a percentage of federal spending minus transfer payments (see Figure 6.2) declined every year from the end of the Reagan era in 1988, when it stood at 68 percent, to 2003, when it reached a half-century low of 49 percent. Since then it has changed direction and has risen again to 52 percent. This naturally closely parallels, although at a higher level, the path for acknowledged national defense spending as a percentage of federal spending (also depicted in Figure 6.2). Acknowledged national defense spending in 2007 was only 29 percent of federal expenditures (minus transfer payments), grossly misrepresenting the share of military spending in federal outlays.

FIGURE 6.2: Actual and Acknowledged Military Spending as a Percentage of Federal Expenditures (minus transfer payments)

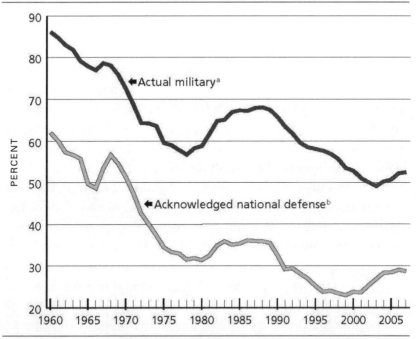

a) For derivation of actual military spending see Table 6.0.
b) Acknowledged national defense equals Office of Management and Budget, National Defense.
Source: See Table 6.0.

The U.S. Imperial Triangle Today

What does the foregoing tell us in relation to my original question? Is it reasonable to argue, as Hobsbawm and others have, that the expansion of U.S. militarism and imperialism in the present period is the result of "a group of political crazies," who have come to power in Washington and constructed a "radical right-wing regime" abounding in "megalomania"? As an explanation of the current phase of U.S. empire this is clearly inadequate. Despite the often neoconservative nature of the Bush administration's top operatives, they have had the broad backing of the greater part of the establishment in the wars on Afghanistan and Iraq, the War on Terrorism as a whole, the huge military buildup, etc.

To be sure, if a Democratic administration under Al Gore had come into power in 2000 it is not at all certain that the United States would have gone to war with Iraq, in addition to Afghanistan, though an attempt would have been made to uphold U.S. imperial interests. The Bush administration from the first was distinguished by the particularly bellicose group of neoconservatives at its helm. But they hardly lacked solid backing within the circles of power. Strong support was extended by both political parties, Congress, the judiciary, the media, and the corporations generally. Disagreements were largely about troop levels, the amount of force to be applied, relations to allies, dates of withdrawal (partial or whole), distribution of forces between the major "theaters," etc. More fundamental questions, even about the use of torture, were avoided. Major dissent mainly came from the bottom of the society.

All of this suggests that expanded militarism and imperialism are deeply entrenched at present, at least within the top echelons of U.S. society. It reflects a general concern to expand U.S. hegemony as part of an imperial grand strategy, including rolling back insurgent forces and "rogue states" around the world and keeping junior partners in line. The war in Iraq is best viewed as an attempt to assert U.S. geopolitical control over the entire Persian Gulf and its oil—an objective that both political wings of the establishment support, and which is part of the larger aim of the restoration of a grand U.S. hegemony.[27] The vast scale of U.S. military spending—encompassing more than 50 percent of the federal budget (excluding Social Security, Medicare, and other transfer payments) and constituting 7 percent of the entire GDP—is thus externally rooted in the needs of the U.S. imperial grand strategy, which continually strains the U.S. system to its limits.

U.S. imperialism has been transformed in recent decades by the absence of the Soviet Union, giving the United States more immediate power (particularly in the military realm), coupled, paradoxically, with signs of a decline in U.S. economic hegemony. It is this dual reality that has led to urgent calls throughout the power elite for a "New American Century," and to attempts by Washington to leverage its enormous military power to regain economic and geopolitical strength, for example, in the Persian Gulf oil region. In recent years, the United States has enormously expanded its military bases and operations around the world with bases now in around seventy countries and U.S. troops present in various capacities (including joint exercises) in perhaps twice that number. Washington is thus not just spending money on the military and producing destructive weapons, or engaging in wars and interventions. It is also building a lasting physical presence around the world that allows for control/subversion/rapid deployment.[28]

As a further reason not to dismiss the new surge in U.S. militarism and imperialism as merely the "megalomania" of a few, my argument points back to Kalecki's imperial triangle, as constituting the principal dilemma facing opponents of imperialism. The creation of a huge military establishment to serve the U.S. empire was understood, in military-Keynesian terms, as a quasi-full-employment strategy aimed at combating economic stagnation. With the help of the media (which, as General Electric Wilson insisted, had the task of "marshalling" public opinion in support of the permanent war economy), the distinctive foundations of post–Second World War U.S. capitalism were laid. The growth of the antiwar movement in response to the Vietnam War, and the end of the Cold War, represented setbacks for the imperial triangle, which showed up in terms of temporary drops in military spending as a percentage of GDP. Each time, in the late 1970s/early 1980s and again in the late 1990s/early 2000s, such temporary lulls in military spending have been followed by a military resurgence.[29]

For Kalecki the weak link in the imperial triangle was clearly the mass media propaganda system, which had the job of selling the permanent war economy to a population that could conceivably opt for other, more rational, just, and egalitarian courses. Unlike the Korean War or the Vietnam War, the Iraq War (like the Gulf War before it) was preceded by a massive antiwar movement in the United States, demonstrating the willingness of perhaps a majority of the population to seek another way, opposed to militarism and imperialism. It was the monopoly media, far more concentrated than in Luce's day and now virtually indistinguishable from monopoly-finance capital (becoming its public voice), that came to the rescue of U.S. war capitalism in its moment of need, giving credence to its obvious lies. "The press," as I put it in 2008, "was [soon] eating out of the Bush administration's bowl."[30]

In a period of economic stagnation, financial crisis, declining hegemony, impending environmental collapse, and new populist insurgencies, Washington, representing the U.S. oligarchy as a whole, was once again able to enlist the media monopoly in the marshaling of public opinion in support of the imperial project through the promotion of war hysteria and combating "the terrorist threat." What made this possible was the prior existence of a well-oiled, privatized propaganda system designed to limit the range of legitimate debate in the mainstream media. In this system even the outer reaches of the quite timid liberal punditocracy were strictly walled-in to fit within the proscribed boundaries of elite debate. Today fundamental dissent against the military-imperial system, no matter how thoughtful or well informed, is decidedly off-limits, except for periodic ridicule. Ours is decidedly a "military-industrial-media complex."[31]

Nevertheless, the imperial triangle is now increasingly confronted with its own contradictions. As Baran and Sweezy foresaw more than four decades ago in *Monopoly Capital*, the U.S. military system faced two major internal obstacles. First, military spending tended to be technologically intensive and hence its employment-stimulating effect was decreasing. "Ironically," they observed, "the huge military outlays of today may even be contributing substantially to an increase of unemployment: many of the new technologies which are byproducts of military research and development are also applicable to civilian production, where they are quite likely to have the effect of raising productivity and reducing the demand for labor." Second, expansion of "weapons of total destruction" and the devastating effects of the use of more powerful weapons could be expected to generate a growing rebellion against the permanent war economy at all levels of society, as people perceive the dangers of global barbarism (or worse, annihilation).[32]

Today the enormous weight of Washington's war machine has not prevented it from being stretched to its limits while becoming bogged down in Iraq and Afghanistan. Although still capable of great destruction, the United States is significantly limited in its ability to deploy massive force to achieve its ends whenever and wherever it wishes. The dream of Pax Americana, first presented by John F. Kennedy at the height of the Cold War, has turned into the nightmare of Pox Americana in the years of waning U.S. dominance. The role the media monopoly has assumed in recent years in the promotion of war propaganda has contributed to the rapid growth of a media reform movement, which is now challenging the concentration of communications in the United States.[33]

There is no doubt that a society that supports its global position and social order through $1 trillion a year in military spending, rivaling that of all the other countries in the world put together, unleashing untold destruction on the world, while ignoring intractable problems of inequality, economic stagnation, financial crisis, poverty, waste, and environmental decline at home is a society that is ripe for change.

7

The Penal State in an Age of Crisis

AS A RULE, CRIME and social protest rise in periods of economic crisis in capitalist society. During these times, the well-to-do become increasingly fearful of the general population and are more disposed to adopt harsh measures to safeguard their positions at the apex of the social pyramid. The slowdown in the economic growth rate of U.S. capitalism beginning in the late 1960s and early 1970s—converging with the emergence of radical social protest around the same period—was accompanied by a rapid rise in public safety spending as a share of civilian government expenditures. So significant was this shift that one can speak of a crowding out of welfare state spending (health, education, social services) by penal state spending (law enforcement, courts, and prisons) in the United States during the last third of a century.[1]

With the U.S. economy now experiencing economic depression/stagnation on a scale not witnessed since the 1930s, the vicious circle of slow growth/expanding inequality on the one hand and increasing state repression of the working population on the other, which has characterized the neoliberal era, is bound to worsen—barring a major change in social relations. The role of penal state spending is therefore crucial to understanding the developing crisis of U.S. class society.

The Civilian Government/GDP Ceiling and Penal State Spending

In chapter 3 of this book I noted that non-defense government spending has more or less hovered around 14 percent of GDP for the past forty years.[2] (See Figure 7.1.) Meaningful progressive policies invariably require an increase in civilian government spending—in fact, this becomes a key barometer to measure the material success of progressive organizing and working-class politics. Civilian government spending as a percentage of GDP reached the 14.5 percent level in 1938–39, at the height of the New Deal. It declined sharply at the time of the Second World War, but returned to about 14 percent in the 1970s, where it has basically remained ever since.

My argument was that serious domestic political pressures—in effect, the capitalist class and corporate special interests—made it

FIGURE 7.1: Non-Defense Government (Federal, State, and Local) Consumption and Gross Investment as a Percentage of GDP, 1929–2008

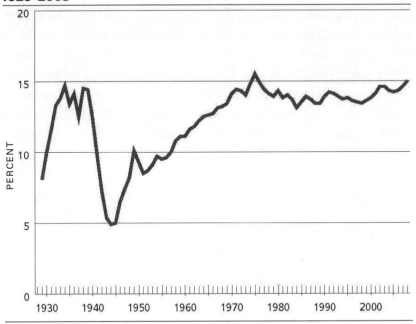

Sources: Bureau of Economic Analysis, National Income and Products Accounts, Table 1.1.5 (Gross Domestic Product), and Table 3.9.5 (Government Consumption Expenditures and Gross Investment).

difficult, nearly impossible, for civilian government spending as percentage of GDP to rise above the 14 percent ceiling for any length of time.[3] I noted that in other advanced capitalist nations, where the labor movement and left were stronger, the percentage of GDP allocated to civilian government spending tended to be considerably higher. Hence, I concluded that it is extremely unlikely to get anything close to a dramatic increase in civilian government spending without an extraordinary increase in popular political organizing—far beyond what has existed in the United States for generations or what the two dominant U.S. political parties would encourage. To believe that Obama would have delivered a new New Deal on his own was nonsensical, even if a significant percentage of his voters, perhaps a majority, would have been delighted for him to do so.

The other main aspect of the government budget, military spending, does not generate the same opposition from elements of the capitalist class or the corporate community—quite the contrary—and therefore has no such ceiling on its growth. Hence military spending has been subject to periodic huge increases (as well as periodic declines), and has remained the main means of fiscal stimulus of the economy for the past seventy years. I chronicled the under-recognized extent of military spending in the U.S. economy in chapter 6.[4]

But there was a lingering problem I had with the argument on civilian government spending. If the past three decades have been ones of retrenchment for labor and the left, growing inequality, increased power of capital over the government, and massive and successful attacks on government programs that serve the poor and working class, how could civilian government spending as a percentage of GDP have remained stable at around 14 percent? Should it not have declined?

A good part of the seeming paradox is explained by other sources of spending with very strong political backing, such as various subsidies going to agriculture, highways, and business, and the need to maintain at least the basic services and workings of civilian government. Though much of civilian government spending as a percentage of GDP has been constrained over the past thirty-plus years—especially social services—other areas that benefit the ruling order directly have increased.

FIGURE 7.2: Public Safety as a Percentage of Civilian Government Spending

Sources: Bureau of Economic Analysis, National Income and Products Accounts, "Government Consumption Expenditures and Gross Investment," Table 3.9.5, and "Government Consumption Expenditures and Gross Investment by Function," Table 3.15.5.

One area in particular that has been on the receiving end of ever increasing public funds has been police, courts, prisons, and jails—what is euphemistically termed "public order and safety." As Figure 7.2 demonstrates, the share of such penal state spending has nearly doubled as a percentage of civilian government spending over the past fifty years and now stands at 15 percent of the latter. Because total civilian government spending stayed pretty constant as a portion of GDP, this sharp increase in penal state spending has had the effect of crowding out other forms of civilian government spending.

Penal state spending is much closer to military spending than it is to other forms of civilian government spending, not only in its commitment to control via state violence (particularly where the police have themselves become increasingly militarized), but also in its freedom from barriers erected by vested interests blocking its further expansion. It faces no powerful domestic constituency that opposes expenditure in this area, as does spending on the environment, public housing, public health, mass transit, or public education. It

FIGURE 7.3: Adult Incarceration Rates per 100,000 Population

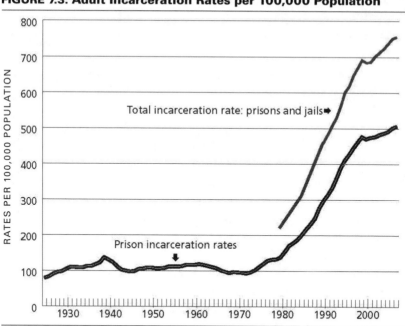

Sources: U.S. Census Bureau, Statistical Abstract of the United States: 2009 (128th Edition), No. HS-24, "Federal and State Prisoners by Jurisdiction and Sex: 1925 to 2001," http://www.census.gov/compendia/statab/; Bureau of Justice Statistics, "Prisoners" and "Prison and Jail Inmates at Mid-year," various issues in series, http://www.ojp.usdoj.gov/bjs/pubalp2.htm.

has therefore evolved into a huge industry in its own right—one that incessantly demands that the government open the spigot ever wider. And, like military spending, it is uniquely positioned to play on jingoism and fear, with no small amount of racism for good measure. For a politician to oppose increased prison spending routinely is to invite career suicide. The public statements critical of the prison-industrial complex by Senator Jim Webb (D-Virginia) toward the end of his political career are striking, not only for their insight and courage, but for their isolation from virtually all other political commentary on the matter emanating from the mainstream. The penal state is as off-limits in official U.S. politics as empire; in this sense it can be regarded as the domestic side of a militarized society and an empire in decline.

The emergence of the penal state in U.S. society is striking and catastrophic. For much of the twentieth century, the United States imprisoned roughly the same proportion of its population as other nations. This is no longer the case. Figure 7.3 demonstrates the

FIGURE 7.4: World Incarceration Rates per 100,000 Population, Select Countries

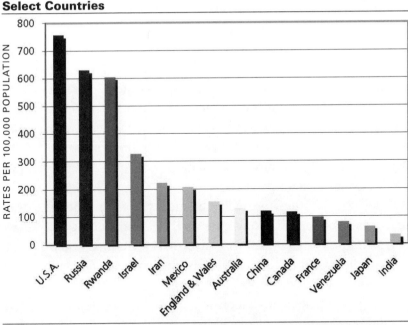

Source: Roy Walmsley, International Centre for Prison Studies, "World Prison Population List (8th edition)," January 2009, http://www.prisonstudies.org.

astonishing increase in incarceration rates for all adults, which began to skyrocket in the 1970s.

This growth becomes more dramatic when the U.S. incarceration rate is compared to that of other nations, as Figure 7.4 demonstrates. The United States accounts for 5 percent of the world's population, and almost a quarter of the world's prisoners. It is number one when it comes to locking up its own people. No thug dictator, no psychopathic madman, anywhere in the world can touch the United States in this department.[5]

The figures for the United States are based on the jail and prison population totaling 2,293,157 in 2007. This doesn't even include the 119,955 reported detainees held in territorial prisons, jails in Indian country, U.S. Immigration and Customs Enforcement (ICE) facilities, military prisons, and juvenile detention centers.[6]

The neoliberal offensive that followed the economic slowdown and the social protests of the 1960s and early '70s resulted in an expanded definition of crime and increasing sentences. The change was most evident in the epidemic incarceration of the population for drug-possession offenses in the 1970s and '80s, which, combined with onerous mandatory sentences, was the dynamite for the prisoner explosion. Incarcerated drug offenders have soared 1,200 percent since 1980.[7] Those in prison due to drug possession now account for 53 percent of all federal prisoners and 20 percent of state prisoners.[8] These offenses were victimless, and nonviolent. "When I started as a police reporter," David Simon, former *Baltimore Sun* journalist turned creator of the TV program *The Wire*, said, "33, 34 percent of the federal inmate population was violent offenders. Now it's like, seven to eight percent."[9]

The "war on drugs" proved to be most successful when the drug users were poor and working class and, especially, nonwhite. "I saw more drug use at Georgetown University Law Center when I was a student there than I've seen anywhere else in my life," Senator Webb said. "And some of those people are judges."[10]

The plot thickens as I look at Figure 7.5. The crime rate per 100,000 population—calculated in the official series based on property and violent crimes, taken as indices of crime in general—peaked some two decades ago, yet the incarceration rate, as we have seen, continued to shoot up. The "prison-industrial" complex thus took on its own logic. It required additional bodies to justify the expanding budgets and profits. A prison has come to serve the same function as a military base in the economic lifeblood of numerous communities across the nation. "I can get $600,000 from the state for a new jail," one Virginia mayor recently said, "but I can't get $40 for Healthy Families," a public health program for infants.[11]

Neoliberalism and the Punitive Turn

It was not a mere coincidence that the explosion in the prison population coincided with the emergence of neoliberalism as the reigning philosophy in the United States. Neoliberalism, in essence, is capitalism with the gloves off, a political regime in which the interests of capital are elevated and the interests of the working class are demonized and demolished. It was the main political-economic response of the system to the slowdown of economic growth in the early 1970s,

FIGURE 7.5: Crime Rate per 100,000 since 1960*

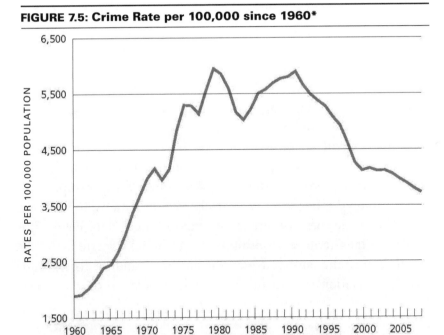

*Note: The FBI's Uniform Crime Report uses property and violent crimes, which are referred to as "index crimes," to construct the crime rates.

Sources: U.S. Census Bureau, Statistical Abstract of the United States: 2009 (128th Edition), No. HS-23, "Crimes and Crime Rates by Type of Offense: 1960 to 2002," http://www.census.gov/compendia/statab/; U.S. Federal Bureau of Investigation, "Crime in the United States," various issues in series, http://www.fbi.gov/ucr/ucr.htm.

which has persisted and indeed worsened since. It was also meant to counter the 1960s and early 1970s era of social protest. To some extent the drug war can be understood as a classic case of the phony moralism that thrives as a distraction in neoliberal times, covering up the real failures of capitalist society. But there are two other, even more direct ways in which neoliberalism is crucial to explaining the expansion of the penal state.

First, neoliberalism, although initially a response to economic slowdown, represented a kind of revolution-in-reverse in U.S. society, promoting social control and profitability on behalf of society's overlords through a "war on crime," among other means. The rise of neoliberalism, in response to economic stagnation tendencies, has been marked by a shift of income and wealth to the very top and increased impoverishment the further one goes down the economic pecking order. Studies show that those nations with the highest rates of inequality also tend to have higher rates of incarceration, with the United States representing an extreme on both counts.[12] Inequality and prison admission are so closely correlated that a recent study of U.S. wage, employment, and incarceration rates concluded: "Empirical analysis suggests that if levels of economic inequality that were observed in the mid-1980s prevailed through the 1990s, prison admission rates among black and white men without college education would be reduced by 16–25%."[13]

Bernie Madoff notwithstanding, prisoners come almost entirely from the poor and working class. Rising incarceration rates reflect in the first instance a rising industrial reserve army of the unemployed/underemployed. Thus there is normally a close relationship between inequality, joblessness, poverty, crime, and incarceration. Figure 7.6 shows the long-term relationship between the jobless rate for civilian, non-institutionalized men on the one hand, and the federal and state incarceration rate for the adult male population on the other, from the early 1950s until the present (1948 = 100, five-year moving averages). The jobless rate in this sense should not be confused with the common use of "joblessness" to refer to unemployment, which includes only those who are officially counted as belonging to the labor force and who are also without jobs. Rather, the jobless rate looks at the overall share of adults who are jobless, thereby capturing the larger economically marginalized population.[14]

Up until the mid-1980s, as can be seen in the chart, changes in the jobless rate for men and the incarceration rate for men follow a similar pattern. The close relationship between trends in joblessness and incarceration evident in this period reflects both economic fluctuations and that prisoners tend to come from the most economically vulnerable populations in society. As Berkeley sociology professor Loïc Waquant, known for his research on the U.S. penal state, has noted, "Fewer than half of inmates [in U.S. prisons] held a full-time job at the time of their arraignment and two-thirds issue from households with annual income amounting to less than *half* of the so-called poverty line."[15]

Yet, beginning around 1985, as Figure 7.6 also shows, incarceration soared off into the stratosphere, quite apart from joblessness, which rose much more slowly. This reflected what Glenn Loury, Merton P. Stoltz Professor of Social Sciences in the Department of Economics at Brown University, has referred to in his *Race, Incarceration, and*

FIGURE 7.6: Changes in Jobless Rate for Males (20 Years and Older) and in Males in Federal and State Prisons as a Percentage of Adult Male Population

1948 = 100, 5-year moving averages

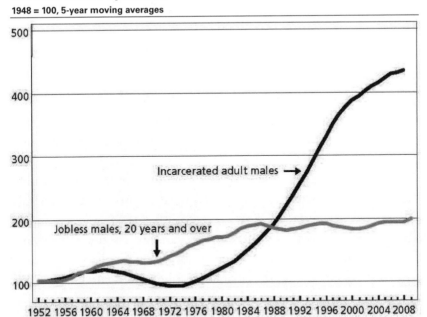

Sources: U.S. Census Bureau, Statistical Abstract of the United States: 2009 (128th Edition), No. HS-24, "Federal and State Prisoners by Jurisdiction and Sex: 1925 to 2001," http://www.census.gov/compendia/statab/; Bureau of Justice Statistics, "Prison and Jail Inmates at Mid-year, 2008," http://www.ojp.usdoj.gov/bjs/pubalp2.htm; U.S. Census Bureau, "Annual Population Estimates by Sex and Age," various releases (population data for 2008 are projected), http://www.census.gov/popest/estimates. html; Bureau of Labor Statistics, (figures not seasonally adjusted), http://www.bls.gov.

American Values as the "punitive turn" in the mid-Reagan period. The key change was the passage of the 1984 Sentencing Reform Act implementing new "federal sentencing guidelines." These were, in fact, not so much "guidelines," but new mandates that compelled judges to implement maximum sentences. Subsequently, there has been a continual stiffening of sentences for offenders. The passage of "three-strikes" legislation in most states in the 1990s constituted a further intensification of this punitive turn, resulting in much higher levels of incarceration.[16]

As Marx noted in 1859 in the *New York Daily Tribune*: "Violations of the law are generally the offspring of economical agencies beyond the control of the legislator, but it . . . depends to some degree on official society to stamp certain violations of its rules as crimes or transgressions only. This difference of nomenclature, so far from being indifferent, decides on the fate of thousands of men." Thus what were previously minor transgressions, such as drug use charges, became in the 1980s full-fledged crimes. This, together with increased use of maximum sentencing provisions, led to a vast increase in the incarceration rate in U.S. society.[17]

The harsh reality of neoliberalism's "punitive turn" in the 1980s and '90s remains below the radar of a majority of people in U.S. society. The devastated population that fills our prison cells has little commercial or political influence, buying relatively little and voting infrequently—if even permitted to do so. Hence the news media almost never cover this issue. Imagine the press coverage if the prison population was drawn almost entirely from the upper-middle class! Politicians with rare exceptions regard prisoners as dangerous animals to be contained and coerced rather than fellow humans. Rehabilitation has thus gone out the window. As the conservative Harvard professor James Q. Wilson openly declared in 1975 in his *Thinking About Crime*, the goal should be to "isolate and punish" since "society really does not know how to do much else."[18]

Second, neoliberalism is devoted to turning any public-sector undertaking that can be profitable over to capitalists. Here we see the seamy underside of the system: beneath all the highfalutin lectures on hard work, efficiency, free markets, competition, and accountable government is the deeper reality of routinized corruption, of public monies diverted into rich people's pockets.

The booming prison sector has been increasingly privatized to support the needs of capital. In the 1970s, along with growing reliance on private contracts to provide prison services (like meals, transportation, and health care), the first completely privately owned and operated high-security institutions came under contract with the state. Juveniles and immigrants were the first to be locked up in such facilities. Testing privatization on the most vulnerable and politically disenfranchised groups gave private companies the foothold necessary to become part of the conversation about what to do with the rising costs of imprisonment. The increasing costs, of course, were themselves predicated upon skyrocketing incarceration rates, translating into booming demand for the prison services industry.

Because privatization of prisons is objectionable to many on ethical and moral grounds, even to those who support capitalism otherwise, corrections were attacked as grossly inefficient, requiring intervention by the more streamlined private sector. The most common fantastical figure bandied around by privatization advocates was that private prisons would save the state as much as 20 percent in costs. Consequently full privatization of prisons, though still far from constituting a majority of facilities, began in earnest.

The actual truth is that privatization of prisons produces almost no savings, as a 2001 study under the aegis of the U.S. Department of Justice titled "Emerging Issues on Privatized Prisons" demonstrated.[19] The study added that what savings the private firms did generate came almost entirely through lowering wage costs; i.e., smashing the prison guard unions. The similarity to efforts to privatize other public services, like education, is evident.

What is clear, however, is that the private prison industry has tremendous incentive to increase the use of prison labor in the marketplace, and derives much of its force from this fact. Already thirty-seven states have legalized the contracting of prison labor by private firms.[20] Nor is the private sector alone exploiting prison labor; already a significant portion of military equipment is produced in federal prisons.

Much like the military sector and the health insurance sector, the prison-industrial complex, both private and public, has become a major industry, with the standard accoutrements of conventions, trade shows, and Wall Street investment analysts devoted to it. It has its golden revolving door from public to private sector. Most important, it has become a tremendously powerful lobbying force in Washington and state capitals across the nation. It requires, as we have seen, not only public money, but bodies to justify that money. It has taken on a life of its own.

Prison Conditions and Racism

Fyodor Dostoevsky once observed that "the degree of civilization in a society is revealed by entering its prisons."[21] So what would we find?

By nearly all accounts the conditions in U.S. prisons are deplorable and getting worse. Prisons do a better job of converting first-time offenders into seasoned criminals than in assisting prisoners to become gainfully employed. This plays into the nineteenth-century meme (going back to the New Poor Law of 1834) that prisons should be a horrific experience for prisoners. The goal seems to be to abuse them to such an extent that they will do anything to avoid them. It did not work in Dickens's time, and it does not work today.

The latest national study of U.S. recidivism revealed that of prisoners released in 1994, within three years 67.5 percent were rearrested for a new offense, 46.9 percent were reconvicted for a new crime, 25.4 percent were resentenced to prison for a new crime, and 51.8 percent were back in prison, "serving time for a new prison sentence or for a technical violation of their release, like failing a drug test, missing an appointment with their parole officer, or being arrested for a new crime."[22] These rates of recidivism are among the highest in the world, with Britain being the only possible rival for the top position.

Along with losing productive time in prison and not gaining the necessary skills and tools to reenter society in a positive way, many prisoners exit prison with even less of a life intact, no safety net, no place or means to survive while trying to get their lives in order. To make matters worse, research shows that the legal status of people with conviction records makes it improbable that many released prisoners will ever make it in society.

One important report, titled *After Prison*, indicates that "rather than helping them successfully transition from prison to community, many current state and federal laws have the opposite effect, interfering with the rights and obligations of full citizenship in nearly every aspect of people's lives. These laws diminish public safety and undermine the nation's commitment to justice and fairness, creating roadblocks to basic necessities for hundreds of thousands [even millions] of individuals who are trying to rebuild their lives, support their families, and become productive members of communities."[23]

"Post-incarceration reentry programs are haphazard and often nonexistent," Senator Webb noted, "making it extremely difficult for ex-offenders to become full, contributing members of society."[24]

Prisons have had to take up much of the brunt of cutbacks in spending on the mentally ill in the neoliberal era. Four times as many mentally ill people are in prisons as in mental health hospitals.

FIGURE 7.7: Projections of Likelihood to Be Incarcerated for Children of Various Age Cohorts

	Percent ever going to prison during lifetime, born in:		
	1974	1991	2001
TOTAL	**1.9**	**5.2**	**6.6**
Male	**3.6**	**9.1**	**11.3**
White	2.2	4.4	5.9
Black	13.4	29.4	32.2
Hispanic	4.0	16.3	17.2
Female	**0.3**	**1.1**	**1.8**
White	0.2	0.5	0.9
Black	1.1	3.6	5.6
Hispanic	0.4	1.5	2.2

Source: Bureau of Justice Statistics, "Prevalence of Imprisonment in the U.S. Population, 1974–2001," (2003). http://www.ojp.usdoj.gov/bjs/abstract/piusp01.htm.

One-sixth of all prisoners suffer from mental illness of one sort or another.

More than 20 percent of prisoners report they have been sexually assaulted by guards or fellow inmates.[25]

Were Dostoevsky to witness such barbarism he would undoubtedly pronounce civilization long dead in the United States, and regard the self-congratulatory tone of U.S. society as a supreme irony.[26]

Yet none of the above captures the greatest ignominy of the prison crisis in the United States: the prison population is disproportionately African American and Latino. By disproportionate, I mean not only in relation to the population as a whole, but also in relation to the population of poor and working-class people. It is impossible to look at the prisoner explosion without seeing racism in all its fury. Fully three-quarters of all prisoners locked up for drug-related charges are African American.[27] In the late 1990s, for black men in their thirties, prison records were nearly twice as common as bachelor's degrees. "Among all men, whites in their early thirties are more than twice as likely to hold a bachelor's degree than blacks. Blacks are about 50 percent more likely to have served in the military. However, black men are about 7 times more likely to have a prison record."[28] And the likelihood of imprisonment is increasing.

In 2003, the U.S. government's Bureau of Justice Statistics issued an updated report titled "Prevalence of Imprisonment in the U.S.

Population, 1974–2001." As Figure 7.7, based on this report, indicates, if incarceration rates remained at the 2001 level, 32.2 percent of black males born in 2001 would be expected to go to prison, as would 17.2 percent of Hispanic males, and 5.9 percent of white males. For women, all things remaining the same, 5.6 percent of black females would go to prison, 2.2 percent of Hispanic women, and only 0.9 percent of white females. Of course, all things have not remained the same; incarceration rates have continued to climb. And, these figures do not include jails, which house close to a third of all U.S. inmates. Combining expectations for jail experience and the continued increase in imprisonment rates, I can only assume that these figures are major underestimates of the foul life chances and dim futures on offer to so many of the children we now see playing on underfunded school grounds.

Although recent trends are alarming, they were a long time coming. The best report furnished by the Bureau of Justice Statistics for looking at the long-term racial disparities between whites and blacks in prison runs from 1926 to 1986 (see Figure 7.8). Due to changes in the Bureau of Justice data, I had to finish the series (after 1986) using percentages of the actual prison population, rather than the race of those admitted as in the original statistics. The dotted vertical line in the chart reflects this discontinuity in the official data. Nevertheless, the long-term trend presents a coherent picture. As you can see, from the time the data was first reported until the present, the trend has been toward minorities making up a larger and larger percentage of persons admitted to state and federal prisons, now constituting about two-thirds of the total. Blacks now make up more than a third of the prison population, and the percentages of Hispanic and "other" are on the rise in relation to whites.

In 1926 the federal and state imprisonment rates per 100,000 population were estimated at: whites, 36; blacks, 106; and other, 62. (Local jail detention figures are unavailable.) Today, the total incarceration rate per 100,000 individuals, including federal and state imprisonment and local jail detention, is: whites, 820; blacks, 5,126; and Hispanic, 1,907. Latinos represent the fastest growing segment of the minority prison population, rising from 5 percent of federal and state inmates in 1978 to 21 percent in 2007.[29] "The incarceration rate of American Indians and Alaska Natives," as noted

FIGURE 7.8: Percent of State and Federal Prisoners by Race, 1926–2006*

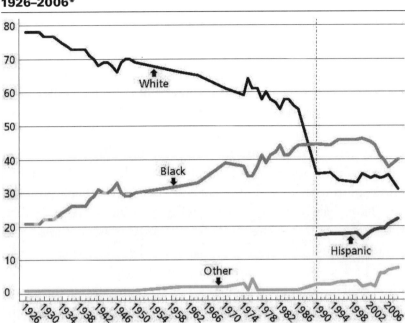

*After 1986, the categories white, black, and other exclude Hispanics.

Sources: Bureau of Justice Statistics, "Race of Prisoners Admitted to State and Federal Institutions, 1926–86," (1991), http://www.ncjrs.gov/pdffiles1/nij/125618.pdf; Bureau of Justice Statistics, "Prisoners," various issues in series, "Correctional Populations in the United States," various issues in series, and "Prison and Jail Inmates at Mid-year," various issues in series, (older issues are not available online), http://www.ojp.usdoj.gov/bjs/pubalp2.htm.

in a 2007 article in *Criminal Justice Studies,* "is 19 percent higher than the national rate."[30] In the last decade, according to Amnesty International, the number of immigrants in detention has tripled from 10,000 in 1996 to over 30,000 in 2008.[31]

To add insult to injury, the United States is one of the few nations that prohibits prisoners from voting, and in some states the ban is lifelong. Nearly 2.5 percent of U.S. adults and fully 14 percent of black men are now disenfranchised because of criminal convictions. In the crucial Florida election of 2000 that resulted in George W. Bush becoming president, at least 11 percent of that state's adult black population was disenfranchised as a result of felon disenfranchisement laws as opposed to around 4 percent of the non-black population. Altogether current laws disenfranchise over five million U.S. voting age citizens, according to the Sentencing Project.[32]

Smashing the Penal State

In my view, as depressing as the picture is, it is not hopeless. The worsening economic crisis, the failure of neoliberalism's punitive turn, *and rebellion from below* could, in a reversal of fortunes, create the basis for radical change. Penal state spending could be crowded out by renewed welfare state spending—or by more fundamental changes in the social structure of power in U.S. society.

We may be approaching a moment in which it will be possible to open up a debate on the obscenity and absurdity of the present order and its punitive social control mechanisms. The current economic crisis is putting states and municipalities in a very difficult position. They have sharply declining revenues but the social needs of their struggling populations are escalating. If today's state and local governments follow business-as-usual and use their shrinking revenues to cut back on necessary social programs to bankroll their bloated prison systems, support for public safety spending among the overall population may falter. More and more people may conclude that the United States cannot afford its prison-industrial complex any more than its military-industrial complex, given pressing social needs.

Already, there are cracks in elite opinions that were quiet heretofore on the prison crisis. Smashing the penal state is job one not only for socialists and progressives, but for any sentient beings who are worth their salt. The words of Eugene V. Debs from 1918 have never rung more true: "While there is a lower class, I am in it, and while there is a criminal element I am of it, and while there is a soul in prison, I am not free."

PART THREE

Media and Politics

8

The State of Media and Media Reform

MEGAN BOLER: In your 2004 book *The Problem of the Media* you pose the question, "Is the media system a democratic force?" This focus frames the questions I'll be asking today, and I'm excited to get an update from you on this crucial topic. You're a scholar with expertise in many areas—history, policy analysis, and communications—and I've been indebted to your work for many years. To begin, I thought I'd ask about your intellectual and political roots—about your background, your vision of change, your thoughts on democracy and its future. Who do you recall reading in your early formative years, and who do you look to now for inspiration?

ROBERT W. MCCHESNEY: I graduated from high school in 1971 and was deeply influenced by the social movements of the times. I was also a bit of a hippie. I dropped out of college for a year, and when I returned in 1973, I was committed to studying economics—mainstream economics—to understand how capitalism works from a capitalist perspective. I also wanted to study history and politics: I was very serious about understanding the world. This was a very different moment historically from anything subsequently. It was a time in which radical social theory and critical scholarship were really increasing in importance at universities across the world, so there was a space opened for critical work. I went to college exactly at this moment and used it as an opportunity to really immerse myself in social theory, history, and economics in a very productive manner.

There were many authors I read during that period who have been the foundation of everything I've done since then. I discuss this period at length in my 2007 book *Communication Revolution*. I had the privilege of reading Marx thoroughly and pretty systematically after doing a study in European history and classical economics and philosophy. It was exhilarating to read him and Engels, and then later to study the twentieth-century Marxists. You know, I rarely quote Marx, he's never really played a noticeable role in my subsequent research, but that experience was so extraordinary intellectually. It certainly had an effect on me, on how I put things together and think about the world. Specific authors that I read then that really stuck with me include C. B. Macpherson and C. Wright Mills, the legendary American sociologist. His books *The Power Elite* and *The Sociological Imagination* were two cornerstones of my development. Mills was an active scholar in the fifties, and he was a genuine public intellectual long before that term was in vogue. Mills was the sort of figure I was familiar with in high school. I think it would be unusual for a scholar of that nature to be known to high school students today. That says something about the times as much as it does about C. Wright Mills.

The most important intellectuals forced upon me during that period were the economists Paul Sweezy, Leo Huberman, Paul Baran, Harry Magdoff, and Harry Braverman. They were loosely called the Monthly Review School, after their magazine, the *Monthly Review*. I stumbled across their work when I was a college dropout in 1972 and living with friends in a dump over some bar in Cambridge, Massachusetts. I was browsing in a bookstore when I came across their books. I think I was working as a night watchman at a Christmas tree stand that winter, and I had plenty of time to read. It was the first time I gained a coherent understanding of capitalism that avoided left-wing jargon and posturing but did not water down the critique. It was empirically driven. I devoured those books, and they really changed everything in terms of how I view capitalism, history, scholarship, and politics. There is no question that the education I received from them was a foundation that's been central to my work, the scholarship you talk about, and my understanding of the world.

MB: That's a wonderful description of how you came to some of the major theory—your training in economics isn't often commented upon, but it really shows in much of the focus of your work. Is there anything you'd like to say about your early experiences in media production?

RWM: Well, I've been working hands-on in media going back to 1962, when I became a paper deliverer for the *Cleveland Plain Dealer*. Then I worked, of course, on school and college papers. I also worked at my college radio station, as the news anchor! When I moved to Seattle in the late seventies, I worked as a volunteer at the local alternative newspaper for a while, and I worked on the paper of the Tenants' Union in Seattle—it was a pretty significant movement in the seventies in the U.S.A. I was always doing media-related stuff—it was something I gravitated to fairly naturally.

In fact, I didn't go to graduate school until I was thirty, and I spent a good five years in my twenties working in commercial media. Following in my father's footsteps, I started selling advertising for a weekly alternative paper in Seattle in 1979. And events being what they were at that time, within six months I was made the publisher. That was the middle of 1979, and then the following year a bunch of us who worked at the paper broke off and started a monthly rock-and-roll magazine, *The Rocket*. I did that for several years in Seattle. It was actually a very extraordinary experience for me and very helpful for my later research because I was in charge of running a magazine. By the time I left that in '83 to go to graduate school, I think we had a staff of seven or eight, a fairly large payroll, and we were a significant and recognized force in Seattle and the Puget Sound area. Later, when I was going through graduate school and studying political economy, this experience informed my thinking because some of the questions I was asking I had firsthand experience addressing—they weren't abstract issues to me.

MB: Questions, for example, around how advertising shapes content or how business shapes publication?

RWM: Absolutely. How advertising shapes content was a central issue I had to deal with directly as a publisher. One of the big issues for us as a publication—and this isn't something I'm especially proud of, but I'm not going to run from it—was that the central advertisers were cigarette companies. My general manager, Greg Feise, and I spent an inordinate amount of time cultivating the big tobacco companies and their ad agencies to get them to make ad buys, because if we could get a contract with them, it would make us economically solvent. We had a shot at getting their accounts because they weren't permitted to advertise on radio and television and we were delivering exactly the market they wanted. My skin crawls as I say these words. I mean, I was delivering teenage eyeballs to this death industry. But that's the context I worked in, and it gave me a rich appreciation for real business situations, real markets, and how people ethically deal with these situations.

I remember how triumphant Greg and I were when we finally got R.J. Reynolds to sign a huge year-long contract for something like four full-page ads in every issue, in full color, no less. That meant we would get to use full color throughout the entire magazine, paid for by R.J. Reynolds. Upon hearing the news, one of our editors, Karrie Jacobs, said, "OK, now it's time for *The Rocket* to do a cover story on the harmful effects of cigarette smoking." She was serious. I looked at her like she was absolutely insane, when in fact she was the only sane person in an absurd situation, and I said, "Of course we're not going to do that. If we do, the contract is void and we may go out of business." That's the dilemma—a real-world dilemma—I faced. There were scores of incidents like this. As a result, I have been very critical of how the system is set up, while being sympathetic to the people doing their best within that system.

MB: Right, a central contradiction of capitalism. I wonder if that perhaps leads to the question of how you came to establish a media reform movement through Free Press?

RWM: My work as a scholar crystallized when I stumbled across my dissertation topic in the mid-eighties, which eventually became my first book. I say stumbled because I was just reading Ben Bagdikian's *Media Monopoly*, and I sort of had an epiphany and it occurred to me what I needed to study. I realized that commercial media was not a natural American system that was embraced all the time without any qualms. My dissertation and the resulting book addressed the movement in the United States in the early 1930s to oppose commercial broadcasting and to establish a much stronger nonprofit, noncommercial media. I didn't realize it at the time, but it became clear that selecting that topic had put my career on a certain trajectory.

Telecommunications, Mass Media and Democracy came out in 1993, and it got a lot of popular public interest, even though of all my books it was the most academic. Because when people heard about the book and then read it, the response was always the same: "You mean it didn't have to be this way?" For a surprising number of people, it was like the sky had opened for them, the idea that media wasn't a natural system you were stuck with like the Rocky Mountain range.

I ended up giving lots of public talks, and doing more media than many professors get to do. Invariably people were asking me questions like, "How does this relate to today, when journalism has collapsed and our democracy is struggling?" I used my historical training to look at more contemporary issues. Everything I've done since then has fallen pretty much into that category, and that was because the moment of that first book demanded it. I didn't think it was right for me to say, "I'm the historian—you figure it out. I'm going back to the archives; see you later." I wrote that first book because I was concerned about today; I didn't write the book because I only cared about 1932. And so I felt I had to come up with answers. I had to participate in that discussion. I needed to talk to many people and draw people into this conversation—to make it a public issue.

The argument that I made in my books and articles in the nineties was that the media system wasn't natural—it was the result of policies and extensive subsidies. And that the problem in the United States was that these subsidies and policies had been made in the public's name, but without the public's support and consent. I used the example of the 1930s as a case study to show how that has worked historically and the type of journalism we get as a result. The whole unavoidable conclusion is that we need to have some sort of political campaign to increase participation in these policy decisions. The argument received a great deal of momentum with the emergence of the Internet, which again drew attention to the key role of policies. The Internet forced a rethinking of regulations and rules surrounding media structure. For some, especially those on the political right or those who had commercial interests, the emergence of the Internet simply signified that technology was reigning supreme and we could let free markets do their magic. But that was really more a rhetorical ploy. In the real world of media, it actually forced a whole number of important policy questions to the fore, questions about how industry is structured, what sort of subsidies are given, and what sort of regulations apply.

So the issues that I was interested in would be coming to the fore no matter what, because of the technological revolution and because of a deep concern about the quality of journalism and the quality of the cultural content being delivered by the corporate media system. You put those two things together, and throughout the 1990s you saw a tremendous increase in popular dissatisfaction with the media status quo. This was an issue that people needed to organize around; they wanted to win, it was that important. But for people to organize around media issues was an extraordinarily difficult thing to do compared to most other issues. It was very difficult to get popular attention for an issue when you had to rely on the news media to organize for you, because this was not an issue that the media were going to cover. Or if they were going to cover media policymaking, they would do so in a way that would fit the interests of the dominant media firms that had a stake in the outcome of these media policy debates. That was one of the factors explaining why the people lost in the 1930s and why it was difficult to get something up and running in the 1990s.

So my work naturally led to the idea that there had to be a movement to do this. There had to be an organized campaign to draw people in, to link up to other organized groups, to put grassroots heat on policymakers to actually serve the public interest and not the corporate interest. There was a recognition that this would be extraordinarily difficult to do because of the power of lobbyists and their control over the media. This made it hard to get more than a very small fraction of the population to understand that it was their right, and I would argue their duty, to engage in media policy.

By the beginning of this decade, I think we saw a qualitative shift. I think the crucial factor was that I was contacted by a campaign finance organizer, Josh Silver, in 2002, and we got together and began discussions with my friend the journalist John Nichols about starting a group that would organize public support for media reform. It would be called Free Press, and Josh would run it; and John and I would be on the Board and lend what support we could. And when we started it, we thought this was going to be a long, slow ramp-up. We thought it was going to take us ten or fifteen or twenty years to make this a really big issue, and we'd have a lot of digging to do and a lot of seeds to plant, so to speak.

Then in December 2002, I think, Josh was sleeping in a closet in Massachusetts somewhere—we had almost no budget—and this media ownership fight hit the United States. The Federal Communications Commission decided to revisit its media ownership rules, which it had to do by law, and the Republican majority was expressly committed to getting rid of the rules or relaxing them as much as possible. It was a blatant giveaway to the big media companies. The corruption was so thick it was impossible not to see, and we came in just as this was taking place. And you know, I think my initial response, and most people's response, was that the fix was in, the Republicans were going to get this change through, and we were screwed. They were going to allow one company to own most of the media in any given town around the country, with all that that would suggest for the quality of journalism and community involvement in media.

And then the anti-concentration in media ownership movement just exploded. I'd like to say Free Press was responsible for it, but it wasn't. Free Press was still just getting started; there were a lot of existing public interest groups in Washington that played a crucial role. Consumers Union's media project, the Media Access Project, and Jeff Chester's Center for Media education really did a lot of the heavy lifting. Other groups got involved for the first time, like Common Cause, the National Rifle Association, and MoveOn, and this thing just took off. It was astonishing. For those of us at Free Press, it collapsed what we thought would have taken ten years to do into one year. It showed us that we actually had an issue you could organize heterogeneous communities around. You could take what seemed like complex issues and draw popular attention to them, and people genuinely cared—the soil was very fertile.

By the end of 2003 we had our first media conference. It was really great to get everyone with an interest in this issue together in one room, talk things through, and get a sense of what sort of movement we had. We planned this conference in January of 2003, and we thought we might get 200 people. Well, thanks to the ownership fight, the conference exploded like a volcano. We had 1,700 people there, we had to close down registration, and it was extraordinary—it was like a Woodstock-type event for us. For everyone it was a revelation to have this conference. So by the end of 2003, it was clear there was actually a movement. It has continued to grow ever since through our next two conferences, and moved into a wider range of important policy issues. Now, in April 2007, we have a staff of 25 to 30, almost 400,000 members, and we've really developed a lot of skills and the ability to do stuff. I'm not on the staff—I'm a board member, and I'm the president—but I'm still quite pleased and delighted and shocked by the success. It's not just the group, though, it's really about the movement. The stars were aligned and the timing was just perfect. There are a number of other activists outside of Free Press working on this issue who are the heart and soul of this movement—we're just one part of it—and it's an extraordinary movement.

MB: Having been at the most recent Media Reform conference [Memphis, January 2007], I can say that it seemed to me it was a record turnout and a very historic event. My experience on the ground was that there was a diverse group of media activists, journalists, and policymakers on hand—primarily, if not all, from the United States—but with quite diverse agendas. I wonder about your experience there in Memphis, and the evidence that you're part of building a movement. Does it give you some sense of hope?

RWM: Oh, it can't help but give me hope. The politics of this movement are different from a lot of social movements, and it produces very interesting outcomes as a result. It makes the politics easier and trickier at the same time. What I mean is that media reform is both a nonpartisan movement and a progressive movement. It's nonpartisan in the sense that the sorts of reforms we're working for are not, for example, to censor certain types of political speech and enhance others, or to air our viewpoint more than other viewpoints. That's not at all what this movement is about. This movement is about building a media system that does justice to the democratic needs of a self-governing people. We just want to expand the range and quality of media, not favor one group over the other in a zero-sum game. It's not about censorship. So almost all the reforms we work on—network neutrality, media ownership, public broadcasting, getting rid of government propaganda—are nonpartisan issues, and apply to Republican, Democrat, liberal, conservative. They aren't meant to favor one group over another. This is about expanding the range and quality of the media system so that it's not in the service of a relatively small number of commercial interests. What we found in issue after issue is that when you are out of Washington and away from the party bosses, we have immense support from rank-and-file Republicans on a lot of these issues. They don't like their kids' brains marinated in advertising, they don't like political advertising on TV; they don't want one company to own all the media in their community; they don't want their cable and phone company to privatize the Internet and determine which websites they can and can't see. What we found is that these issues cut across the political spectrum. In that way this movement is similar to voting reform groups or campaign finance reform or electoral reform groups who are simply trying to make the system work more efficiently and have a viable democracy.

On the other hand, though this isn't purely a nonpartisan movement, it's very much a progressive movement. Despite the rhetoric that you hear from people in power in the United States or in other countries, not everyone really wants democracy. Not everyone in this country wants to make it easier for people without property to have influence over policies. There are people, or interests, who currently have significant power in our government and our society who like the status quo. They don't want an informed, participating population. To Thomas Jefferson, the press system was necessary because unless poor people had information to govern their lives they were left with a corrupt system that couldn't be democratic. Because the wolves, as we call them, will eat the sheep, the rich will plunder the poor. I think that's why so many of the people associated with this movement come from liberals, progressive ranks, the political left, because that's what gets you into the movement, that's what gets you fired up.

MB: What vision underlies the *kinds* of change you've been part of? Your work evidences a commitment to legislation and policy as one front for change, and I wonder how you came to decide on those as a focus for the social movement.

RWM: Well, I think the media reform movement actually has four different components. Working on policies is one of them, and that's the one we focus on at Free Press. I think it's the most important one for social and political organizing, and the most important overall. The next two are doing independent media, which is especially important in the digital era, and providing media education and critique. This is something that we have a lot of skill at from years of academia and being on the outside looking in. Groups like Fairness & Accuracy in Reporting (FAIR) and the tremendous Media Literacy movement are making people informed about how the media system works so they can participate in changing it. And criticism of bias in the news from groups like Media Matters for America is another component of critique. A fourth component is the movement among media producers, especially workers, journalists, and creative people. Their interest in taking a larger role in the media process could just shift some of the power from Wall Street, from advertisers, managers, and corporate interests. That's the fourth leg of the table.

I think all four parts work together, and I've argued this at length in *Tragedy and Farce,* the book I wrote with John Nichols. They really aren't competing approaches to solving the problem; they're entirely complementary and need each other. None of them can succeed without the other. Now, we put most emphasis at Free Press on legislation and policy for a number of reasons, but the primary one is that our media system is not a natural free-market system. It is a system that's created through policies and subsidies by the government and has been that way since the beginning. It's a profit-motivated system, but it's not a free-market system. United States media firms—and I think this is pretty much true in every major nation—I'm sure it's true in Canada—receive extraordinary subsidies from the government, way beyond what other traditional industries receive. Every private firm gets benefits from the government: they get to use the roads, the water system, public education; they get employees who are trained by the state. Media firms get those same benefits, and theoretically they pay taxes to earn those benefits. But what I'm talking about in terms of subsidies for media firms goes way beyond that. Media firms are receiving direct and indirect subsidies from the U.S. government, especially the federal government, and also state and local governments, totaling in the tens of billions of dollars

every year. These include monopoly franchises to radio and TV stations and cable and telephone systems; copyright provisions that
protect content providers and give them monopoly markets; government postal subsidies; government work to enhance sales overseas;
and subsidies for audiovisual productions. You put all these things
together, and you have an enormous public subsidy. These subsidies
are made in the public's name without the public's informed consent.
That's really what drives the policy side. The government created this
media system to no small extent, and it's done so based on policies
that the public's played no role in drafting but they're paying for out
of their wallets. So to me that's really where the rubber hits the road
in this movement. Ultimately we have to change the system, and
that means going through the policies. I'm not opposed to subsidies,
by the way; I just think the public should get something in return
for these enormous gifts. I think we have to consider all the options
for how we must deploy our resources, and maybe giving monopoly
privileges to AT&T to run the Internet isn't such a smart idea.

MB: That's a good segue to my next question. Your scholarship and
movement with the Free Press reflect to me a combination of conviction and principles, alongside a kind of pragmatism in your choice of
where to push for media democracy. Which does leave me with the
question: What about the micro level? For example, where do small-
scale initiatives such as pirate TV or community radio fit into the
vision you've just described of challenging corporate media?

RWM: Well, one of the pleasant surprises of the last five years is that
unlike other social movements, the media reform movement doesn't
have one goal that you either get or you don't get. For example, in
the United States, the election campaign finance reform movement,
which took off in the 1990s, has pretty much died off. It has died
off not because the issue is no longer important—the issue is more
important today than ever—but because the organizers realized either
you win publicly funded elections, or whatever reform you get short
of that will leave a crack in the edifice that will allow big money to
come in and take it over and destroy the spirit of your initial reform.

In the media reform movement, what you have are a broad range
of areas that you can work in, and you can win tangible discrete victories that can't be taken away. That's what gives it a lot of its vibrancy.

For example, you raised the issues of community radio or TV; you know, we're going to have hundreds and hundreds of new low-power FM radio stations in the United States due to a large extent to public activism forcing Washington to deliver these signals. New stations are going up around the country. They're getting licensed now as a result of this activism, and these stations can't be taken away—it's a real victory. There are a number of instances like this. The micro stuff is a very important part of the big picture. It's not just about winning some huge fight—although there are huge policies, like network neutrality, that are absolute thumbs up or thumbs down for the whole media system, where we need all hands on deck.

MB: Let me just follow up on that question about small-scale developments with some examples. I'm wondering if you have any thoughts about, say, for example, Andy Bichlbaum and the Yes Men's interventions, and how they've gotten content onto the BBC. I'm talking about tactical media as an intervention—it's one of the themes of this book. How do you see these types of activities? Are they effective? Do you see them as part of media reform or not?

RWM: Oh, they're good, the Yes Men are terrific. We're big believers in using humor and creative mechanisms to draw attention to our movement because it's not like the news media are racing out to cover our story. There's going to be a study done at some point about media coverage of this movement compared to similar movements in size and magnitude. I think it will be an interesting study because my sense is that the news media run from the media reform story for a variety of reasons. And I think what that means is that it puts the onus upon us to come up with creative ways to communicate with the public.

One of the things that this movement's done has been to use new media—podcasting, blogging, YouTube, MySpace—to popularize the issues and to bypass the traditional media. We've really worked on this in the last year with the Save the Internet campaign, and in some ways, the media reform movement has been among the pioneers of developing the Internet as a grassroots organizing tool. It really goes back to 2003, when e-mail and the Internet were so crucial to organizing the media ownership campaign. We've gone through a whole new phase today of how we work that, but a lot of it is putting together catchy, entertaining, informative podcasts and video that then go viral and get communicated outside those channels. And if they're powerful enough, they might get picked up by the traditional media and noticed. So I think that one of the things that this movement works on is creative ways to use media to publicize issues, and going back to the Yes Men, creative ways to get attention. While the Yes Men aren't talking about media issues per se—oftentimes they talk about issues of social justice—I think their existence is a testament to the fact that our media system has fundamental problems.

Let me tell you one story about that. I heard a talk Ralph Nader gave a few years ago. He was running for president in 2000, and he was being introduced by Michael Moore, who gave a great talk to introduce Nader. Moore was very funny, he told jokes, everyone was jumping up and down and laughing. And then Nader comes up to talk. And you know Nader isn't going to win any awards as a stand-up comedian—he's a very serious guy. Nader says, "Isn't it great to have someone like Michael Moore giving this great political talk to introduce me?" And everyone agrees. And then he says, "You know, we should really think about that for a second—the only critical ideas that our media systems get out and circulate are funny ideas. There are comedians—you know, Bill Maher, Michael Moore—but there are no serious voices." Nader said he once traveled in the Soviet Union in the 1960s as a young man, and he was struck by the fact that it had the best political humor he'd ever seen. There was an underground political humor that was simply off the charts. That didn't mean they had a healthy society or healthy media systems—the official media system was actually so atrocious that humor was the only way people could survive. And I think he was trying to make a point that this is the situation we have in our society, that the official media is so atrocious as a rule that the only way you can get in edgewise is through satire and humor. And that while that is an understandable approach, we shouldn't romanticize it, because it really points to the fundamental crisis. If we had a legitimate or decent media, you wouldn't have to put on a clown suit to get noticed. You could just talk about an issue and be taken seriously—you wouldn't be automatically dispelled to the lunatic fringe.

MB: I want to pick up on an argument in your book *The Problem of the Media,* which I heard you reiterate at a journalism education conference in Toronto in 2005. I was going to say, at that panel in 2005, "Bob, can you say more about your lack of faith in the uses of Web 2.0 as an intervention? Don't they in any way offer viable alternatives or challenges to corporate media?" Ironically, you have the Save the Internet campaign, which is high on your list despite the sense of discounting those small-scale interventions. But overall, I hear you express very little faith in the promise of the Internet as an alternative to corporate-owned media. Is that accurate?

RWM: The way I would frame it is this: Can the technology offered by the Internet be sufficient to unleash popular power such that the system can be overturned independent of any other policy actions? There are some who actually believe that now that the Internet exists, we can all go out and blog and do our thing and we're going to take over, the corporate interests are doomed, and we're going to have a much better media system. I don't agree with that. I just don't buy it. That doesn't mean those micro-actions aren't very important, but their importance is part of a broader movement that works on a number of different fronts.

Unleashing the free market with the magic of the Internet does not magically produce great journalism. The technology does a lot of great things, as I've talked about already. We used the Internet and new technologies with our organizing, and they're a foundation of our success. But I have no illusion that that means that you can just go online and have great journalism. Journalism requires resources and skilled people getting paid salaries. It requires institutional support so that if you offend someone in power, you will have support and you won't get hassled or arrested. These things don't happen magically just by having the Internet; they require public decisions, distribution of resources, creation of systems. In the United States, it's clear that merging profit seeking with the Internet has not done anything to improve our journalism, or very little. If anything, it's part of the process of seeing it continue to unravel.

And so we need to come up with constructive policies to take advantage of these technologies, in order to create community journals and community media. It won't happen organically on its own, and that's really my argument. Now, that doesn't mean you don't do the little stuff, it just means you don't have the illusion that the little stuff is sufficient and therefore you can let the big guys continue to get the ten-billion-dollar subsidies, privatize the Internet, run everything. That's my argument.

MB: Following up on that, I think about the examples that exist despite the fact that we haven't achieved our ends yet necessarily. You've written that "good journalism and good media requires money and institutional support," but what about the exceptions to this: Pacifica, Democracy Now, Indy Media. I assume that, given your lack of optimism about poorly funded interventions, you see some limitations to these independent media?

RWM: Oh, absolutely there are limitations. For one thing, let's take community radio stations like Pacifica. These stations depend upon federal support. I'm in Madison now, and WORT, a wonderful community station, maybe the most popular radio station in this community, gets 20 percent of its money from the federal government. It gets as much of its money from the government in broadcasting subsidy as does any NPR station in the United States. It desperately needs that money or it can't survive—it's already hanging on by the skin of its teeth despite its popularity. You know, we need enlightened policy so that stations that are this popular actually can have equipment that doesn't look like it was air-shipped out of London after the Blitzkrieg of 1943. And so I think the examples you gave are exactly why we do need coherent policies in addition to independent media.

MB: Right. Turning to the broader landscape outside of North America, do you have any thoughts about the recent launching of Al Jazeera English?

RWM: Well, not specifically, because I haven't seen it.

MB: Which is another interesting aspect of new media—how and if it is known, where it is and isn't broadcast, and all these questions. I think it is very significant that access to the web now allows many in the international community to access Al Jazeera in English. That is one example that stands out in terms of the significant difference the combination of web-based communication has helped establish.

RWM: I think in the next three to five years, the really interesting developments are going to be at the global level. In every country and region around the world, people are battling with these issues, and they're really the same issues everywhere. There are differences between countries, and concerns are different, but there's so much common ground and there are so many issues now, like Internet governance, which transcend national governments. I think the next stage is going to be drawing people together, like the Memphis conference, but also people from around the world, in some sort of global summit to put pressure on leaders and global institutions to serve the public. The problem we see in the United States with corruption is only magnified at the global level, where institutions are even one step further removed from grassroots pressure.

MB: Picking up on the Save the Internet campaign: I was talking to some colleagues who work in these areas, and they noted that people working in open source and open access movements have been inspired by your critiques—but they are also concerned to develop an alternative non-proprietary, non-market, networked information economy. I wonder if you have any thoughts on the possibilities of a non-proprietary, non-market information economy to see possibilities of democratic politics and economy online.

RWM: My belief right from the beginning of seeing digital communication was that there's a fundamental conflict between the potential and logic in digital communications systems and the sort of traditional intellectual property/copyright rules that increasingly butt up against and make no sense with the new technologies. This is exactly why we need an enlightened policymaking to pursue policies that don't just serve the entrenched interests of commercial powerhouses but actually go beyond that to what sort of policies regarding information are needed to encourage a more vibrant market media system. The one thing I know for sure, though, is that winning that fight, especially in the United States, is going to be really hard because there's so much money on the other side of the table. And the key to getting there is building up popular awareness and support; it's the only way you're going to win that fight.

MB: So this is a huge question, but I know you're up to it, given the historian and philosopher that you are. I wondered if you could say something about the particular vision of democracy that underlies a project like the media reform movement or Free Press.

RWM: I think that the vision is actually pretty elementary—this movement doesn't require a very elaborate one. Self-government is impossible without a viable press, and this is not a controversial idea, this is a foundation of the democratic theory. And it's also foundational to *anti-democratic* theory that you need a press system that manipulates people, keeps them in their place. You don't really have to have much more of an understanding beyond that to know the importance of this movement and of these issues.

MB: And do you see democracy as a strictly formal process, or would you want to say something about democracy as a way of life, a right to know, that's broader than formal process?

RWM: Well, I think the way democracy has evolved in the United States, and arguably in other nations to an extent as well, it has become a formal entity in which the actual participation of citizens is pretty minimal. In fact, Macpherson's work that I referred to earlier was very instrumental in helping me to grasp this understanding of democracy and its limitations. What we need to do is try to invigorate public life, to put people in a position to actively participate in their communities and their world—as governors, not simply as consumers going through formal bouts of voting every three years for candidates and parties over which they don't have very much control and about which they know very little. That form of democracy is better than nothing to a certain extent, but it's not sufficient. And the media are part of that problem in that it's become so hollow that public life has been largely demoralized.

MB: Do you see new platforms such as YouTube, MySpace, blogging, and other kinds of new media or tactical interventions as part of that kind of invigorated participation, as showing signs of impacting what is counting as democratic process?

RWM: It seems to me the evidence so far is very positive about the ability of the new technologies to help generate popular awareness that wouldn't be there otherwise and get people engaged and involved, but at this point I'm uncomfortable extrapolating because I think we're still early in the game. We're doing everything we can to push that, but I think there's a tendency to get so tied to a technology that it's like when you fall in love with someone—you don't see their warts for a few days. I think there's an element of that with the fascination with YouTube and MySpace and things like that, which doesn't mean there isn't any reason to fall in love, but rather that we have to always be careful not to jump into the deep end—to make sure there's enough water in there.

MB: In *The Problem of the Media* you address the hype that the Internet will set us free and you write, "In one sense this is a blatant ideological ploy by powerful media firms to distract attention if they gobble up more media so they may be better poised to crush competition generated by new technologies."

RWM: There is no question about that; it isn't even a debatable point. I mean, the Internet is this enormous propaganda device employed by industry and their PR people and their lackeys. Every time they want to do anything, they wave the Internet flag, and say, "Well, there is always new content on the Internet, so you've got to do whatever we want. Everything's changing; you can't regulate it, you have to keep giving us subsidies on our terms, you have to do whatever we tell you because of the Internet." There's no question that's going on. There's not an issue we're dealing with where we don't get that argument—argument number 1-A that's used by industry at every turn in the United States.

MB: And what's the logic there?

RWM: Well, the logic is that with the Internet now here, every market is blasted off, open, it's completely competitive. So you don't have to worry about whether one company owns all the radio stations, TV stations, and newspapers in the community because you know people can go online and blog to their heart's content. You don't get that argument in Canada? Your capitalists ought to come down here for a PR lesson.

MB: Well, I'm a native of San Francisco, and I've only been here a few years, but a big bone I have to pick is that there is even less attention to media ownership concentration here in Canada than there is in the United States. When I've tried to research even a media map—you know how in the United States there are some pretty good media concentration maps—it's almost impossible to find. In terms of concentration, I would say we are nearly worse off in Canada than in the States, and there's less regulation as far as I can tell.

And then I get students who, even after spending a long while deconstructing notions of objectivity, fairness, and balance, will say, "Well, at least there's the CBC, and the CBC is objective." What do you say to that?

RWM: Yeah, the CBC plays a big role in my historical research. It looks good today by comparison to the sort of horse manure that's served up by the balance of the press system. But that's like saying someone is the best ice hockey player in Malaysia. [Megan laughs] You've got to look at the context. I think the value of looking at something like the CBC is that you see, as Marc Raboy puts it in the title of his famous book, the missed opportunities—what it could be that it isn't, what's been lost over the years. And in that context, you know, the possibilities are much greater than the realities.

MB: We actually haven't talked about your feelings about government's role in media. What are your thoughts on the BBC and CBC, and on the Public Broadcasting Service and the Corporation for Public Broadcasting in the United States, in terms of content, and in terms of your hopes for media democracy?

RWM: I'm a believer in public media as a big part—not the only part, but a big part—of a vibrant media system. By public media I mean subsidized through the public, noncommercial, nonprofit media. There's been so much frustration by progressives around the world with their own domestic public services, frustration with the content, the bureaucracy, the lack of democracy, that there have been schools of thought saying, "Let's just throw them all under the train. We don't need them anymore; we'll just go online and blog each other. We don't need those guys." I think that's the anarchism of fools, so to speak. I would argue that with the new technologies, what we now have is an opportunity to have a much more heterogeneous structure for a noncommercial, nonprofit media than we've had in the past. We should view it as an opportunity to expand and radically enhance nonprofit, noncommercial media so that it's not a centralized operation with one institution controlling the entire thing, but rather you have local community media, some national media, but competitive nonprofit media. Multiple nonprofit, non-commercial media operating independently.

But I do think the need for public funding to support media, which has been the premise of the process in the United States since 1791, is not going away, and one of the great campaigns in the United States today is to find resources and funding to enhance non-commercial, nonprofit media into the digital area and build vibrant institutions that can be accountable, that can serve the public. And so I'm a big believer in public media, and the need to make that a central issue in our organizing.

MB: Glad I asked you that. Moving to some of the last questions: What might be the kinds of questions that are most important to you as you teach the next generation of communications studies students? What's most important to you to convey to them or get them to engage in?

RWM: My experience is that at the undergraduate level, most students are pretty much ignorant of everything that you and I have just been talking about. When they hear about this and learn about it and read about it and talk about it, it's sort of a litmus test for them. The vast majority of them get really interested and really engaged, and it's very exciting as a teacher to see this process take place. I see it every year, and it makes me really enjoy going into the classroom. I see these students who are starved to engage with this world, who are frustrated with the sort of corporate culture that they're immersed in, and when they get some perspective on it and can see some of the limitations and some of the alternatives, they get energized and excited.

MB: I was giving a talk at a major university on some of my work in the area of media and philosophy and democracy, and somebody in this audience of top education scholars asked with hostility, "What does media have to do with conventional education?" I have to say I was a bit taken aback because I wondered, where does one begin in answering that question? But I wonder what your response would be to a question like that.

RWM: Well, for me, media is the number one department of education in the world today. So I think a better question would be, what does school have to do with education? [Megan laughs] I'd turn it around, because for a lot of people coming of age in the United States today, their education is coming through media on fundamental matters and issues as much as through schools. I think I can understand why you would find the question bizarre since the connections between the two institutions are so strong, as are the premises of education and media. To no small extent, the media system is the educational system of our society, certainly as much as school if not more. To view it as divorced from education is to me a very formalistic view of education that is not connected to the actual lived experiences of people on this planet.

MB: I wanted to ask you about the recent headlines about the satellite company merger and any thoughts you had on that.

RWM: Well, we're still formulating our response to that. What is lost oftentimes in the shuffle is that we have two satellite radio companies instead of ten or twenty, not because the market per se can only have two, but because there's only enough spectrum right now allocated to have two. It's a government-created duopoly in effect, and now the two players are saying that, considering that the government created a duopoly, this could be turned into a government-sanctioned monopoly. By sanctioned I mean that if the merger does go through, it would be impossible for a new competitor to start up, not just for economic reasons—it's tough enough to go against a monopoly—but because there wouldn't be spectrum to do it.

The firms are going to argue, of course, that they'll go broke unless they can have this monopoly, they can't survive otherwise. And traditionally in the United States, the way issues like this are then resolved is that the merger goes through, they allow the monopoly, and then in exchange the monopoly is supposed to do all sorts of public service stuff. The public gets squeezed because the corporate lobbyists are a hundred times stronger, and the politicians and regulators are really half-hearted in their efforts to represent the public. We aren't strong enough now, I think, to stop this merger necessarily, but we'll see if we're strong enough to at least put much stronger terms in the merger proposal, much greater teeth than would be there otherwise. It's going to be an interesting test of the strength of our movement.

MB: This is sort of going back, shifting again the focus to the micro: as you describe corporate capitalism as it defines and shapes the potential of media and democracy, I want to return once again to the question of where the individual fits in this scheme of change.

RWM: The question is what the individuals do—it's how you regard yourself as an individual. Do you regard yourself as sort of a solo operator who basically came out of the woods 100,000 years ago, on your own, and made contracts with all the other people who came out of the woods, so you're basically a single unit on your own, or do you regard yourself as part of an evolving social organism with tremendous dependency on others for survival? And I view the human condition as very much the latter. I view us as fundamentally social creatures, where the individual exists and is defined by relationship to other people, and in that sense, then, the key is to look at what seem like individual problems to try and see if there's a social link there. There might not be for every issue, but for many issues, lots of people have similar concerns, and if they try to treat them all individually, they won't really find satisfactory results. But if they come together and treat them socially, they can actually solve the problems.

And those are the sort of problems we're dealing with in media reform. Everyone can sit around and whine about the fact they don't like all the advertising in media, they don't like the crappy journalism, but they think it's an individual problem—they've just got a problem with the media personally, and then they just try to solve it by finding a website to go to and they can do their thing. That's really not ultimately a satisfactory solution, a rational solution. A much smarter solution is for all those individuals to find their common interests and ground, understand how the system works, and create a system that works to their satisfaction. That's called media reform.

9

Walter Lippmann and the Crisis of Journalism

THE UNITED STATES IS now widely acknowledged to be in the midst of a stunning collapse of journalism as it has been known for the past century, if not the entire nation's history. The number of paid working journalists per capita declined gradually over the past two decades and then fell off a cliff beginning around 2007. Advertising, which provided the vast majority of revenues to news media for a century, has many new options in the digital era and is in the process of jumping ship. The prayer that new technologies would magically create a business model for a sufficient and viable democratic journalism is not panning out. There is no turnaround in sight, nor any reason to expect one. The United States—and indeed every nation in the world to varying degrees—faces a fundamental problem: how to create a viable independent news media, or consider what the world will look like without a Fourth Estate.

In *The Death and Life of American Journalism*, John Nichols and I argue that an important understanding of how to generate solutions to the current crisis of journalism can be found in our own rich and largely overlooked press history.[1] The framers of the Constitution—most famously Thomas Jefferson and James Madison—and the first several generations of Americans had no illusions that the "market" would provide sufficient journalism. They deployed massive public subsidies to spawn an independent free press, and these subsidies were crucial for the survival and growth of American democracy and the liberties we cherish. In this era in which the market has too little interest in producing sufficient journalism, it is a rich legacy we need to appreciate and study. In our view, the fate of self-governance and our Constitution hang in the balance.

As Americans grapple with their current crisis, they would also be wise to turn to the work of Walter Lippmann, one of the great journalists and most distinguished public intellectuals of the twentieth century. Although he has played an outsized role in scholarly assessments of journalism for decades, based on his classic works *Public Opinion* (1922) and *The Phantom Public* (1925), the choice of Lippmann as prospective sage might surprise some contemporary media scholars. Based on these works, in the past two decades Lippmann has sometimes been caricatured as one who was skeptical, if not downright hostile, toward popular democracy. At the most extreme, he is seen as a proponent of having experts guide the "bewildered herd" and use the news media to "manufacture consent" for political positions that served elite interests. By this reasoning, Lippmann's work might be the last place to look if we wanted to learn why and how to establish news media that would throw logs on the fire of democracy.

Although I recognize Lippmann's growing skepticism toward democracy in the 1920s, following Michael Schudson's defense of Lippmann, I do not think a close reading of *Public Opinion* or *The Phantom Public* supports such crude generalizations.[2] These works raised important concerns about the problems facing democracy and the capacity of journalism to generate the informed self-governing citizenry postulated in democratic theory. Some, perhaps much, of the writing and concerns in these books—for example, Lippmann's discussion of depoliticization in the opening of *The Phantom Public*—is nothing short of brilliant and has survived all too well to the current era.

Concerning journalism and the news, however, these books do not age especially well. Journalism is but a supporting character within a much broader plotline in both books. Moreover, the context for these books was the historical moment when professional journalism was in ascension and the commercial news media system was functioning. In our current crisis, the approach Lippmann takes is somewhat orthogonal to the great journalism issues before us.

It is therefore to our considerable good fortune that Lippmann authored two largely unknown pieces in 1920 that deal directly with journalism and its relationship to self-government. These are "A Test of the News," a long essay co-authored with Charles Merz that appeared in *The New Republic*; and *Liberty and the News*, two of the three chapters of which had been published in *The Atlantic Monthly*.[3] "A Test of the News" systematically evaluated the coverage of the Russian Revolution from 1917 to 1920 by the *New York Times*. It was trailblazing research that anticipated by decades some of the best news media content analysis of recent times. *Liberty and the News* is Lippmann's only direct encounter with the relationship of journalism, democracy, and liberty. It is some of his most astonishing prose and by any reckoning an extraordinary work, with many dimensions of analysis. One cannot read these works and dismiss Lippmann as an anti-democratic elitist.

These works are even more important because they were written at the climax of the last truly great defining crisis for journalism. It is during times of crisis and upheaval that a disproportionate number of our greatest breakthroughs in social science have been made, as tried-and-true formulations are subject to far greater scrutiny. (Consider John Maynard Keynes and the Great Depression, for example.) Faced with a crisis, our greatest thinkers often become more critical, creative, and original and provide us with insights and lessons for the ages. So this specific period was an extraordinarily fecund time for the development and crystallization of Lippmann's thinking about the press and self-government. As times changed, his work would rapidly move in somewhat different, and more politically conservative, directions. He turned from structural concerns to greater emphasis upon human psychology as the key independent variable, with the institutions of society taken more or less as a given; but that does not alter the power or importance of what he wrote in 1919 and 1920. Indeed, Lippmann never renounced the research and arguments in "A Test of the News" or *Liberty and the News*, even if he never quite returned to them in letter or in spirit. They were of a moment.

For contemporary observers, it is often underappreciated that by 1919 and 1920 the credibility and legitimacy of the news was very much in question by much of the American public. "It is admitted that a sound public opinion cannot exist without access to the news," Lippmann and Merz stated. "There is today a widespread and a growing doubt whether there exists such an access to the news about contentious affairs. This doubt ranges from accusations of unconscious bias to downright charges of corruption, from the belief that the news is colored to the belief that the news is poisoned."[4] The primary, though not exclusive, factor explaining the threat to the news and democracy was the rapid emergence of organized propaganda, or what today would often be called public relations. During World War I, Lippmann saw firsthand the successful use of such propaganda by the U.S. government and a compliant press to warp public opinion. He argued that propaganda made much worse an already "extremely refractory" and "increasingly disserviceable" commercial journalism of the times.[5]

Nowhere was this more apparent than in Lippmann and Merz's detailed examination of the *New York Times'* coverage of the Russian Revolution. Though hardly sympathetic to the revolution, they were appalled at what they found: the nation's most prestigious newspaper was basically conveying the wishes, distortions, and lies of anti-revolutionary forces as the gospel truth. The biggest liar was the United States government itself. The *Times*, they wrote, was being "seriously misled" by "its reliance upon the official purveyors of information."[6] They concluded: "The reporting of the Russian Revolution is nothing short of a disaster. On the essential questions the net effect was almost always misleading, and misleading news is worse than none at all." Journalists "were performing the supreme duty in a democracy of supplying the information on which public opinion feeds, and they were derelict in that duty. . . . Whatever the excuses, the apologies, and the extenuation, the fact remains that a great people in a supreme crisis could not secure the minimum of necessary information on a supremely important event."[7]

Lippmann emphasized the way government propaganda altered the traditional democratic equation. He found the emergence of such propaganda nothing short of frightening; it created an existential crisis for the entire notion of a free press, and therefore self-government. "Government tends to operate by the impact of controlled opinion upon administration. This shift in the locus of sovereignty has placed a premium upon the manufacture of consent. . . . Without protection against propaganda, without standards of evidence, without criteria of emphasis, the living substance of all popular decision is exposed to every prejudice and to infinite exploitation."[8]

The implications of the corruption and degradation of the news could not be more severe. As Lippmann put it, people increasingly "are baffled because the facts are not available; and they are wondering whether government by consent can survive in a time when the manufacture of consent is an unregulated private enterprise. *For in an exact sense the present crisis of western democracy is a crisis of journalism.*"[9] News media were therefore institutions of singular importance. "For the newspaper is in all literalness the bible of democracy, the book out of which a people determines its conduct.... Now the power to determine each day what shall seem important and what shall be neglected is a power unlike any that has been exercised since the Pope lost his hold on the secular mind."[10] Hence what Lippmann and Merz termed "a fundamental task of the Twentieth Century: the insurance to a free people of such a supply of news that a free government can be successfully administered."[11]

What is striking in these works is the conviction that journalism and the institutions that produce journalism are to be thought of not as private enterprises, but as public institutions. "A great newspaper is a public service institution," Lippmann and Merz wrote. "It occupies a position in public life fully as important as the school system or the church or the organs of government."[12] Lippmann noted: "The news columns are common carriers. When those who control them arrogate to themselves the right to determine by their own consciences what shall be reported and for what purpose, democracy is unworkable."[13]

In short, the people and the government have a direct stake in seeing that the news media system functions properly, and the owners have no right to claim it as their private property and as of no public concern. In *Liberty and the News* he suggests that public money could be spent to improve the quality of information.

In 1920 Lippmann was not at all certain that this crisis would be resolved satisfactorily. "In a few generations it will seem ludicrous to historians that a people professing government by the will of the people should have made no serious effort to guarantee the news without which a governing opinion cannot exist. 'Is it possible,' they will ask, 'that at the beginning of the Twentieth Century nations calling themselves democracies were content to act on what happened to drift across their doorsteps; that apart from a few sporadic exposures and outcries they made no plans to bring these common carriers under social control?'"[14]

Lippmann had an ambiguous attitude toward the commercial news media system and toward newspaper owners. The first two decades of the twentieth century constituted an existential crisis for them, as brazen partisanship, sensationalism, corruption, and scandal undermined the legitimacy of the commercial system. Some publishers feared for their very existence. Lippmann acknowledged this threat and had little sympathy for most of the owners. "In some form or other the next generation will attempt to bring the publishing business under greater social control. There is everywhere an increasingly angry disillusionment about the press, a growing sense of being baffled and misled." He concluded that "someday Congress, in a fit of temper, egged on by an outraged public opinion, will operate on the press with an ax."[15] He never even entertained the notion that competition in the "free market" would of its own volition provide the journalism necessary for self-government to succeed. Although fiercely opposed to censorship, Lippmann exhibited no apparent concern for how public involvement would infringe upon publishers' First Amendment rights.

That being said, Lippmann did not regard the newspaper owners as a structural barrier to reform that was insurmountable. In his analysis he routinely assumed that the actual power to control the news rested with editors, not publishers. He had little interest in how the commercial and political concerns of owners determined or influenced who became editors and what values guided the editors' work. He had little apparent interest in the collusion of government with big business, nor was he especially concerned with how journalism affected different sectors of the population. Not everyone outside of the highest reaches of government lost if the news failed to create an informed and participating citizenry. Surprisingly, for one who had been a socialist just a few years earlier, Lippmann did not entertain the idea, foundational to Jefferson and Madison, that those with property and privilege greatly benefited by an ignorant and ill-informed populace. He had, to be blunt, no class analysis.

At almost the exact time *Liberty and the News* and "A Test of the News" appeared in print, Upton Sinclair's *The Brass Check* was published.[16] Sinclair excoriated newspaper publishers for the corruption and anti-labor bias of their news. The book is filled with example after example, and makes it impossible to regard actual ownership of media as insignificant to newsroom operations or the content of the news, as Lippmann presupposed. It, too, is a seminal work in journalism history. But Sinclair used a hammer where at times Lippmann's scalpel would have been preferable. Sinclair and Lippmann would each have benefitted mightily from an encounter with the other's work. Regrettably, they mostly spoke past each other, probably due to political differences, as Lippmann's cursory dismissal of *The Brass Check* in *Public Opinion* demonstrates.[17]

Even a socialist like Sinclair had difficulty imagining a different news media system than the private ownership model in place in the United States, so one can hardly chastise Lippmann for internalizing as a "given" the dominant commercial system not only of his time but for the balance of the century. Good publishers were possible and therefore necessary. Lippmann dedicated *Liberty and the News* to C. P. Scott, the legendary owner and editor of the *Manchester Guardian* since 1872. "In light of his career," Lippmann wrote, "it cannot seem absurd or remote to think of freedom and truth in relation to the news."[18] It may be some indication about the importance of commercial pressures upon the news that after Scott's death, his family placed the *Guardian* in a nonprofit trust beginning in 1936. The trust's stated "core principle" was to "preserve the financial and editorial independence of the *Guardian* in perpetuity, while its subsidiary aims are to champion its principles and to promote freedom of the press in the UK and abroad."[19] (The nonprofit course has served the newspaper well. As commercial news media have floundered in the current crisis, the *Guardian*, by many accounts, is arguably a greater and more important source of quality journalism, both traditional and now digital, than ever before.)

In *Liberty and the News*, Lippmann was not taking the radical step of calling for nonprofit newspapers; instead he was primarily cautioning newspaper owners to appreciate that they had to change course. He was hoping that the fear of extinction would encourage those publishers less principled than Scott to do the right thing.

"Wise publishers will not pooh-pooh these omens," he wrote. "The regulation of the publishing business is a subtle and elusive matter, and only by an early and sympathetic effort to deal with great evils can the more sensible minds retain their control."[20]

To Lippmann the solution was clear, and he was emphatic: newspapers needed to embrace professional training and standards for reporters and editors to ensure the highest quality of factually accurate and contextually honest information unpolluted by personal, commercial, or political bias. "Primarily," Lippmann and Merz wrote, "we believe professional standards of journalism are not high enough, and the discipline by which standards are maintained not strong enough."[21] Reporting, Lippmann wrote, needed to be removed from "untrained and biased hands." "The existing news-structure may be made serviceable to democracy along the general lines suggested, by the training of the journalist, and by the development of expert record and analysis."[22]

"How far can we go in turning newspaper enterprise from a haphazard trade into a disciplined profession?" Lippmann asked. "Quite far, I imagine, for it is altogether unthinkable that a society like ours should remain forever dependent upon untrained accidental witnesses." It would require a commitment from press owners and journalists themselves, and public money for institutions like schools of journalism to train a generation of great expert reporters. "No amount of money or effort spent in fitting the right men for this work could possibly be wasted, for the health of society depends upon the quality of the information it receives."[23]

Lippmann had no illusions that the crisis afflicting journalism in 1920 could be solved in-house by owners and editors, or by simply consulting elite intellectuals. He regarded the establishment of professional standards as necessary but not sufficient, and not likely to be done in a satisfactory manner without popular involvement. What is striking is how adamant Lippmann—the oft-chastised elitist—was that the public needed to play a loud and persistent role in creating an adequate news media system. "Only rarely do newspaper men take the general public into their confidence. They will have to sooner or later," he wrote. "The philosophy of the work itself needs to be discussed; the news about the news needs to be told. For the news about the government of news structures touches the center of all modern government."[24] The debate over journalism needed to go before the general public; it was everyone's business. Left to elites and insiders, reform would be improbable. "Those who are now in control have too much at stake, and they control the source of reform itself." It was particularly important for politically organized progressives to take the issue of journalism seriously. "Change will come only by the drastic competition of those whose interests are not represented in the existing news-organization. It will come only if organized labor and militant liberalism set a pace which cannot be ignored."[25]

Job one for the skilled and educated reporter would be to see through the spin and propaganda put forth by governments and powerful interests, or the reporter's own opinions, so that citizens could be given an accurate understanding of the day's events. "In going behind opinion to the information which it exploits, and in making the validity of the news our ideal, we shall be fighting the battle where it is really being fought. We shall be protecting for the public interest that which all the special interests in the world are most anxious to corrupt."[26]

As Lippmann and Merz put it, reporters needed to create and enforce a professional "code of honor," similar to that adopted and enforced by the professional associations of lawyers and doctors, and they needed to "watch vigilantly for infractions of that code."[27] The turn to professionalism, Lippmann argued, could create a "great independent journalism, setting standards for commercial journalism." In short, professionalism could force even recalcitrant publishers to fall in line, much as the "splendid English cooperative societies" had set high standards for commercial enterprises there.[28]

Judging by these works, Lippmann can arguably be regarded as the preeminent visionary who best imagined the role that professionalism would come to play in saving journalism from the lack of credibility it had in the first two decades of the twentieth century. That is no small historical achievement. By the early 1920s, the American Society of Newspaper Editors had been formed, and among its first tasks was to establish a code of conduct. Schools of journalism, which barely existed before World War I, exploded in prominence. For the next generation this would be the major development in journalism, and the exact contours of the professional code were debated and fought over by reporters, editors, and owners.

By the 1950s, few explicitly partisan newspapers remained, as most newsrooms operated in accordance with professional principles. Even longtime partisan holdouts like the *Chicago Tribune* embraced the notion of professionalism and nonpartisanship in journalism—once Colonel Robert McCormick died—and a "separation of church and state" between the business office and the editorial office. The notion that the news should be unbiased and "objective" became common- place, to the point that generations of Americans assumed it was the intent of the First Amendment.

We should not take the notion of Lippmann as the "Founding Father" of American professional journalism too far, as the manner in which professional journalism actually developed in the United States veered dramatically from the core values he prescribed in *Liberty and the News* and in "A Test of the News." Most striking, Lippmann and Merz thought the entire point of professional jour- nalism was to be able to rigorously dissect, fact-check, contextualize, and critique information provided by governments and special inter- ests. "Statements of fact emanating from governments and the circles around governments cannot be taken as judgments of fact by an independent press."[29] How ironic that a primary tendency of pro- fessional journalism as it has evolved in the United States has been to take the claims of government, especially when those in power are in general agreement, at face value, even when there are enor- mous grounds for skepticism. The dreadful coverage of the lead-up to the 2003 U.S. invasion of Iraq is exhibit A, but the list is long and depressing. Contemporary professional news, such as it exists, has flunked the single most important item on the Lippmann test by any honest calculation.

Although Lippmann was obsessed with the provision of objective journalism by trained journalists, he did not think that such objec- tive news would end political arguments and undermine political opinion. He simply thought it should be the basis for them. He was not at all opposed to opinionated journalism—he was, after all, the co-founder of the *New Republic* and for many decades a decorated political columnist. Rather, his argument was that opinion-based journalism required a great deal of news that was primarily dedicated to providing an honest understanding, as opposed to journalism driven by partisan or commercial motives.

We can debate whether such truly objective journalism can ever exist; few people actually believe that it can. Institutional and human biases are unavoidable, and the starting point is to be honest about it. But that hardly eliminates Lippmann's concern. Some journalism can be "more" objective than other journalism, and we need some journalism that attempts to get it as straight as possible, and to be held accountable to that standard. Perhaps the best way to put it is that we need journalists to be scholars, not lawyers. Scholars, if they are honest, seek out criticism of their arguments and contradictory evidence, and address it in the interest of having the strongest and most accurate possible understanding of their subject. Lawyers, on the other hand, just want to win. They cherry-pick facts and quotes and eliminate context where it goes against their position. They only deal with competing positions and disagreeable evidence when forced to, and the point is to discredit it or minimize its impact by any means necessary.

Lippmann's journalism is a journalism of scholars. A journalism of lawyers is no democratic journalism at all.

As we increasingly live in a world where too much of public life is barely covered by working reporters any longer, Lippmann's warnings about the consequences of losing factually based reporting loom large. "The cardinal fact always is the loss of contact with objective information. Public as well as private reason depends upon it. Not what somebody says, not what somebody wishes were true, but what is so beyond all our opining, constitutes the touchstone of our sanity." "The really important thing," he added, "is to try and make opinion increasingly responsible to the facts. There can be no liberty for a community which lacks the information by which to detect lies." Our core liberties lose their basis for support. "When freedom of opinion is revealed as freedom of error, illusion, and misinterpretation, it is virtually impossible to stir up much interest in its behalf. It is the thinnest of all abstractions and an over-refinement of mere intellectualism." "There seems to be no way of evading the conclusion," Lippmann wrote, "that liberty is not so much permission as it is the construction of a system of information increasingly independent of opinion."[30]

A journalism-free world chock full of people free to spout their opinions, therefore, is hardly a free society, and in no sense can it be regarded as democratic. It is far closer to a living hell. "Men who have lost their grip upon the relevant facts of their environment are the inevitable victims of agitation and propaganda. The quack, the charlatan, the jingo, and the terrorist, can flourish only where the audience is deprived of independent access to information." Lippmann was blunt about the course of a journalism-free future: "I am equally convinced that democracy will degenerate into this dictatorship either of the Right or of the Left, if it does not become genuinely self-governing."[31]

Today we are in the midst of a crisis of journalism and of democracy every bit as frightening as that of ninety years ago. To some extent it is due to the degradation of professional journalism, significantly (though not exclusively) owing to the commercial forces that Lippmann failed to account for in his analysis. The feisty independent and fearless professional journalism Lippmann desired was incompatible with a commercial and significantly monopolistic news media system. Even more fundamental, a technological revolution has caused the business model of commercial journalism to disintegrate, leaving what remains of it in shambles. There is no longer the resource base that Lippmann assumed was in place to bankroll the newsrooms of the nation.

What that means is we cannot use Lippmann's 1920 playbook to determine the exact solution to our current crisis. But so what? We cannot necessarily use the same policies and subsidies used by Jefferson and Madison, but they still have crucial lessons for us about journalism and democracy, and so does Lippmann. His understanding of the role and importance of the press system and the news for freedom and democracy is nothing short of sublime. His understanding of the public and political nature of journalism and the crucial role for the public is a necessary rejoinder to the absurd and ahistorical market fundamentalism that has derailed our discussion of the journalism crisis. His critique of a fatuous "freedom" to basically lie with impunity in a fact-free world of spin and propaganda should send shivers down our spines. We have a large foot in that reality already, and we cannot afford to wait and see what happens if and when the other foot lands there as well.

Solving the crisis of journalism, creating an independent Fourth Estate that will make self-government and freedom truly possible, will be difficult, but it is not impossible. It was the Framers' mission, it was Lippmann's mission, and it must be ours. We may not get the perfect solution, but we can get much better solutions than will exist if we do nothing and maintain the status quo. In *Liberty and the News*, Lippmann found optimism in our very nature: "The desire to know, the dislike of being deceived and made game of, is a really powerful motive, and it is that motive that can best be enlisted in the cause of freedom."[32] We can never afford to forget Lippmann's core point: that in an exact sense, the present crisis of democracy is a crisis of journalism.

10

The Personal Is Political: My Career in Public Radio

IN THIS CHAPTER I look at the problems facing progressives and those on the political left in the United States in participating in political analysis and debate in mainstream journalism and the news media. I focus on radio broadcasting, as this is where much of the political discussion in the United States takes place. Radio broadcasting is the least expensive of the media for production and reception, it is ubiquitous, it has adapted itself to the Internet, and it is uniquely suited for locally based programming. I leave aside the matter of the Internet, as this is an issue I address in detail elsewhere; although the digital revolution is of indubitable importance, it does not appreciably alter my basic argument.[1] I also stay away from television, and cable TV news networks in particular. While those channels are important, they too do not affect my core points. I look specifically at my own experience with hosting a weekly public affairs program on an NPR-affiliated radio station in Illinois from 2002 to 2012. This was, to my knowledge, the only series on an NPR station ever hosted by a socialist in the network's history. But before I draw from my personal experiences, some context is necessary.

Background

Considerable scholarship has examined the range of legitimate debate in the U.S. news media. In short, the range tends to be bounded by the range of debate among political and economic elites; when they agree on a topic, it is pretty much off-limits in the news media and various discussion programs.[2] As Jeff Cohen, the founder of Fairness and Accuracy in Reporting, puts it, the range of debate tends to extend "all the way from GE to GM."[3] When non-mainstream views do get attention, they tend to be misrepresented, ridiculed, or trivialized. Occasionally, during periods of social upheaval and powerful social movements, dissident views can get a hearing, even a respectful one; but when the momentum recedes, the coverage declines sharply, both qualitatively and quantitatively.

For those firmly ensconced in the mainstream, this tends to be no more a concern than drowning is to a fish; it barely warrants consideration as an issue. For those outside the mainstream, addressing the too-narrow range of legitimate discourse has been a constant problem, and an issue of almost singular importance. For much of American history, the emphasis was upon creating independent media that could provide a forum for dissident views. By the middle of the twentieth century, the emphasis became gaining access to mainstream media and elite media discourse, as they dominated the political environment; independent media, such as they existed, were increasingly marginal and ineffectual.

For modern societies as a whole, elite-driven media debate may not be an enormous problem in political democracies with high voter participation, relative economic equality, vibrant political cultures, and economic growth and stability. As none of those criteria apply to the contemporary United States—and it is arguable how much the last criterion has applied since the 1980s—the nature of media and media systems is a very big deal.

To be precise, the ideological barriers are stronger in journalism and explicit public affairs coverage than in the balance of the media culture. Commercial entertainment allows a bit more wiggle room for dissident and left-wing ideas, though that point should not be exaggerated. It is striking, too, that celebrities from the entertainment world can get an audience in mainstream media to discuss ideas outside the mainstream with an ease that scholars or activists could only dream about. But again, that point should not be exaggerated. It is "open" only in comparison to the lockdown in place for the range of debate in the news media.

Much of the explanation for the constricted range of debate in mainstream journalism points to the commercial basis of the industry: private ownership supported by commercial advertising as the revenue base. This gives journalism an implicit small-*c* conservative bias. Such news media, especially as the firms get larger, the owners richer, and the markets less competitive, tend to have a built-in bias toward the status quo; this point has been understood for a good century. Even those analyses that emphasize the crucial role of professional ideology in setting the values for the field often acknowledge that the professional values emerged in an environment where the commercial and political values of the owners were internalized. This critique began with newspaper journalism and was extended to commercial broadcasting as it became pervasive by the middle decades of the twentieth century.

Indeed, from the 1930s through the 1970s, commercial radio and later television broadcasting tended to be almost devout in their commitment to staying close to the middle of the road and not veering outside the boundaries of elite debate. (This is what is meant by "neutrality" or "objectivity" in journalism.) The principle was encapsulated in the Federal Communications Commission's Fairness Doctrine, which was formally adopted in the 1940s.

Those on the political right found such journalism insufficiently sympathetic to their worldview and political program, and a detriment to their prospects of political success. In the 1970s they launched an intense campaign to make the mainstream news media more sympathetic to the right, specifically seeking to overturn the Fairness Doctrine, which required stations to provide balance in their coverage of public affairs.[4] They got their wish when the Reagan FCC overturned the Fairness Doctrine in the 1980s. Soon thereafter, Rush Limbaugh and a legion of charismatic far-right blowhards all but monopolized the commercial airwaves with regard to political chat, generally mouthing the same Republican Party talking points *ad nauseam*. If one were to visit the United States any time after around 1990, and if one assumed that commercial radio provided an accurate reflection of the nation's political temperament, one might logically conclude that the United States was the most extreme right-wing nation since the defeat of fascism in 1945. An outsider might be surprised that Pat Buchanan or Michele Bachmann did not win the presidency with 90 percent of the vote.

Moreover, with regard to structural and core economic issues, the range of political debate has shifted far to the right in the United States since the 1970s. This has been driven to a large extent by aggressive campaigns by moneyed and corporate interests to assert their domination of the political process.[5] Issues that once were accepted as mainstream—for example, public education, progressive taxation, labor unions, social security, and the need for full employment—are now subject to withering criticism, and their future is in jeopardy. Inequality has increased sharply, and the political system is awash with institutionalized corruption. As both parties have followed the money trail, the flag of centrism has been pushed toward the right-field foul line. This has accentuated the problem of journalism and media for progressive activists, and for citizens who wish to assert democratic values and practices. As may be evident by now, I fall under that heading.

Ironically, mainstream discussion of the parties emphasized how they have "polarized," with each party moving further to extremes. That is inaccurate, if not preposterous. The alleged "polarization" refers to the fact that the parties no longer overlap, as white southern Democrats have stopped getting elected, and moderate and liberal Republicans have become extinct; but both parties have moved appreciably rightward on core structural issues. The lack of overlap in a system in which the two parties have made it virtually impossible for an effective third party to gain a foothold contributes to the degeneration of the governing system—an outcome that apparently is of no great concern to the moneyed benefactors who pay for the politicians. Democratic voters, on the other hand, have not moved to the right on most issues—if anything, the opposite is the case—which is a recurring tension in the political system, and a basis for hope.

In the United States, there have been two forms of broadcast media since the 1960s that were created to counter the problems in the commercial system, for journalism, public affairs, and entertainment.

Both were born of a more liberal era, when the notion of generating media to expand awareness and political participation was considered a legitimate public policy objective. The Public Broadcasting Act was passed in 1967, which established the Corporation for Public Broadcasting (CPB) and eventually the Public Broadcasting Service (PBS) television network and National Public Radio (NPR). Beginning in the mid-1970s, scores of community radio stations were created, joining the handful of stations like those of the Pacifica network that were established prior to the 1970s.

Although both NPR and community radio stations depend upon CPB support to help sustain their operations, they each followed a different logic. The NPR stations began in a time when they were envisioned as providing a forum for dissident voices, for those precluded from the commercial system. Political pressures made that an impossibility for public broadcasters early on. NPR stations settled into the role of being a main source of political information and discussion on the air. With the disappearance of commercial radio journalism in the United States by the end of the 1990s, NPR stations often became the only game in town. NPR journalism and public affairs programs tend to avoid the salaciousness, idiocy, and asininity of the commercial broadcasting world—which is no small contribution—but stay resolutely within the boundaries of elite debate. They are perpetually in fear of budget cuts driven by the political right with its endless jihad against "liberal" bias. NPR stations are firmly lodged in a relatively well-established niche of the media system.

Community radio stations, on the other hand, have a more fragile basis for existence. There are fewer of them, they largely rely on volunteer labor, they sometimes struggle to find effective management systems, and many of them are one bad pledge drive away from catastrophe. At the same time, the community stations as a rule have a much broader range of political ideas; they are the broadcast media that are not constrained by the range of elite debate. Community radio is where one can go to get real criticism of corporate capitalism or U.S. foreign policy, or where one can go to get thorough discussion of the environment, which is impossible with NPR or commercial stations. The entertainment, too, tends to be far more eclectic than what can be found elsewhere on the dial. The downside:

with meager resources, the patchwork of stations is barely visible to the great mass of the population.

Enter the Professor

Much of the above is reflected in the critical scholarship on media, journalism, and politics. Some of it draws from my own research on the political economy of communication. As my career advanced and I had published a few books, which attracted considerable attention for academic titles, I was able to experience firsthand how the interview/talk programs worked. Between 1993 and 2013, I did approximately 1,000 guest appearances on radio programs. Only a smattering of these appearances were on commercial radio stations, where, with only a few exceptions, the interviews were brief and/or I was paired with a mainstream person to provide "balance." Such balance is almost *never* required of mainstream guests.

(How I would have adored seeing Thomas Friedman, some retired general who serves as the "expert" on all cable news channels, John McCain, or another mainstream pundit paired with Noam Chomsky or any informed critic for a debate on U.S. foreign policy! It never happens, even on NPR stations as a rule, even when history demonstrates, as with the 2003 Iraq invasion, that the closer one gets to war, the closer the mainstream explanations come to being adulterated half-truths and lies. Someone like Christopher Hitchens was *persona non grata* in the mainstream media when his views were stridently critical of U.S. foreign policy; when he became a firm proponent of U.S. military intervention in the Balkans and Iraq and a loud critic of the antiwar movements, he became a household name. The quality of his writing and thinking did not change—only his political views.)

The rest of my 1,000 radio interviews were split between community stations, NPR affiliates, and interviews with foreign public service broadcasters. The community stations were hit-and-miss; some interviewers were unprepared and unfocused, while many of the shows were absolutely first-rate. Those interviews were respectful and serious, and perhaps the best I have ever had. The NPR stations tended to be more professional, but the hosts were and are much more cautious. Again, many of the programs were tremendous, and the callers on the NPR call-in programs were sympathetic and discerning. There was nothing whatsoever like this on commercial radio in the United States. That is where ideas and thoughtful discussion go to die.

In 1995 I began my own career as a radio host. At the time I was teaching in Madison, Wisconsin, and I was asked to do a shift hosting a public affairs program every second week on WORT-FM, the local community station. I was a volunteer. I sought out guests who had little exposure in the media but whom I knew had a good deal to say. Many were academics whose work had a political orientation. I had complete liberty to select guests, and the responsibility to do so. When I accepted a teaching position at the University of Illinois in 1998, I stepped down from the show. I soon realized that I missed doing it; it was fun being on the other side of the table.

What I especially enjoyed about doing hour-long interviews on noncommercial stations was that I could give guests an opportunity to really lay out their positions and explain themselves. This is something that is rare for critical scholars and progressives, who invariably struggle with the sound-bite cliché Olympics on commercial media. Critical ideas outside the mainstream need time to be explained. Mainstream views can generally invoke deeply ingrained cultural references: free enterprise, entrepreneurs, markets, America, and choice, for example. I wanted to give those dissident voices—often the truth-tellers—an opportunity to speak, and give a starving audience the opportunity to hear them.

Because I had ample time to explain my own views in my own writings and in interviews in which I was the subject, I had little desire or need to use my position as host to make my own views the heart of the show. To the contrary, I treated my guests exactly the way I like to be treated when I am a guest: I read their books and/or articles, I tried to help them get their main ideas communicated clearly, and I let them explain their work and their ideas. Having been interviewed extensively gave me a sense of what a good interview entailed. I recalled how baseball legend Ted Williams responded when asked whether he—arguably the greatest hitter in the game's history— could possibly manage pitchers. "I was a great hitter because I studied pitching, so I think I can coach it." I developed a great deal of respect for the good hosts I dealt with over the years. To do the job well was a lot of work: it requires a considerable amount of preparation and the ability to be a good listener. Lots of the radio hosts I met on local stations—including Ian Masters, Marc Steiner, and Sonali Kolhatkar, to name but a few—provided a model for my work. At the national level I learned a lot by listening to Amy Goodman, David Barsamian, Bill Moyers, Terry Gross, and, curiously enough, Larry King.

An incident in the summer of 2000 reinforced for me why my approach to doing public affairs radio was necessary. I began writing a column that year for the *Silicon Alley Reporter*, a trade publication started by Jason McCabe Calacanis that focused on the Internet boom in New York City. My book *Rich Media, Poor Democracy* had just been published, and Calacanis wanted me to provide a critical take on Internet matters, which I gladly obliged. (The column was titled "Homage to Catatonia.") By 2001 the dot-com crash had put the magazine out of business, but before that it was a big deal, and each issue was fat with advertising. In the summer of 2000, at its peak, the *Silicon Alley Reporter* hosted a one-day conference in Westchester County, New York, for the movers and shakers in the New York Internet economy. Several hundred people paid a hefty fee to attend, and I was flown in to be one of the plenary speakers.

Instead of giving speeches in the packed theater, the plenary speakers were interviewed sequentially onstage by Charlie Rose, then as now the host of a daily PBS interview program. Rose apparently had a close connection to Calacanis or others high up at the *Silicon Alley Reporter*. At that point his PBS show was at its peak, and many academics and public figures considered it the premier interview show in American media. It exemplified the constricted range of debate in American mainstream media: corporate CEOs and mainstream thinkers dominated. Thomas Friedman had what seemed like a second residence on the set. It was the voice of the establishment. Dissidents were generally restricted to entertainers and artists, and were often "balanced." I confess I was intrigued by the idea of having thirty to forty-five minutes with Rose by myself. In the back of my mind, I thought that perhaps once he saw what a good interview I was, he would have me on his TV show. I could dream, couldn't I?

My excitement increased when I watched Rose interview the plenary speaker who immediately preceded me onstage—a Yale professor whose claim to fame was having been a victim of one of the

Unabomber's mail bombs a few years earlier. I discovered during the course of the interview that this professor had right-wing views, though I had never heard of him before, nor have I subsequently. At any rate, Rose peppered this guy with softball questions right down the middle of the plate. To hear Rose, one might think this man was the greatest genius of the twentieth century. Most of Rose's questions were seemingly prefaced with something along the lines of "Because you are such a great genius and wonderful human being . . ." I suspect some people in the audience contemplated naming their next child after the Yale professor. I was salivating at the thought of getting a round of those questions and smacking the answers over the center-field fence to the thunderous applause of the audience. Yee haw!

Instead, Rose's tone changed perceptibly the moment I came onstage for my interview. Batting practice was over, and the questions were more like brushback pitches or beanballs. Rose had little apparent sympathy for my position, and even less interest in allowing me to explain myself in my own terms. He was civil, don't get me wrong, and the interview went smoothly. But I was dealing with his trip—being the border policeman for the range of legitimate debate—and never got much of a chance to explain what I was about. It confirmed what I already knew: there needed to be a place for progressives and those outside the mainstream to have their voices heard and reach a larger audience than that provided by the smattering of community radio stations. It did not exist in America.

To some extent, that impulse motivated my political work in the subsequent years. In 2002 and 2003, John Nichols, Josh Silver, and I formed the media policy reform group Free Press. It exploded into prominence during the Iraq War in 2003, when it became public knowledge that the same media conglomerates whose news divisions had uncritically reported the official lies that got the United States into the war were attempting to change rules so they could own even more media outlets. Free Press has been active since then on a number of issues that are all about democratizing the media system and expanding the range of legitimate debate beyond that sanctified by Wall Street, political elites, and corporate America.

But as important as policy activism was for reforming the system, in the meantime there was work to be done, or else the prospects for structural reform on any issue, including media, would lessen.

In 2001 I approached officials at WILL-AM, the NPR affiliate associated with the University of Illinois at Urbana-Champaign, and broached the idea of my doing a weekly public affairs program, with an emphasis on media issues. I knew it was a long shot, as no other NPR station had a program like the one I was proposing. But I was also familiar with the saying that the farther one got from salt water, the better were the chances that an NPR station would be open-minded. That was certainly the case with WILL. The management responded positively and listened to tapes of my WORT program from the 1990s, and when a spot opened up in the schedule, I went on the air in April 2002. The program, *Media Matters*, ran every Sunday from 1 to 2 p.m. central time for the next ten and a half years, until the final episode in October 2012.

The reason the show worked was that WILL gave me carte blanche to do as I pleased. I was solely responsible for selecting (and procuring) guests. The station provided an engineer to be in the studio, but I provided my own labor for free, and I was responsible for getting my own producer at my own expense. My guests over the 500-plus weeks included a who's who of progressives: Andrew Bacevich, Sherrod Brown, Sundiata Cha-Jua, Noam Chomsky, Barbara Ehrenreich, Bill Fletcher Jr., Thomas Frank, Janine Jackson, Chalmers Johnson, Lawrence Lessig, Toby Miller, Michael Moore, Ralph Nader, Bernie Sanders, Norman Solomon, Gore Vidal, and Howard Zinn, among others. I had many of the finest journalists of our era on the program on a routine basis, people like Robert Scheer, Amy Goodman, Juan Gonzalez, Katrina vanden Heuvel, Jeremy Scahill, Michael Hastings, Naomi Klein, John Pilger, Glenn Greenwald, Chris Hedges, Salim Muwakkil, Matt Taibbi, and Alexander Cockburn. Despite their accomplishments, many of those people could not get an hour-long audience on an NPR station. Nearly all of them appeared at least twice on my show, and many of them appeared at least once every year or two. My occasional co-author, the journalist John Nichols, was a guest thirty-three times, in part because he always co-hosted my twice-annual pledge drive shows.

Probably half of the programs were with more obscure guests I wanted to bring into the public eye. Occasionally I was able to increase the visibility of an important writer making an original argument with compelling evidence. In 2009, for example, I had Wendell

Potter as a guest. Potter was a former health insurance executive who provided an inside account of the nefarious practices in the industry. He would later gain national attention. In 2011 I had Michelle Alexander as a guest to discuss her astonishing book *The New Jim Crow*. At the time, barely anyone knew about it; within a year, it would be a bestseller. I was also delighted to have Diane Ravitch on the program to present her eloquent defense of public education and her critique of school privatization efforts. It was a voice rarely heard in the mainstream media. In all of these cases, I received a flood of feedback in the days following the broadcasts.

A recurring theme among my guests was the state of the economy, the nature of economic policy debates, and how the news media covered the economy. The guest roster included multiple appearances by Paul Krugman, John Bellamy Foster, Joseph Stiglitz, Dean Baker, Mark Weisbrot, James K. Galbraith, Michael Perelman, Robert Reich, Robert Kuttner, Juliet Schor, and Robert Pollin. There were scores of other times I knew the program was providing material not available elsewhere, and that it was having an effect. It reinforced for me the importance of blasting open the media system.

The show was surprisingly noncontroversial. I suspect part of that was due to my approach: I did not use the program to push my own views and ideas; it was about the guests. Casual listeners who did not know of my work otherwise would have been unlikely to glean much about my specific political positions or writings. I disliked interviewers who inserted themselves into the limelight. I tried to let the guests speak about what they knew best, and I gently guided them. Nor were my guests doctrinaire; they ranged all the way from Democratic Party liberals and progressives to socialists and beyond. I even had a few nonpolitical and mainstream guests when the topic was appropriate. If all my guests had appeared in the same room at the same time, some explosive arguments would have certainly ensued. Only on a few occasions did I really challenge a guest to back up a statement I found farfetched. I figured that was the listeners' job, as this was a call-in show. And most weeks the phone lines lit up at WILL; the callers often asked better questions than I did.

This is not to say that WILL did not get complaints about my show, especially its political orientation. In the first few months, the station management kept me apprised of the criticism; thereafter they kept me in the dark, saying there was very little to worry about. So I will never know how much flak the station received. The only serious attack came in 2008 or so, when a prominent far-right-winger who makes a career red-baiting progressives (and who has never lived in Illinois) tried to raise a ruckus about the left leanings of my guests. He claimed this was an abuse of public broadcasting, and that any NPR show should have what he deemed to be balanced guest lists or be pulled off the air. I explained to the right-winger and my station manager that my bias was toward guests who were otherwise mostly unavailable in the commercial and public media. Since one could listen to endless far-right-wingers on AM radio coast to coast twenty-four hours per day—they were almost impossible to avoid—there was no need for me to offer them a slot on my measly show. My program, in fact, *was* the beginning of a real balance at NPR and in the broader media culture. The station manager at WILL gave me unconditional support. It made it a pleasure for me to work there.

This support gave me added incentive to help raise money for the station. As it developed, *Media Matters* became a barnburner during pledge drives, invariably raising far more money than any other program on the station. Listeners wanted to send an emphatic message to station management that the show had a strong following, and the message was received loud and clear. Moreover, at one point the WILL person responsible for such matters told me that *Media Matters* was the top-ranked program in the area in its time-slot for listeners aged 25–54. I was told at another point that a full half of all the Internet traffic and downloads for the station could be attributed to *Media Matters*. Thanks to podcasting, the audience for the program was national, even international, and a significant portion of that audience did not listen in real time. We got callers from all over the nation and the world. When I decided to discontinue the program to have more time for other projects in 2012, I was inundated with e-mails and letters and messages from fans across the planet—literally hundreds of them within a few weeks. By just about any measure for an NPR program, it was a hit.

I was especially moved by the significant number of young people who contacted me to describe how they had stumbled across *Media Matters* and to say it had introduced them to a world they did not know existed. It changed their lives. It reminded me how, when I was fourteen years old, I saw a TV interview with Gore Vidal in which he described the United States as an empire. Later that same year, I saw another interview on local TV in which someone described racism in Cleveland, Ohio, where I grew up. Those two events shook the foundations of my world and helped push my life in a very different direction. Media *matters.* The right wing gets it, the mainstream gets it. Progressives have got to get in the game. Except for the various incarnations of Bill Moyers's superb programs on PBS—which are still going strong in 2014—progressive voices are all but nonexistent in public media. In commercial television—including MSNBC—political viewpoints are on increasingly shaky ground as one heads to the left of the leadership of the Democratic Party.

Therefore, perhaps the most sobering aspect of the *Media Matters* experience has been that no other NPR station—not a single one—has attempted to emulate it. One might think that, given its popularity by all measures, other NPR stations might be looking to do something like it in their own communities. It is not like these stations are setting the world on fire with their present offerings. If anything, programs like *Media Matters* can be moneymakers, possibly cash cows, because they reach a large underutilized and appreciative audience. Nor is it the case that I am the only person capable of hosting such a program; the country is crawling with talented people who could do a bang-up job. And as I discovered, there are extraordinary guests—I barely scratched the surface of what is out there—who richly deserve to be part of the public conversation in the United States. Our media and our nation are much weaker for their absence. Yet there has been zero interest by anyone else in doing such a show; indeed, there was no interest by other NPR stations to pick up *Media Matters* when WILL management briefly pursued the matter a few years into the show's run, after they had seen how popular it was with listeners. I am left with the conclusion that the left politics scared the pants off NPR officials outside of Champaign-Urbana. If there is an alternative explanation, I am—to invoke Ross Perot—all ears. My program was the exception that proves the rule.

PART FOUR

Bringing It All Back Home

11

The Cultural Apparatus of
Monopoly Capital

THE PAST HALF-CENTURY has been dominated by the rise of media to a commanding position in the social life of most people and nations, to the point where it is banal to regard this as the "Information Age." The once-dazzling ascension of television in the 1950s and 1960s now looks like the horse-and-buggy era when the Internet, smartphones, and the digital revolution are taken into consideration. For social theorists of all stripes, communication has moved to center stage. And for those on the left, addressing the potential of communication in achieving social change and then maintaining popular rule in the face of a reactionary backlash is now a primary concern.[1] The Arab Spring and the media battles of the elected left governments in Latin America are exhibits A-1 and A-2. Any serious left critique or political program must account for, and embrace, communication or risk being irrelevant.

To address these emerging concerns, "the political economy of communication" has emerged as a dynamic field of study over the past four decades, and one in which considerable radical scholarship has been undertaken. The field addresses the growing importance of media, advertising, and communication in advanced capitalist societies, examining how the capitalist structure of communication industries shapes media content, as well as the role of media and culture in maintaining the social order. In particular, the field explores the way media "depoliticizes" people, and thereby entrenches the privileges of those at the top. It highlights the importance of government policies in creating the communication system, and the nature of the policymaking process in capitalist societies. In North America, the decisive founders of this area of research were Dallas Smythe and Herbert Schiller. In Europe, a generation of scholars coming out of the 1960s launched the field, and there the work was more closely attached to a rereading of Marx. Perhaps the most visible manifestation of the research in the United States has been the stellar critique of journalism produced over the years by Edward S. Herman and Noam Chomsky.[2] Countless left activists are versed in the material today, a testament to the field's value and importance.

To no small extent, political economists of communication, including myself, identified themselves as in the tradition of radical political economy, but with a sophisticated appreciation of media that had escaped their predecessors, locked in the past as they were. Paul Baran and Paul Sweezy were occasionally held up by political economists of communication as representing the sort of traditional Marxists who underappreciated the importance of media, communication, and culture.[3] Because of the preeminent role of their 1966 book *Monopoly Capital*, Baran and Sweezy tended to receive more criticism than other radical economists who were likewise seen as negligent in this area. Smythe's seminal 1977 essay, "Communications: Blindspot of Western Marxism," though acknowledging *Monopoly Capital*'s strengths and importance, devoted more criticism to it than to any other work.[4] The pattern has persisted in subsequent writings.[5]

I was never especially impressed by this criticism.[6] To me, *Monopoly Capital*, and the broader political economy of Baran and Sweezy, far from ignoring communication, provided key elements for a serious study of the subject. Its emphasis on the importance of giant corporations operating in oligopolistic markets offered a very useful way to understand media markets. Specifically, Baran and Sweezy's take on the "sales effort" and the role of advertising in monopoly capitalism was, and is, the necessary starting point for any treatment of the subject.[7] Few other economists came close to them in making advertising a central part of their political economy of capitalism. In doing so, they made the media and communication industries central components of modern capitalism.

Along these lines, one of my favorite pieces by Baran and Sweezy was their 1962 written testimony to the British Labour Party's Advertising Commission, headed by Lord John Reith, the iconic former director general of the BBC. The Advertising Commission was established as part of the Labour Party's reconsideration of the use of commercial advertising on British radio and television. Later published in *Science and Society* as "Theses on Advertising," and largely unknown to this day, Baran and Sweezy's testimony took the political-economic arguments concerning the role of advertising in contemporary capitalism that were later developed in *Monopoly Capital* and applied them foursquare to understanding media.[8] Their analysis of the deleterious effects of advertising on media operations and content, as well as society as a whole, is powerful and ages well. The piece also suggests that Baran and Sweezy, far from being determinists who thought any struggle for reform was a waste of time unless or until capitalism was overthrown, had a keen sense of the importance of media policy fights in the here and now. The Advertising Commission Report was finally published in 1966, and reflected the views of Baran and Sweezy with respect to the key roles played by oligopolistic markets, the decline of price competition, and the role of "the monopoly power of established firms" in the rise of modern mass media advertising.[9]

In addition, Baran and Sweezy demonstrated a sensitivity to the importance of technology and its capacity for changing the nature of capitalism and the nature of society that was mostly unrivaled among economists left, right, and center. Their work placed emphasis on examining "revolutionary" technologies like the steam engine, electricity, and the automobile, which provided the basis for capitalist expansion for generations and turned the world upside down in the process. In 1957 Sweezy characterized the United States as being in the midst of a sweeping "scientific-industrial revolution," due to the confluence of the corporate expansion into directing research and the rise of permanent militarism in the 1940s. In a careful review of economic history and contemporary scientific and technological developments, and with a look toward the horizon, Sweezy put the invention of the computer and the emerging communication revolution at the center of a technological revolution that would be every bit as profound as that wrought by the steam engine. To those who found this hypothetical, if not preposterous, Sweezy responded: "Come back in another thirty years. The transformation of society implicit in the new technologies will then be in full swing and you will be able to see signs of it on every hand."[10]

Yet in reading *Monopoly Capital,* one was left, somewhat paradoxically, with little sense that communication per se was of much interest to its authors.

This changed in 2011, when a missing chapter was discovered that had been written for *Monopoly Capital.* Originally drafted by Baran and titled "The Quality of Monopoly Capitalist Society II," it was focused on culture, communications, and mental health.[11] It had been intended to appear as the book's penultimate chapter, and Baran had planned to add more material related to the mental health section, which was only loosely related to the culture section.[12] But in March 1964 he tragically died of a heart attack, leaving the redrafting of this chapter undone. Sweezy was therefore left with the task of editing and completing it. He worked extensively on the chapter in November 1964 and perhaps later, editing the manuscript, cutting out considerable material from the original draft, and adding some new material related to communications. He gave this later version the title "The Quality of Monopoly Capitalist Society: Culture and Mental Health." In the end, however, he elected to leave it out of the book, recognizing that there were issues that the two of them had not sufficiently worked out together.[13]

When I read this missing chapter, however, I immediately saw that the portion on culture was based on serious research and important theoretical insights. It also demonstrated a commitment to a "political economy of communication" before the field had even crystallized, and far beyond what almost anyone had imagined possible. It also provided a quite different perspective on Baran and Sweezy's goals for *Monopoly Capital.* Focusing on monopoly capital's creation of a mass society culture, it was in some respects intended to be the logical culmination of the book's argument. Its point was to provide an understanding of the political culture of monopoly capitalist society, and the implications for radical social change.

As I reviewed the work of Baran and Sweezy on culture and communication, as well as other pieces that appeared in *Monthly Review* in the late 1950s and '60s, it became clear that the culture chapter that

was missing from *Monopoly Capital* was not an isolated occurrence or
an anomaly, but rather part of a broader emerging intellectual school.
I discovered that some exceptional related work was done during this
period by several major radical and Marxist intellectuals—people like
C. Wright Mills, Herbert Marcuse, E. P. Thompson, Ralph Miliband,
Eric Hobsbawm, and Raymond Williams, who were in regular communication with one another. All of these thinkers contributed to
the critique of the cultural apparatus.

On the one hand, the work of this period demonstrates a creative and open-minded Marxism or radical social criticism that
embraced the issue of communication and plunged into the problems it posed for social theory. It animated much of what would be
most impressive about the New Left, which was about to explode
into prominence. On the other hand, the examination of communication gravitated from criticism of capitalist culture to being
concerned with the politics of culture, and how control of communication systems was becoming a necessary political battlefield for the
democratic left. As early as 1961, Thompson observed: "The task of
creating an *alternative* means of communication has, from the start,
been a major preoccupation of the New Left."[14] In this sense these
works anticipated many of the issues that concern the left today, and
the approach offers clarity and insight that has considerable value for
activists worldwide.

These works can also be seen as providing some of the crucial
foundation for a political economy of the media, helping us to construct the critical responses we need today in the age of the Internet,
social media, and the ongoing attempts in Latin America and elsewhere to repossess the cultural apparatus of society.

Brecht, the Frankfurt School, and the Concept of Cultural Apparatus

In retrospect, the basis of Baran's, if not Sweezy's, concern for, and
awareness of, culture and communication issues is obvious. Baran
worked as a researcher under Friedrich Pollock, the associate director of the Institute for Social Research in Frankfurt before fleeing
Germany in 1933, following Hitler's accession to power. Baran's experiences and associations in Frankfurt were to exert a strong influence

on his writing, so much so that he is sometimes characterized as the foremost political economist associated with the Frankfurt School.[15] During the 1950s and early '60s, when he was a professor of economics at Stanford, Baran met and corresponded with other figures he had known at the Institute for Social Research, including his close friends Herbert Marcuse and Leo Lowenthal, and kept up with the writings of Erich Fromm, Max Horkheimer, and Theodor Adorno.[16]

Central to the Frankfurt School's concerns was the relationship of mass culture to politics and social change. Baran read widely and carefully in this area, and it was his passion for the subject that likely was the impetus for the prospective chapter in *Monopoly Capital*. He approached culture and communication as encompassing art, literature, entertainment, education, media, and the role of intellectuals.[17] His main concern was the undermining of affirmative culture, as a necessary form of human development, due to the relentless process of commodification promoted by monopoly capital. As he stated in 1950:

> We have to understand the ideologically overpowering impact of bourgeois, fetishistic consciousness on the broad masses of the working population. . . . The heartbreaking emptiness and cynicism of the commercial, competitive, capitalist culture. The systematic cultivation of devastatingly neurotic reactions to most social phenomena (through the movies, the "funnies," etc.). The effective destruction in schools, churches, press, everywhere, of everything that smacks of *solidarity* in the consciousness of the man in the street. And finally, the utterly paralyzing feeling of solitude which must overcome anyone who does not want to conform, the feeling that there is no movement, no camp, no group to which one can turn.[18]

In Baran's view, commodified culture comes to play a preeminent role under monopoly capitalism. The overarching critique is of the massive and growing gap between the actual quality of culture in the United States and what the society is capable of producing. This gap is both cause and effect of the absurdity of monopoly capitalism and evidence of its increasing destructiveness. It is a political-economic critique because it assesses the cause of the gap as the capitalist nature of society and, more specifically, the capitalist nature of the "cultural apparatus." Baran and Sweezy took seriously the close examination of the structures of media and communication industries.

It was the concept of the cultural apparatus, derived from Bertolt Brecht, Fromm, Horkheimer, Marcuse, and Mills, that formed the central organizing principle in Baran's drafting of the discussion of culture and communications in *Monopoly Capital.* The earliest outlines for the "Quality of Monopoly Capitalist Society II" chapter covered the realms of the "mass media" and "mental health."[19] Baran was to transform this, however, into a treatment of specific media, particularly book publishing and broadcasting, as manifestations of what he and Sweezy called the development of "the cultural apparatus of monopoly capitalism." Indeed, their analysis in the missing chapter begins and ends with the concept of the cultural apparatus.

To understand the significance of this, it is important to know something of the history of this crucial Marxian concept. The notion of the cultural apparatus owed its centrality in Marxian theory primarily to the work of Brecht beginning in 1932.[20] Brecht saw what he referred to as the cultural "apparatus" or means of production and of technical control of cultural processes as applying to every realm of cultural production, including the theater, opera, radio, book publishing, and film. The crucial problem for the artist, who did not control the cultural apparatus in capitalist society, was thus to find ways to gain control or to subvert the apparatus in order to promote critical, dialectical, and revolutionary ends. However, Brecht was under no illusions, and in his view the dominant role of the cultural apparatus in bourgeois society was to reinforce existing power relations. As Rowitha Mueller has stated: "Thus the terminology itself points up the connection between culture and politics." In Brecht's view, the cultural apparatus functions, among other things, to stabilize the existing social relations both politically and economically. He "saw this in terms of a selection process: 'Society absorbs via the (cultural) apparatus whatever it needs in order to reproduce itself.'"[21]

In Brecht's view, artists and intellectuals are not masters of the cultural apparatus, but rather their work is completely subordinated to it and to capitalist objectives, and thus "they are supporting an apparatus which is out of their control." "The intellectuals . . . are completely dependent on the apparatus, both socially and economically; it is the only channel for the realization of their work. The output of writers, composers and critics comes more and more to resemble raw material. The finished article is produced by the apparatus." The capitalist order got in the "general habit of judging works of art by their suitability for the apparatus without ever judging the apparatus by its suitability for the work." The result was that "work amounts to so much merchandise, and is governed by the normal laws of merchandise trade. Art is merchandise, only to be manufactured by the means of production (apparati)."[22]

Brecht concretely explored various forms of the cultural apparatus—theater, radio, film—with the idea of carrying out a kind of guerrilla war that would end up appropriating them for purposes of revolutionary change. He believed that ultimately "the socialization of these means of [cultural] production" was "vital for art." The goal, then, was to develop strategic approaches to asserting control over the various apparati, which were currently "wholly capitalist." This required empirical research and a deep understanding of the various ways in which the artist and intellectual could employ leverage. Brecht's drama was explicitly designed to subvert the apparatus of the theater in this way. As he wrote: "When I read Marx's *Capital* I understood my plays."[23]

The artist and the intellectual in this perspective had a crucial role to play in the struggle over the cultural apparatus that was so vital to society. In Brecht's plays this took the form, to use a phrase of Baran's, of "the confrontation of reality with reason," through various dialectical devices. Brecht employed the concept of "inploitation" (a kind of reverse or internalized exploitation) to describe the complex, contradictory role of the consumer of the products of the cultural apparatus, who was simultaneously both a victim and a kind of complicit exploiter in the context of the struggle of the cultural producer or artist with the owners.[24] The role of the artist and intellectual as revolutionary was to reestablish the relationship between the consumer and producer of cultural work by undermining the estrangement from human needs and capacities enforced by the bourgeois society.

As Walter Benjamin, who was enormously influenced by Brecht, argued, the question of "the author as producer" was not so much a question of the "position [of the artist's work] vis-à-vis" the various forms of the cultural apparatus, as "what is its position *within* them?"

The fundamental problem in cultural change then became "adapting the apparatus to the ends of the proletarian revolution."[25]

Brecht argued that the struggle over the cultural apparatus was not confined to those forms such as film and broadcasting that were new, but extended to the entirety of communication forms, all of which were being increasingly mechanized, commodified, and transformed. This included traditional forms such as printed books and the theater. "The changes wrought by time leave nothing untouched, but always embrace the whole." A crucial aspect of this was "the mechanization of literary production," which could not "be thrown into reverse." The goal then has to be to reconstruct the existing cultural apparatus to prevent these increasingly complex media from being removed further and further from the development of human needs and capacity and "the new possibilities of communication."[26]

The concept of the cultural apparatus played a formative role in the work of the Frankfurt School. As early as 1932, it occupied a central place in Fromm's article "The Method and Function of an Analytic Social Psychology"—published in the *Zeitschrift für Sozialforschung* and seen as the foundational work integrating historical materialism and psychoanalysis. As Axel Honneth explained the importance of this piece: "Within the intellectual circle of the Institute for Social Research, Fromm was entrusted with the task of working out a psychology that could be linked with economics without any fissure."[27]

Fromm wrote that "the creation of the [governing] norms" in society was "not left to chance," but rather, "one whole basic part of the cultural apparatus serves to form the socially required attitude in a systematic and methodical way." The "cultural apparatus" was depicted as driving, in the language of psychoanalysis, the "libidinal structure of society"—or what Fromm later called "social character"—channeling it so that it was no longer a threat to the status quo. With respect to the working class, the cultural apparatus played a key role in forming what Fromm termed the social cement meant to counter the effects of alienation.[28]

Writing in a similar vein in 1936 in "Authority and the Family," Horkheimer discussed how revolutionary periods remove some of these cultural controls, depriving them of power, while in periods of restoration and reaction an "outmoded cultural apparatus as well as the psychic makeup of men and the body of interconnected institutions acquire new power. Then there is a need to investigate the culture thoroughly." As a structure of power, the cultural apparatus seeks to bond the population to the status quo by means of the promotion of particular ideas and ways of life, which are internalized within the psyche. In Horkheimer's words:

> One function of the entire cultural apparatus at any given period has been to internalize in men of subordinate position the idea of a necessary domination of some men over others, as determined by the course of history down to the present time. As a result and as a continually renewed condition of this cultural apparatus, the belief in authority is one of the driving forces, sometimes productive, sometimes obstructive, of human history.[29]

But it was in Marcuse's "33 Theses" (written in 1947 and found in draft form in Horkheimer's archives, appearing only posthumously in Marcuse's *Collected Works*) that the issue of "the cultural apparatus of monopoly capitalism" was first raised. There Marcuse wrote, in thesis 15:

> The phenomenon of cultural identification demands that the problem of "cultural cement" (*Kitt*) be discussed upon a broader basis. One of the most important factors involved here is the leveling of formerly avant-garde oppositional forces with the cultural apparatus of monopoly capitalism (the transformation and application of psychoanalysis, modern art, sexuality, etc., in the work and entertainment process). First and foremost, the effects of "*Kitt*" within the working class should be investigated: "scientific management," rationalization, the interest of the worker in increased productivity (and with it, in the intensification of exploitation), strengthening of nationalistic sentiments.[30]

The concept of cultural cement as articulated here by Marcuse followed Fromm and Horkheimer. For Horkheimer it was this cement that was at all times the crucial object of analysis, since it "artificially held together the parts tending towards independence."[31] The intent of Marcuse's fifteenth thesis was to underscore the necessity of empirically researching how this cementing of workers to the dominant order was actually accomplished (in contradictory fashion) by the cultural apparatus of monopoly capitalist society.

This reflected the central problem governing the research program of the Frankfurt School. As Honneth has put it:

> A major portion of the theoretical construction and social research of the Institute during the 1930s was an attempt to provide an empirical answer to the problem expressed in this tension [between exploitative socioeconomic conditions and cultural stability]. Its guiding motif is formed by the question "What psychic mechanisms have come about that enable the tension between the social classes to remain latent, even though it borders on conflict as a result of the economic situation?" The program of an interdisciplinary social science, outlined by Horkheimer at the beginning of the 1930s, is tailored to the investigation of this phenomenon.[32]

Erich Fromm was later to describe the "cultural apparatus" as a "filter" conditioning what entered society's "social unconscious."[33] As he wrote in *The Sane Society* in 1955 (a book that strongly impressed Baran): "Eventually, he [the alienated industrial worker] is under the influence of our whole cultural apparatus, the advertisements, the movies, television, newspapers, just as everybody else, and can hardly escape being driven into conformity, although perhaps more slowly than other sectors of the population."[34]

Mills, Thompson, and Williams

Similar considerations led Mills, beginning in the late 1950s, to commence writing what was to be a major work but was left unfinished at his untimely death, *The Cultural Apparatus*. The historically specific context of Mills's entry into this sphere is powerfully described by Stanley Aronowitz:

> Mills had come to the conclusion that it was not the economy or even self-interest in general that drove contemporary social agents to action or inaction. Mills concluded that in the epoch of what he

termed "overdeveloped" capitalism, the masses were moved more broadly by "culture" than reason. He had become convinced that the cultural apparatus played a central role in reproducing the entire "setup." But it is not the anthropological conception of culture—a whole way of life—that he believed determined politics or secured the domination by the leading institutional actors. Mills's invocation of the cultural apparatus ... signaled that culture was no longer the spontaneous creation of the people but instead was an aspect of the organization and reproduction of social and political domination. If social transformation was at all possible, its protagonists were obliged to understand the process of production and distribution of key cultural forms, especially the mass media. Clearly, the implication of his projected study was to argue for a new counterhegemonic strategy of the Left that matched the force of the culture industry.[35]

Mills delivered three university lectures at the London School of Economics (LSE) in January 1959, utilizing a manuscript titled "The Cultural Apparatus, or the American Intellectual." These three lectures were later published as "Culture and Politics: The Fourth Epoch," "The Cultural Apparatus," and "The Decline of the Left." Together they constitute the main extant materials of his projected book on *The Cultural Apparatus*—left behind at the time of his death from a heart attack at age forty-five in 1962.

Mills did not get very far in this unfinished work in defining what he actually meant by the cultural apparatus. His approach was broader and more obscure than the way the concept was being used in Marxist theory, in which it was essentially equivalent to the cultural means of production, including the technical means themselves. In contrast, Mills used the notion of cultural apparatus somewhat ambiguously in terms of "observation posts, interpretation centers, and presentation depots" and went on to say that it was "composed of all the organizations and milieux in which artistic, intellectual, and scientific work goes on." His emphasis was more on processes than on structures, and he dwelled on the role of the intellectual, writing: "I have been studying, for several years now, the cultural apparatus, the intellectual—as a possible, immediate radical agency for change."[36] This tended to downplay the power dimension and reduced the question of the cultural apparatus itself to the question of the intellectual, rather than emphasizing the dialectical relation between cultural producer and the capitalist cultural apparatus as in Brecht and the Frankfurt School. Nevertheless, Mills went on to make the critical point that

> what intellectuals now confront is the expropriation of their cultural apparatus itself. We do not have access to the means of effective communication, but more than that, many of us are losing control of the very means of cultural production itself. The situation of the serious movie-maker—is not this the prototype of all cultural work-men? We are cut off from possible publics and such publics as remain are being turned into masses by those businessmen or commissars who do control and manage the effective means of communication. In their hands, these are often less means of communication than means of mass distraction. . . . What we ought now to do is repossess our cultural apparatus, and use it for our own purposes.[37]

Mills's approach had a big impact on the New Left Marxists in Britain. E. P. Thompson attended the last of Mills's three LSE lectures on the cultural apparatus, and called it "absolutely splendid."[38] But there was friendly criticism from a Marxist standpoint. In a long letter to Mills, Thompson wrote: "You argue that intellectual workers must repossess their cultural apparatus and use it for their own purposes. In what sense have they ever possessed it?"[39] For Thompson it was a question not of repossession of the cultural apparatus but of the construction of a left cultural apparatus. "The problem presents itself," he wrote in 1959, "as one of constructing (however painfully slow the process may seem—though steady progress is being made) an *alternative* 'cultural apparatus' which bypasses the mass media and the party machinery, and which opens up direct channels between significant socialist groupings inside and outside the labour movement." Thompson was deeply involved in communications issues in the late 1950s and early '60s, and submitted a memorandum (as did Raymond Williams) to the 1960 Committee on Broadcasting (the Pilkington Committee). The Pilkington Report was presented to Parliament in 1962.[40]

Williams shared with Mills and Thompson a concern to translate the critique of the cultural apparatus into a political strategy and program for the left. The starting point for his analysis was "the subordination of a general communications process to an increasingly powerful system of advertising and public relations."[41] In 1961 he argued:

> Instead of the ritual indignation and despair at the cultural condition of "the masses" (now increasingly uttered even by their supposed friends) it is necessary to break through to the central fact that most of our cultural institutions are in the hands of speculators, interested not in the health and growth of society, but in the quick profits that can be made by exploiting inexperience. True, under attack, these speculators, or some of them, will concede limited policies of a different kind, which they significantly call "prestige"; that is to say, enough to preserve a limited public respectability so that they will be allowed to continue to operate. But the real question is whether a society can afford to leave its cultural apparatus in such irresponsible hands.... We should be much clearer about these cultural questions if we saw them as a consequence of a basically capitalist organization, and I at least know no better reason for capitalism to be ended.[42]

Again it was Thompson who asked the hard question, observing in 1961 that Williams had failed to consider "the contrary problems of 'utopia' . . . and of an intellectual tradition associated with social groups opposed to established interests—which must make its way without the benefit of institutions or cultural apparatus of its own, and which is exposed to the dangers of sectarian aridity or of losing its best men in the institutions of the 'other side.'"[43] Indeed, it was Thompson's lifetime struggle as a historian (in works such as *The Making of the English Working Class*) to show how the working class in England had sought to construct its own class consciousness and culture, despite its exclusion from the dominant cultural apparatus, i.e., the main means of intellectual production of the society.[44]

Toward a Wider Political Economy of Communication: The 1960s Critique

This was the state of the discussion in 1962 when Baran first set about drafting the analysis of culture and communications for

Monopoly Capital. Baran and Sweezy's intention in this planned penultimate chapter of their book was to uncover the way in which the cultural apparatus of monopoly capitalist society was increasingly owned and controlled by the vested interests, undermining the critical and "intellectual side of civilization" and the possibilities for effective social change. Both the publishing and the broadcasting industries, they wrote, demonstrated "the striking extent to which culture has become a commodity, its production subject to the same forces, interests, and motives as govern the production of all other commodities."[45]

Their analysis focused on "the cultural industries" as distinct forms of production, which as they "moved from handicraft to mass production" increasingly fell "under the sway of corporate business" geared to maximum profits and catering "to all the frailties and weaknesses of human nature." Under monopoly capitalism, "cultural output . . . turned into its opposite," embodying a further fracturing of human reason and human action, and impeding rather than enhancing human development and historical change.[46]

Noting that book publishing had already lost out to newspapers and magazines as the "predominant form of reading," Baran and Sweezy nevertheless insisted on its "unique importance in society's cultural apparatus." From their experience, literacy, and access to literature and a broad range of political books, was foundational to popular democratic politics. They were aware that progressive U.S. government policies and subsidies in the 1940s aimed at increasing literacy and expanding the publication and distribution of books had proven highly effective. They also were unsurprised that Senator Joseph McCarthy had singled these policies out as pro-Communist and anti-American.[47] Indeed, Leo Huberman, Sweezy's co-editor at *Monthly Review,* had been subpoenaed in 1953 by McCarthy's own Senate committee due to the inclusion of several of his books in the State Department's overseas libraries. Huberman defiantly told the McCarthy committee: "A manifesto voted by the American Library Association on June 25 [1953] and concurred in by the American Book Publishers Council, opens with these words: 'The freedom to read is essential to our democracy. It is under attack.' Everyone knows that the main attacker is this committee of Congress and its chairman."[48]

Baran and Sweezy also saw firsthand that the changing nature of the book industry meant that the broad range of critical books that had proliferated in the 1930s and '40s was becoming a thing of the past.[49] Without policies pushing in a different direction, the commercial book-publishing industry was undergoing enormous expansion, and although it was still "highly competitive," characterized by decreasing rather than increasing profit margins, it was rapidly becoming more and more concentrated, taking on the character of an "emerging oligopolistic . . . industry."

The mass production and concentrated nature of the industry meant that books were more and more standardized and sold in the same manner as cars or cosmetics. This affected content, leading those who controlled the book-publishing apparatus to emphasize: (1) conformist views, albeit a sophisticated conformity that could include severe criticisms of the status quo as long as they did not extend to the underlying structures or the possibility of radical actions; (2) selectivity in the issues discussed; problems of sex, individual psychology, and even race were more admissible than the questioning of the economic and social order; (3) a focus on celebrities; and (4) imitation of new successful fashions.

From there Baran and Sweezy went on to examine the character and content of the leading bestselling books, from religious books to cookbooks, to crime and detective novels, to general bestselling novels. They also included a short discussion of comic books. The general conclusion pointed to the "steady and methodical debasement of the book itself over the last few decades. Transferring to the sale of books the methods used in marketing 'sex apparel' and cosmetics, of liquor and cigarettes and nostrums of all kinds, undermines all respect for literary work, and annihilates the book as a cultural medium."[50]

They paid close attention to the bestselling books of Mickey Spillane—six of which were among the top fifteen bestsellers of the twentieth century—and his vigilante-murderer hero Mike Hammer. Spillane's anti-communism was used frequently to justify his blood-lust and sadism, leading him to have Hammer declare at one point: "But some day, maybe, some day I'd stand on the steps of the Kremlin with a gun in my fist and I'd yell for them to come out and if they wouldn't I'd go in and get them and when I had them lined up against the wall I'd start shooting until all I had left was a row of corpses that bled on the cold floors and in whose thick red blood would be the promise of a peace that would stick for more generations than I'd live to see."[51] Spillane's bestsellers were the perfect counterpart to the McCarthy era.

For Baran and Sweezy, Spillane was only an extreme example of the degradation of the mass distribution novel, in which an artist's concern with "the representation of individual and social conflicts, of human passion, joy, and suffering" had been replaced by books providing "a minute account of the hero's (frequently improbable) overt behavior without any attempt at the discovery, elucidation, and comprehension of the underlying causes and motivations. The purpose is merely to thrill."

Under monopoly capitalism, Baran and Sweezy argued, the cultural apparatus increasingly controlled the artist, "with the writer becoming more pronouncedly an employee of the publishing corporation and his independence increasingly turned into a sham." A few individual artists, of course, managed to struggle with this cultural apparatus and by various means transcend it. But the general tendency toward conformity and degradation within book publishing was not to be denied.

As Hobsbawm observed in a similar way in the *Times Literary Supplement* in 1964:

> The economic facts are conclusive. The professional writer of books is in the position of the hand-loom weaver after the intervention of the power loom: two thirds or three quarters of his profession can earn less than a typist's income, and the number of writers who can live entirely by the sales of their books would fit into a single, not excessively large room. . . . In certain branches of literature, such as utilitarian fiction, craft production can persist, not only because the demand for it is smaller, more lasting and more intermittent, but also because the market can rely on large quantities of casual, part-time labour and the readiness of professional writers to turn themselves into hacks.[52]

Television broadcasting, in contrast, though a far younger cultural apparatus, was not an emerging oligopoly, as in book publishing, but had already been established by government policies as a tight oligopoly. It was here that Sweezy in his work at *Monthly Review* had written two essays on American television with Huberman in 1958 and 1959. The first of these, published in April 1958, was a critique of the Federal Communications Commission (FCC) and its role in facilitating the concentration of broadcast media, both radio and television. The licensing of television stations, the facilitation of the dominance of oligopoly, the deliberate squelching of competition, and the handing out of the airwaves for free to particular corporations (which Huberman and Sweezy compared to the handing out of western lands to the railroads in the nineteenth century) constituted an enormous "swindle" on the public, and the basis of monopoly capital in this area. The fact that this was often accompanied by outright corruption was not surprising. Profit margins from television, they showed, had been strong and increasing, reaching 22 percent by 1956. Sweezy and Huberman dug into the financial data of the television industry as few, if any, other scholars had ever done before, and systematically debunked the notion that regulation of private economic power in the public interest could ever be effective under monopoly capitalism; instead, the only logical solution if one desired democratic media in the public interest was social ownership.[53]

By the early 1960s, it was already clear that the dominance of the three great networks had created a "tightly controlled oligopoly" in television.[54] Baran and Sweezy, who presented their "Theses on Advertising" to the Labour Party's Advertising Commission in 1962, the same year that Baran first drafted their treatment of culture and communication for *Monopoly Capital*, were under no illusion about what drove television broadcasting. They quoted 20th-Century Fox Television president Peter Levathes's statement that "the sponsor buys a show to sell his product. That is the basic purpose of TV. To sell someone's product." The logic of this was clear. Monopoly capital (encompassing corporations as a whole, and more specifically the TV networks and stations) was "interested in maximizing sales and profits by reaching the widest possible audience." This created the conditions for FCC chairman Newton Minow's famous remark in 1961 that television was "a vast wasteland."

This "wasteland" was exposed for all to see in the 1959 quiz show scandal, which demonstrated the corrupt and mendacious way in which television broadcasting was organized with the aim of duping the public, and the moral and intellectual degradation of its content as a result. This was the basis for Huberman and Sweezy's second *Monthly Review* media piece on "The TV Scandals" in December 1959. The problem, they argued, lay not simply in moral decline, as so many commentators argued, but in a system that enforced such moral decline. "Can you imagine," they asked, "a morally responsible campaign to sell a remedy for 'tired blood'? A fantastic example perhaps? Not quite—it just happens to have been the product that Charles Van Doren was selling by his great intellectual feats on 'Twenty-One'"—the quiz show at the center of the TV scandals. The whole point, they went on to argue,

> was put in a nutshell by Professor Seymour E. Harris, Chairman of the Harvard economics department, in an article entitled "Can We Prosper Without Arms?" which appeared in the *New York Times Magazine* of November 8th: "A high rate of investment would increase the nation's productive capacity.... But our private economy is faced with the tough problem of selling what it can produce. This is the reason for Madison Avenue." Quite so, and it is also the reason why neither Madison Avenue nor the [corporate] clients of Madison Avenue can afford the luxury of integrity or moral responsibility.

Adam Smith argued, with some degree of cogency for his day, that if everyone pursued "his" own private interests, "he" would be led, "as if by an invisible hand," to serve the public interest. Nothing could be further from the truth today. When the giant corporation pursues its own private interests—as it must by the very law of its being—it is led by a not so invisible hand to degrade and corrupt the moral standards of a public that is completely dependent upon it not only for jobs and material goods but also for the "food of the mind." This is the plain lesson of the TV scandals.[55]

Huberman and Sweezy went on to argue for

> the creation of a nationwide, government-owned radio-television network under an authority representative of the best elements in the worlds of education, the arts, and entertainment. That this is no revolutionary proposal goes without saying. Both Britain and

Canada have long had government-owned networks, and in both cases they were founded by conservative governments. Their performance has been infinitely superior to that of the private American networks. *The creation of an American counterpart should become one of the leading demands of everyone who recognizes the seriousness of the present situation* and understands the futility, or worse, of relying on the TV industry or its man Friday, the Federal Communications Commission, to initiate and carry through serious reforms.[56]

Huberman and Sweezy (together with Baran) thus followed Brecht, who contended that "the socialization of these means of [cultural] production is vital for art" and the development of communication.[57]

In their later analysis of the quiz show scandal in their chapter on culture, Baran and Sweezy referred to the sordid details exposed in the congressional investigations, which showed that all elements of the television industry were caught up in the scandal. They responded not by calling for greater regulation, but by turning to the British government's 1962 *Report of the Committee on Broadcasting* (the Pilkington Report), which engaged in serious critique of the TV fare in the United States, and which characterized it—pointing to westerns—as containing "excessive violence and sadism." The Pilkington Report recommended an expansion of the BBC's role in television at the expense of further development of private programming—i.e., of the Independent Television Authority, with its channel, Independent Television (ITV), set up in 1955 as a commercial competitor to the BBC.[58]

In Baran and Sweezy's view, there was no effective form of regulation of the content of commercial broadcasting, since

it is not the particular form of swindle and deception that is important but the basic fact that it *is* swindle and deception that incessantly fill the air.

The dominance of the lie is not confined to explicit advertisements. The lie also permeates most of the television day. The world presented on TV is not the real world with its conflicting interests, its irrationalities, its destructive tensions, but also with its unending struggles and tremendous potentialities for betterment. It is an artifact which conjures up a tendentious, utterly misleading image of reality.[59]

For Baran, who was a devoted reader of Kafka, the lesson to be drawn was clear. As Kafka wrote in *The Trial*: "'No,' said the priest, 'it is not necessary to accept everything as true, one must only accept it as necessary.' 'A melancholy conclusion,' said K. 'It turns lying into a universal principle.'"[60] Quoting Adorno, Baran and Sweezy referred to the dulling of the "capacity for life experience" promoted by most television broadcasting. In this respect, "television and other mass media," they wrote, "contributes to a crippling of the individual's mental and emotional capabilities. By helping to instill in him a phantasmagoric image of existence it disarms him on the social and the individual plane." Worse still, it gave rise to cynicism, and a sense that public life is a fraud, while undermining any sense that this was open to change.

Unfortunately, "the increasing awareness of the falsehood of what is conveyed by society's cultural apparatus," they noted, "does not result in a heightened search for truth, reason and knowledge, but rather in the spread of disillusionment and cynicism." Turning to Engels's description of ideology as "false consciousness," they interpreted this in a sophisticated fashion as including "a partial, biased view of reality, half truths, reflecting some important aspects of it without encompassing its totality." What was effectively foreclosed by this ideology was "the existing and expanding possibilities for a different more rational, more human existence." Indeed, they argued that "the cultural apparatus of monopoly capitalism" was aimed at the opposite end of making "people accept what is, to adjust to the tawdry reality and to abandon all hopes, all aspirations for a better society."[61]

The political implications of the missing chapter are therefore decidedly despondent about the prospect of social change in the United States, or any other nation with a similar political and cultural apparatus. The reasons for this were readily apparent. Not only had the Progressive Party disappeared in the United States, and with it much of the effective remnants of the New Deal coalition, but by the early 1960s the days of meaningful parliamentary socialism in Britain had essentially come to an end, as recounted by Williams and Miliband in the pages of *Monthly Review*.[62] As Miliband commented on Mills's frequent despondency at the time: "Often, particularly in his last years, the 'politics of truth' which he advocated sounded more like the politics of despair. Hopelessness is a weakness in a social scientist, almost as grave as mindless unconcern or the cultivation of the fixed grin."[63]

Baran and Sweezy's position can be compared to that of Marcuse in his well-known work *One-Dimensional Man*, published in 1964. In the introduction, Marcuse stated that the main characteristics of the "one-dimensionality" of monopoly capitalist society were easily ascertainable if one were merely to subject oneself to "looking at television or listening to the AM radio for one consecutive hour for a couple of days, not shutting off the commercials, and now and then switching the station."[64]

The dilemma was the Brechtian one. In Marcuse's words (paraphrasing Brecht): "The contemporary world can . . . be represented only if it is represented as subject to change." The current formally "rational universe" of monopoly capitalism was such that it, "by the mere weight and capabilities of its [cultural] apparatus, blocks all escape." It invalidated "the cherished images of transcendence by incorporating them into its omnipresent daily reality." Marcuse ended his book by holding out the thin hope that "the spectre is there again, inside and outside the frontiers of the advanced societies. . . . The chance is that, in this period, the historical extremes may meet again: the most advanced consciousness of humanity, and its most exploited force."[65] Nevertheless, Marcuse's *One-Dimensional Man* was a deeply pessimistic book, centering on the containment and assimilation of the forces of social transformation as a result of the technical and cultural apparatus of late capitalist society.[66] "The legendary revolutionary," Marcuse wrote, "still exists who can defy even television and the press—his world is that of the 'underdeveloped' countries."[67]

Baran read Marcuse's book in manuscript in October 1963, in the midst of working on *Monopoly Capital*.[68] Marcuse's work had a profound effect on him. But Baran was also uncomfortable with the pessimistic conclusion that Marcuse reached in his arguments. Baran thought the matter so important that rather than allow this to affect the analysis of *Monopoly Capital* directly, he proposed to Sweezy that they take up this challenge in their next book. In an extraordinary letter to Sweezy on October 10, 1963, Baran went directly at the existential challenge of Marcuse's analysis to Marxist theory and socialist politics:

After having . . . shown how monopoly capital creates the muck that surrounds us on all fronts, we will have placed *this* part of the story "on the record" [in *Monopoly Capital*]. What is at the present time at issue and indeed most urgently so is the question whether the Marxian dialectic has broken down, i.e., whether it is possible for *Scheisse* [shit] to accumulate, to coagulate, to cover all of society (and a goodly part of the related world) *without producing the dialectical counter-force* which would break through it and blow it into the air. *Hic Rhodus, hic salta!** If the answer is affirmative then Marxism *in its traditional form* has become superannuated. It has predicted the misery, it has explained full well the causes of its becoming as comprehensive as it is; it was in error, however, in its central thesis that the misery generates itself the forces of its abolition. I have just finished reading Marcuse's new book [*One-Dimensional Man*] (in MS) which in a laborious kind of a way advances this very position which is called the Great Refusal or the Absolute Negation. Everything is *Dreck* (filth): monopoly capital and the Soviet Union, capitalism and socialism as we know it; the negative part of the Marx story has come true—its positive part remained a figment of imagination. We are back at the state of the Utopians pure and simple; a better world there should be but there ain't no social force in sight to bring it about. Not only is Socialism no answer, but there isn't anyone to give that answer anyway. From the Great Refusal and the Absolute Negation to the Great Withdrawal and the Absolute Betrayal is only a very short step. I have a very strong feeling that this is at the moment in the center of the intellectuals' thought (and sentiment)—not only here but also in Latin America and elsewhere, and that it would be very much *our* commitment to deal with it. . . . What is required is a cool analysis of the entire situation, the restoration of a historical perspective, a reminder of the relevant time dimensions and much more. If we could do a good job on that— perhaps only a shortish booklet of less than 200 pages—we would

---

*The phrase arises from the Latin form of Aesop's Fables: "Here is Rhodes, jump here!" In the fable, a boastful athlete brags that he once achieved a stupendous long jump in competition on the island of Rhodes. A bystander challenges him to dispense with the reports of the witnesses and simply repeat his accomplishment on the spot: "Here is Rhodes, jump here!"

make a major contribution and perform with regard to many a truly "liberating" act.[69]

Baran thus proposed to put into a restored historical context the apparent crisis of Marxism represented by the decoupling of social consciousness and agency from material contradictions and potentials. The perspective would have remained the critique of monopoly capital, but it would have required as an integral part of this critique a direct confrontation with the notion that the cultural apparatus was a permanent and irremovable roadblock to socialist politics, or even democracy. This was the direction that Mills and Williams were also going with their work. As Williams had put it in January 1960 in *Monthly Review*: "The central problem, as I see it, is cultural. The society of individual consumers which is now being propagandized by all the weight of mass advertising and mass publications, needs a new kind of socialist analysis and alternative."[70]

Baran was moving in the definite direction of extending the cultural critique and merging it with political-economic analysis. However, he was unable to work on this project, which he planned to pursue, with or without Sweezy, following the completion of *Monopoly Capital*. On March 26, 1964, while visiting Lowenthal and looking at a copy of Marcuse's just published *One-Dimensional Man* with a glass of brandy in his hand, he suffered his fatal heart attack.[71]

With the decision by Sweezy to leave the chapter on culture out of the published version of *Monopoly Capital*, Baran's struggles, together with Sweezy's, to confront the cultural contradictions of capitalist society, and the existential as well as strategic questions for the political left, were unfinished.

Monopoly Capital avoided the pessimism implied in the unpublished culture chapter. Its conclusion, "The Irrational System," emphasized the tendency of the economic surplus to rise under monopoly capitalism and the necessity of the wasting of this economic surplus, even as human needs remained unfulfilled—pointing to the increasing irrationality of the entire economic and social order. Key to the whole development was the fact that "a tiny oligarchy resting on vast economic power" was "in full control of society's political and cultural apparatus." Under these conditions, "improvements in the means of mass communication merely hasten the degeneration of popular culture." These were hardly conditions, they reasoned, that could prevail over the long run. Such a system was bound to find itself caught in ever more complex forms of irrationality and destruction. Hence they concluded that it was only a matter of time until the contradictions of the social order generated forces of opposition that would overwhelm them: "We have reached a point where the only true rationality lies in action to overthrow what has become a hopelessly irrational system."[72]

There were "even indications," they wrote, "especially in the Negro freedom movement in the South, in the uprisings of the urban ghettos, and in the academic community's mounting protest against the war in Vietnam, that significant segments of the American people are ready to join an active struggle against what is being cumulatively revealed as an intolerable social order. If this is so, who can set limits to the numbers who may join them in the future?"[73] But it was the world revolt against capitalism based in the periphery that was the real agent of change, to which the United States, as the chief bastion of monopoly capital, was not in the end immune. Despite the enormous power of the system that controlled the means of production—and along with it the state and the cultural apparatus of society—social struggle was breaking out everywhere in the 1960s, creating the hope that monopoly capitalism would be both besieged and challenged from within.

The Critique of Culture and the Media in the 1960s

Perhaps the most astonishing piece from this era is a pamphlet by Raymond Williams that was published by the Fabian Society in 1962: *The Existing Alternatives in Communications*. This almost entirely unknown piece drew from his great work *The Long Revolution* (1961), in which he addressed the question of the cultural apparatus, as well as the first (1962) edition of his book *Britain in the Sixties: Communications* (generally called *Communications*).[74] In 1962, Williams was another important figure, alongside Baran and Sweezy, to give testimony to the Labour Party's Advertising Commission, and their analysis clearly concurred on every point.[75] That testimony influences the pamphlet as well. As noted above,

Williams had submitted a detailed memorandum to the 1960 Committee on Broadcasting (the Pilkington Committee). It addressed the entire structure of the broadcasting industry, and may have influenced the 1962 Pilkington Report.

Like Baran and Sweezy, Williams was strongly impressed by the final Pilkington Report, released shortly after the first edition of *Communications*, and discussed it in the second (1966) edition of his book, in which he referred to it as "the classical point of reference for all reform in this field."[76]

In *Communications*, Williams defined communications as "the institutions and forms in which ideas, information, and attitudes are transmitted and received," while communication (without an *s*) referred to "the process of transmission and reception." Williams argued that the spectacular growth of communications in modern times had "created social problems which seem to be of a new kind." Communication, he argued, joined economics and politics as "equally fundamental" to understanding society. "We have been wrong in taking communication as secondary," Williams wrote. "The struggle to learn, to describe, to understand, to educate, is a central and necessary part of our humanity. This struggle is not begun, at secondhand, after reality has occurred. It is, in itself, a major way in which reality is continually formed and changed." This emphasis, he argued, "is exceptionally important in the long crisis of twentieth-century society."[77]

Accordingly, Williams argued that control over communication was of paramount importance, and commercial control of media was a disaster for humanity, not to mention democracy. "The only alternative to control by a few irresponsible men, who treat our cultural means as simple commodities, is a public system." Williams insisted that there was an important place for consumer information and advice in a communication system, "but advertising is a very primitive way of supplying it." He recognized the "genuine difficulties" of establishing a public cultural system, but that did not alter his belief in its central and immediate importance as a political project. What was required was "no direct control by government" over content, but nonetheless a strong public role, along with public debate and deliberation over the "actual allocation of resources." He was emphatic that the Old Left model of state monopoly and censorship was no legitimate or attractive alternative. Indeed, the bankruptcy of the Soviet-style system was demonstrated most decisively in its hideous communications structure and policies. Until socialists "can show a convincing alternative, which is free of these dangers," people would have no rational reason to change. "The idea of public service must be detached from the idea of public monopoly, yet remain public service in the true sense. The only way to achieve this is to create new kinds of institution."[78]

In *The Existing Alternatives in Communications*, Williams sums up these points and argues that the Labour Party needs to make reconstruction of the media and communication system a central part of its political program going forward. Implicit in his argument is that the very nature of a socialist regime can be gleaned by assessing its communication system, for that is where the rubber hits the road and the commitment to genuine democracy moves from words to practice. In Williams's view, what was essential was a well-funded public system with true independence and legitimate access for ordinary citizens, not just for socialism but also for democracy itself. The point was to create a system in which the means of production in this area were held in trust by the public and leased out to individuals without control from the top, in ways that would create a dynamic, popular, decentralized, and democratic media system. Unless the Labour Party—and by extension, the left everywhere—made restructuring communications a high priority, it would increase the likeliness of their irrelevance and ultimate failure.

The New Left and Communication: The 1960s and '70s and Today

The New Left, as E. P. Thompson had said, was in many ways defined from the beginning by its focus on culture and communication—seen primarily in a political-economic context. The fact that there was in the 1960s a historical moment for reform in broadcasting, after which change would become far more difficult (and British broadcasting would begin to move in the direction of the U.S. system with its commercialism and cultural degradation), was made clear in Williams's comments on the Pilkington Report in the second edition of *Communications*. "It is now more than ever certain," he wrote, "that we shall have to get rid of a commercial television structure, and especially of this one, with its close connexions in ownership with our already concentrated commercial press." Although the BBC had gotten a second channel as a result of the implementation of some of the Pilkington Report recommendations, it was already being forced to mimic the commercial system, competing for audiences "on the basis of profit rather than use" with the ITV channel of the Independent Television Authority. If another commercial channel were to be established, he predicted, "we shall have lost for a generation any chance of making a genuinely public system." The real goal, he insisted, ought to be "to start dismantling both the present commercial structure of ITV and the present centralization of BBC," replacing them with a system of public control over the technical and transmission apparatus, holding it in trust, coupled with "genuinely independent programme companies" that would lease the technical facilities and take responsibility for policy and content.[79]

Williams in many respects captured the core arguments of all the other writers from this period. He took elements of the critique initiated by Baran and Sweezy, the Frankfurt School, and Mills about the growing importance of the cultural apparatus under monopoly capitalism and developed it into a broader and more coherent intellectual vision. More important, he used this as a gateway not to despair over the duping of the masses, but, to the contrary, as a new crucial political battleground where the political left could rejuvenate itself and create a truly democratic socialism. It was no small accomplishment. At the same time this work was being done, Jürgen Habermas had just completed his dissertation in Germany. When one reads what became *The Structural Transformation of the Public Sphere* today—it was not available in English until 1989—one is struck by the manner in which the analysis and arguments are complementary with those of Baran, Sweezy, Miliband, and especially Williams and Mills. Indeed, Habermas closes the book by invoking Mills approvingly.[80]

By the early 1970s, accompanying the global upsurge in political activism, there was considerable attention given to communication issues on the left. In the global South, the newly liberated nations organized for a New World Information and Communication Order in conjunction with a New International Economic Order to redress the global imbalances in control over communication networks and media resulting from centuries of imperialism. It was the first time in global politics that communication was put on the same level as the economy, or better yet, seen as being integral to the political economy.

In Britain, Nicholas Garnham, who would go on to be a central figure in the political economy of communication, wrote a manifesto for media activism in 1972 that drew directly from Marcuse and Williams. "The media of mass communication clearly play a vital role and the control of those media is a matter of central political concern," he wrote. "The media are not neutral in the struggle for democracy. In the Long Revolution the pen may indeed turn out to be mightier than the sword. The outcome of that battle will therefore depend upon which side gains control of the pen." In Garnham's view, a problem with much of the "counterculture" media activism of the times was the belief that "alternative cultures, lifestyles and the institutional forms to go with them could be constructed within the existing social formation and alongside the more traditional social forms."[81] Williams shared this concern, noting in 1975 that the commercial system had succeeded in "incorporating large areas" of alternative popular culture into its own domain.[82]

In his 1975 retrospective look at the preceding fifteen years in British (and, to a certain extent, Western) communication, Williams found some hope that the counterculture that had developed in that period might have lasting progressive value. But he was also skeptical:

> The idea of an alternative culture is radical but limited. It can very easily become a marginal culture; even, at worst, a tolerated play area. It is certainly always insufficient unless it is linked with effective opposition to the dominant system, under which the majority of people are living.

Williams was especially heartened by the emergence of cooperatives to generate communication and culture, but here, too, direct political confrontation with the powers-that-be was unavoidable: "One of the key developments, that of the workers' or producers' or contributors' cooperative, depends, in the high-capital areas, on active support by a reforming government, and that takes us back to one of the central areas of conflict."[83]

In the United States, there was an explosion in developing such "alternative" media in the form of community theater and, especially, alternative newspapers and periodicals. But policy activism also emerged. In the early 1970s, African American groups and other community and civil rights organizations participated in hundreds of license challenges to existing commercial radio and TV broadcasters before the FCC in a failed effort to claim their channels for community use. By the mid-1970s, this activism contributed to the creation of scores of new community FM radio stations and public-access TV channels. The activism was a testament to the vision that Williams and the others had laid out a decade earlier.

By the end of the 1970s and in the final decades of the twentieth century, that vision faded with the collapse of the left and the rise of neoliberalism. As Garnham acknowledged in 1978, the "need" for radical media reform was growing "more acute" at the same time that the prospects for such reform were much further away.[84] The new fields of the political economy of communication and cultural studies downsized their immediate political ambitions and crystallized as academic undertakings, finding a toehold in a handful of universities where they provided a muscular critique while maintaining a tenuous institutional existence thereafter. Williams regarded the emergence of academic media studies as "significant," though he added that it was "ironic that this work should have developed in the same period in which the general situation was so sharply deteriorating."[85] Much of critical communication research subsequently turned away from the structural issues that were central to the work of the 1960s as institutional reform, not to mention socialism, appeared impossible. At its most extreme, this devolution ended up in the varieties of post-structuralist, post-modernist, and post-colonial schools. In such an environment it was easy for this 1960s political-economic and structural-reform tradition to be forgotten, even by some of the people associated with it.

In the past decade, with the emergence of global corporate media empires and the Internet, radical media reform has returned as a major political issue in countless nations. At times the reform efforts can be marginal, especially when they are not associated with popular movements and an organized political left that can provide vision and courage. But what is more important—since it represents a precondition of any forward movement—is how the left has now come to embrace the central importance of structural media reform and communication issues as never before. Never is this more apparent than when one looks at Latin America today, where many of the great struggles concern how progressive forces can get elected left governments to create truly independent media systems free of the traditional domination of a few capitalist clans in every nation, as well as the state. The capitalist forces are determined to use their media power to maintain their class privileges. The fate of these governments and socialist politics writ large may well ride on the outcome.

"Lies had destroyed Latin America. People lie too much, from the press, the politicians, and on the street," Ecuadoran president Rafael Correa said in a 2013 interview. "I think one of the main problems around the world is that there are private networks in the communication business, for-profit business providing public information, which is very important for society. It is a fundamental contradiction." Consequently, the battle to establish a media system that serves democratic values has been a defining issue in each of the Latin American democracies with elected left-wing governments. As nations in other parts of the world turn to similarly popular governments, the issue of media likely will emerge there as well. To Correa, one solution is clear: "I think there should be more public and community media, organizations that don't have that conflict between profits and social communication."[86]

It has been said that Beethoven's late string quartets were so far ahead of their time that we have not yet caught up to them. So it is with this work by Williams as well as that of the other writers from the late 1950s and 1960s concerning the importance of the cultural apparatus to socialist politics that have been all but lost to history until now. Activists today still have much to learn from this visionary work about how to think about communication. All of these writers, for example, were aware of the radical changes that new communication technologies were going to create in the decades to come, but none of them thought these technologies would magically solve fundamental political problems on their own. If anything, the left has been too timid with regard to communication politics, and needs to go big, as Williams advocated more than fifty years ago. The moral of the story: with regard to the political economy of communication, the present is history.

12

A Sharp Left Turn for the Media
Reform Movement

THE CONTEMPORARY MEDIA REFORM movement exploded into prominence in the United States in 2003 as a response to the effort by President George W. Bush's Federal Communications Commission (FCC) to weaken media ownership regulations. Three million people signed petitions opposing the rules changes, many of whom were fresh from the antiwar movement and were appalled by the idea that the same media conglomerates that assisted in the propaganda campaign for the Iraq invasion might be able to gobble up what remained of independent media. The success of this popular uprising was enough to contribute to the federal court's decision to toss out the FCC's ownership scheme. It was a testament to the power of activism to thwart the plans of the powerful in seemingly hopeless conditions.

In subsequent years the U.S. media reform movement blossomed, led primarily by a group I co-founded, Free Press. On a number of major issues, from the broadcasting of "fake news" created by corporate PR agencies and the protection of public and community broadcasting to the battle for an open, accessible, and uncensored Internet, Free Press led the charge in Washington, D.C. The thinking behind the group and the movement was to have one foot in the battles of the day as they were being fought in the capital, while the other foot was organizing in the field, with the idea of expanding popular awareness and involvement in the movement. We realized that for most people the range of media policy outcomes then countenanced in Washington seemed abstract or inconsequential. We needed to capture their imagination with bold and radical proposals. The strategy was to create an army for structural media reform, so the options expanded beyond what was then permissible in Washington, where, as FAIR's Jeff Cohen once put it, the "range of debate extends all the way from GE to GM."

With no small amount of irony, the media reform movement, relatively speaking, enjoyed considerable success inside the Beltway in the second term of the Bush administration. The Obama campaign in 2007 and 2008 expressed interest in media reform and worked closely with members of the movement to design what was, by the standards of Washington policy debates, a progressive platform. Except for Obama's speech against the Iraq War invasion, it was arguably his communication platform that most distinguished him as a progressive in the 2008 presidential primaries. He had the blogosphere all atwitter, so to speak. For the media reform movement, the gravitational pull of the Beltway was getting stronger, and it was intoxicating. The movement shifted its emphasis from the field to working in the corridors of power. Around the world, media activists looked to the United States as the place where organizing was getting stuff done. Again, there was irony: as recently as 2002, John Nichols and I had written a short book on how the United States trailed most other nations in media activism, and needed to get its act together.[1]

One can debate whether this was an appropriate strategic shift, but there can be no debate that the strategy failed. The Obama administration abandoned its platform almost immediately, and repudiated the movement, except for those people who carried its water. For whatever reason, it decided not to put any of its political capital in this area. A few activists argued that they had been more effective in the Bush years at winning their objectives. A deep and pervasive depression clouded the struggle, a depression that remains to this day.

In my opinion, the media reform movement needs to abandon its recent history and turn in a new direction altogether. On the one hand, it needs to return to its roots and the core principles on which the movement was founded. On the other hand, the movement needs to recognize that the world has changed dramatically in the past decade. Specifically, capitalism is in the midst of a prolonged crisis, with no end in sight. This changes the political playing field and opens up new requirements and opportunities for democratic reformers. In what follows I elaborate on these points and offer three policy proposals that might provide vision and direction for the media reform movement. These are radical ideas, far outside the existing range of debate inside political circles or even the academy. Unless ideas along the lines of what follow get "mainstreamed," it will be not just the media reform movement but the political left more broadly that will be guaranteed irrelevance and failure.

The Context for Radical Media Reform

The major premises of the media reform movement remain unchanged: communication systems develop largely as a result of policies, since there is no such thing as a natural "default" course of development. From the development of copyright and postal subsidies for newspapers at the dawn of the Republic to the licensing of telephone, broadcasting, and cable TV monopolies, the state has been in the middle of the creation of the media.[2] For example, the Internet's shift from an anti-commercial, egalitarian institution in the early 1990s to a "whoever makes the most money by any means necessary wins" undertaking was not foreordained by the gods. It was the province of politics.[3]

In a capitalist society, including one with formally democratic practices, the policy debates will be weighted, at times heavily, toward commercial interests, especially in a matter like communication, where there is tremendous profitability as well as political power attached to dominance. But the debates persist nonetheless, and organized popular forces have won media policy victories. In Europe, for example, the same political left that made labor unions, single-payer health insurance, and subsidized higher education possible was the decisive force that established well-funded nonprofit and noncommercial broadcasting systems. U.S. history is riddled with examples of the rich getting their way with communication policy debates, but there have also been victories for popular forces. From free postage for the delivery of small weekly newspapers in the 1840s (which included most abolitionist publications) to the creation of community radio stations in the 1970s, organized people have on occasion defeated organized money.

One thing that has changed over the past forty years is that it has become more difficult for popular forces to influence policy. The corruption of the media policymaking process was one of the founding concerns for Free Press, and if it is possible, the process has grown even more corrupt in the past decade. The U.S. political system has become what John Nichols and I characterize as a Dollarocracy.[4] The vast majority of the population has no influence over core policies, regulations, taxation, or the budget, which are the province of large corporations and the very wealthy who dominate U.S. governance.[5] Systemic corruption is the order of the day. The election system has been rendered largely ineffective as a means for citizens to engage in self-government. As former president Jimmy Carter said in 2013, the United States is no longer a "functioning democracy," even by the weak standards of its own history.[6] This means that the chances of winning media policy battles of any great consequence inside the Beltway with the existing array of forces are all but nonexistent.

A second change from 2003 concerns the Internet. Many people knew then that it would just be a matter of time until the Internet overwhelmed and subsumed not only "old media" but much of social life; nobody, myself included, really knew exactly how that would occur. Well, we now have a pretty good idea. The Internet has become a, if not *the*, dominant force in modern capitalism. Not only that, but the benefits of the Internet economy accrue to a very small number of gigantic firms that all enjoy what economists traditionally characterize as monopoly status. Three of the four most valuable publicly traded corporations in the United States are Internet-related firms, and fourteen of the thirty-two most valuable firms are primarily Internet firms. Several more of the thirty-two largest firms have significant digital operations.[7] By contrast, only three of the "too big to fail" banks—which Senator Richard Durbin, in reference to Congress, conceded "frankly own the place"—rank among the thirty-two most valuable firms in the economy.[8] What that means is that these Internet giants control the outcomes of all policy debates that affect them, which increasingly covers most issues of fundamental importance, like taxation, regulation, privacy, labor and consumer rights, and trade.

The third great change from 2003 is that U.S. capitalism is in the midst of what Paul Krugman refers to as another Great Depression. Unemployment remains very high, corporations are sitting on some $1.7 trillion they are not investing in new plants and equipment, and downward pressures on wages are extreme, particularly for the young and the working class.[9] This is part of a long-term problem of stagnation for monopoly-finance capitalism, as John Bellamy Foster and I wrote about in *The Endless Crisis*.[10] Stagnation, combined with political corruption, means that poverty rates have returned to levels not seen for nearly a century in the United States, and inequality is trending toward that found in Malaysia or the Philippines.[11] Nothing in the range of current debates on economic policy proposes anything that will change this dynamic. For the bulk of the population, the future is grim.

The political-economic situation in the United States is therefore unstable and ultimately untenable. When one factors in the environmental crisis, this becomes an even more calamitous and desperate period.[12] What is striking is that all the paeans to the genius of the market, which remain commonplace in policy or academic debates on communication from the respectable left to the right, now increasingly smell like month-old fish left out on a table. Though the news has yet to hit the corrupt elites in Washington, academia, or the mainstream news media, it is increasingly understood by a beleaguered citizenry.

It is also understood by Pope Francis, who delivered a condemnation of capitalism, and capitalist media, in November 2013 that was unsparing and radical: "Today everything comes under the laws of competition and the survival of the fittest, where the powerful feed upon the powerless. As a consequence, masses of people find themselves excluded and marginalized: without work, without possibilities, without any means of escape." He continued:

> While the earnings of a minority are growing exponentially, so too is the gap separating the majority from the prosperity enjoyed by those happy few. This imbalance is the result of ideologies which defend the absolute autonomy of the marketplace and financial speculation.

. . . A new tyranny is thus born. . . . The thirst for power and possessions knows no limits. In this system, which tends to devour everything which stands in the way of increased profits, whatever is fragile, like the environment, is defenseless before the interests of a deified market, which become the only rule.

"No one else," the journalist Robert Scheer wrote, "has put it as powerfully and succinctly."[13]

What is taking place is little short of a sea change. As John Nichols notes, "Thirty-nine percent of Americans surveyed for a November 2012 Gallup poll said they had a positive image of socialism. In a 2011 Pew survey, 49 percent of Americans under 30 said they felt positive about socialism, while just 46 percent felt positive about capitalism. Among African Americans, 55 percent had a positive reaction to socialism, versus 41 percent to capitalism. Among Latinos, it was 44 percent for socialism, 32 percent for capitalism." This is especially notable since few Americans have ever heard anything positive about socialism; it would be like a survey in the Soviet Union in 1955 asking people to compare the merits of capitalism versus communism. What Americans do know today from firsthand experience is that really existing capitalism, to employ the vernacular, sucks. In 2013 the "socialist alternative" candidate Kshama Sawant won a citywide election for the Seattle City Council over a liberal Democrat opponent in a two-person race. A decade ago, a radical like Sawant—who called for the use of eminent domain to allow workers to assume control of abandoned factories—would have been unlikely to nudge 1 or 2 percent of the vote.[14]

In this political-economic environment, it is imperative that activists of all stripes speak boldly and truthfully about the problems of our times and the need for radical change. If activists assume that radical change is impossible and deem it unmentionable—not because it is wrong, but because the entrenched forces are so powerful that to challenge them might undermine short-term legitimacy—by our very actions we increase the likelihood that it will be impossible. In view of the centrality of communication to the political economy, media reform activists have to pull their heads out of the Beltway and start talking to the people who voted Sawant onto the Seattle City Council and elected Bill de Blasio the mayor of New York City.

We need to capture the imaginations of people such that they believe politics can lead to radical improvements in their lives, and the lives of those they know and love. Then we can build an army that will be able to shake the foundations of this rotting system.

The First Proposal: End the ISP Cartel

Back in the 1990s, much verbiage was expended about how the Internet would unleash such a ferocious wave of competition between the Baby Bell telephone companies, the long-distance providers, and the cable TV companies that government regulation (of what were mostly licensed monopolies) in the public interest would no longer be necessary. The market could work its magic in combination with the digital revolution, and competition would be seemingly endless. There were roughly fifteen major Baby Bell, long-distance, and cable/satellite TV companies in 1996, and it was said that they were raring to take each other's business if they were freed from government regulations. These firms also said that they needed to be unchained because scores of new competitors were about to capitalize on the possibilities of digital technology and come after their markets.

These claims constituted one of the largest piles of horse manure in U.S. political history. The dominant firms that pushed this line of reasoning knew they could game the system sufficiently to all but eliminate the threat of real competition, and they could use the relaxation of rules to greatly increase their market power.[15] In 2014, there are only a half-dozen or so major players that dominate the provision of broadband and wireless Internet access. Three of them—Verizon, AT&T, and Comcast—dominate the field of telephony and Internet access, and have set up what is in effect a cartel. They no longer compete with each other in any meaningful sense. As a result, Americans pay far more for cellphone and broadband Internet access than most citizens in other advanced nations and get much lousier service. "They're making a ton of money," one telecommunication executive said about the cartel members in 2013. "They're picking the pockets of consumers."[16]

These are not "free market" companies in any sense of the term. Their business model, going back to pre-Internet days, has always been capturing government monopoly licenses for telephone and cable TV services. Their "comparative advantage" has never been customer service; it has been world-class lobbying. It was that power that made it possible for them to merge endlessly into corporate goliaths and permitted them to quietly overturn existing regulations a decade ago so that they could monopolize their networks for broadband Internet access. That killed competition once and for all. The remaining public interest regulations these behemoths face today are laughable.

The public interest community has responded to the cartel in a number of ways. One policy response has been to press for the maintenance of "Network Neutrality," which is a legacy of the common carrier rules from telecommunication regulation. Net Neutrality provisions prevent the cartel from using its monopoly power to discriminate among websites and users; i.e., all websites are treated equally. There is tremendous commercial gain for the cartel to be able to shake down Internet websites and users for additional money if they wish to have high-speed service. Abandoning Net Neutrality means the cartel has a strong incentive to maintain a dirt road for deadbeats who won't pay more to scare others into paying the cartel for better service. It is inane public policy—the goal should be, as in other nations, to have high-speed service ubiquitous, not artificially scarce—but it is crony capitalism at its best. The American people roundly support Net Neutrality whenever they are queried, but that is not a voice the regulators or cartel members have any interest in activating.

Another response has been for communities to set up their own local municipally owned and operated broadband services to provide an alternative and competition to the cartel. Some four hundred American communities have done that and a 2014 report by the United States Government Accountability Office (GAO) concluded that municipally owned ISPs offered higher speeds at lower prices than the cartel. Wherever these systems exist they have proven very popular across the political spectrum, and especially with small business owners.[17] The cartel has responded to municipally owned ISPs the same way the health insurance giants responded to the proposal for a "public option" in Obama's initial health care reform proposal. In state after state the cartel has pressed its coin-operated politicians to pass laws to crush this competition by making it illegal or impossible for municipally owned ISPs to exist. But some 30 states have refused, because the municipally owned ISPs are so successful and popular.[18] Nonetheless, they are in a constant battle for survival as the cartel uses its considerable lobbying muscle to try to eliminate them, because the existence of these public systems provides tangible evidence that there could be a much better future.

The cartel has passed its historical expiration date. These firms are parasites that use their government-created monopoly power to exact economic "rents"—by which economists mean undeserved income—from consumers and other businesses. Let's cash them out at a price that reflects actual investments, not speculative frenzy. Then let's make cellphone and broadband access ubiquitous and as close to free as possible. (And then people could stop paying through the nose for satellite and cable TV services as well.) We have a terrific proven model to start from with municipally owned broadband systems. How to structure a publicly owned nonprofit network, a digital post office if you will, is exactly where study, debate, and discussion should be directed. It is a solvable problem, and one that demands immediate attention.

Ironically, although socialists have traditionally liked this approach to telecommunication, it is an idea with occasional resonance among conservatives and in the business community as well, as other firms are tired of paying a ransom to the cartel for crappy service. Google launched its own broadband service in Kansas City, if only to demonstrate that it would be possible to have a vastly superior broadband network if the cartel simply got off its butt and invested some of its megaprofits into it. In 2008 then-Google executive and legendary Internet architect Vint Cerf asked publicly whether the Internet might not be better if the data-pipe infrastructure were "owned and maintained by the government, just like the highways."[19] It is a serious question that demands a serious answer.

The Second Proposal: Treat Monopolies like . . . Monopolies

One of the reasons the Internet boom has not led to a golden age of investment and prosperity in contemporary capitalism—unlike, say, what followed from the emergence of the automobile and all of its many related industries in the twentieth century—is that much of the wealth generated by the Internet has been funneled into a very small number of hands. Aside from the cartel, which was an outgrowth of the old telecommunication monopolies, the Internet has produced monopolistic titans like Google, Apple, Amazon, Facebook, eBay, Microsoft, Intel, Cisco, Oracle, and Qualcomm.

These firms take advantage first and foremost of network effects, which tend to produce "winner-take-all" markets with almost no middle class of midsized firms. In addition, patent law and traditional economies of scale contribute to insurmountable advantages over potential adversaries. Indeed, increasingly the Internet seems like a walled garden where these giants are battling with each other for domination in existing and prospective markets, and no one else has a prayer, except to get bought out by a giant. In 2013 the head of the Wikimedia Foundation, which operates the ubiquitous nonprofit and noncommercial Wikipedia, stated that it would be impossible for Wikipedia or anything like it to be created today and thrive on the Internet due to the dominance of the Internet monopolies.[20] The system has become locked down over the past decade.

In combination, these firms have virtually unassailable power in Washington, and the only time they face any regulatory threat is when the giants find themselves on opposite sides of an issue, as has happened with Net Neutrality and intellectual-property debates. These firms tend to get glowing press coverage, and their executives and largest investors are regarded as celebrities or championship athletes. The idea that these firms' legitimacy might be challenged probably seems preposterous to all but a few. Academics trip over one another as they sing the praises of the digital titans. "I am blown away by what I see coming out of the private sector today," an MIT professor of digital economics stated.[21] And indeed, the technological innovations are mind-blowing. But the problem is that these technological advances are all developed to advance the profitability of firms regardless of their social effects. Hence, for example, the obsession with developing amazing surveillance technology that makes the commercial Internet so profitable. Great for them, but not necessarily a benefit for the human race. The Internet brings one of the core contradictions of capitalism to the fore—what is good and rational for those who control the economy is bad and irrational for society as a whole.

These Internet behemoths are all monopolies in the sense that economists use the term: they control sufficient market share—usually at least 50 or 60 percent—to determine both pricing and how much competition they have. As such they pose a direct threat not only to smaller enterprises but to democratic governance. This, again, is not exclusively a belief held by socialists and progressives; it has been at various times a staple belief of conservative free market economic theory.

No less a figure than Milton Friedman argued that capitalism was superior for political freedom and democracy because it separated political power from economic power, unlike feudalism or communism, where the people who controlled the economy also controlled the politics.[22] One of Friedman's mentors at the University of Chicago, the laissez-faire champion Henry C. Simons, said it was imperative that private firms not be allowed to become too large and monopolistic for this argument to hold. Giant monopolistic firms kiboshed the ability of capitalism to remain democratic, because the large firms would overwhelm governance. Here Simons was in agreement with his periodic adversary President Franklin Roosevelt, who in a 1938 message to Congress stated: "The first truth is that the liberty of a democracy is not safe if the people tolerate the growth of private power to a point where it becomes stronger than their democratic state itself. That, in its essence, is fascism—ownership of government by an individual, by a group, or by any other controlling private power."[23]

Simons argued that it was imperative—for both genuine free enterprise and democracy—that monopolistic firms be broken into smaller competitive units, or, if that was impossible, as with utilities and railroads, that they should be "socialized" and directed by the government in a transparent manner.[24] He dismissed the idea of effective government regulation of private monopolies to produce the results that competitive markets would bring, because the monopolies would dominate the regulatory process. Since network effects make it nearly impossible to imagine the effective breakup of the Internet giants, Simons's analysis points squarely in one direction. It is high time we take seriously his concerns and think about how the monopolized Internet services could be put in the public domain and guided by open-source protocol. The late Andre Schiffrin was arguably the first person to grasp this point when he called in 2011 for public debate about whether Google should be converted to a nonprofit entity.[25]

One immediate benefit of this approach: the incessant commercial pressure to collect every possible bit of information on users to better manipulate them would be undermined. It would be far easier to have a regimen with standards closer to what was imagined by the engineers who created the Internet: power would be in the hands of the users, who would control their own digital fate, rather than in the hands of giant firms that are mostly unaccountable ... except to their investors.

The Third Proposal: Treat Journalism like a Public Good

Perhaps the greatest irony or unexpected consequence of the Internet has been that, notwithstanding all its democratizing contributions, it has not ushered in a golden age of journalism and culture. Instead of unlimited quality and quantity, the Internet has eliminated most of the resources that once went to support content production. What I write in this section applies to the entirety of culture, but I will focus specifically on journalism.

As an institution, journalism is in free-fall collapse in the United States. There are vastly fewer paid reporters and editors than there were a generation ago, and it is especially striking when you consider how much the population has grown in that time. Most newsrooms look like the Polish countryside in 1945. Most of what government does receives much less coverage than it did in the past. Many elections are uncovered, and the campaign journalism that remains hardly makes one pine for more of the same. This process began before the Internet, but the Internet has accelerated the process and has made it permanent.

Why is this a problem? All democratic theory, as well as the specific history of the U.S. Republic, is premised on the idea that democracy requires an informed participating citizenry, and such a citizenry can only exist with a strong and vibrant journalism. If that type of journalism does not exist, then our republic and our freedoms cannot survive in any meaningful sense. It is not an exaggeration to say that this point was an obsession for the nation's founders, in particular Thomas Paine, Thomas Jefferson, and James Madison.[26]

This is an issue of particular importance for the mass of the citizenry: those without appreciable amounts of property. The 1 percent, if you will, tend to have access to the information they need to run the world to their benefit. The issue is whether everyone else will have the information they need to participate effectively; this is why the battle for popular journalism is the quintessential democratic struggle. This also explains why in the United States today, those atop the economy appear quite content to have a journalism-free environment, and are the forces that oppose reform. The less people know about how those in power operate, the better.

Why is journalism disintegrating? Commercial interests have decided that journalism is no longer a viable investment, and they are jumping ship. When Jeff Bezos reached into his spare change jar to purchase the *Washington Post* for $250 million in 2013, he paid perhaps 5 percent of what the purchase price would have been in 2000. Ironically, for the past two decades, as commercial interest in journalism has shriveled, the conventional wisdom has been that the Internet would eventually replace dying old media with digital commercial journalism that would likely be far superior to what it replaced. We just had to be patient and let good old Yankee ingenuity, magical technologies, and the profit motive solve the problem.

But that has not happened, nor will it. Indeed, what remains of paid journalism in the United States is disproportionately in "old media." The Internet has been a total flop. If anything, by giving the illusion of an information rainforest with every Google search, it has made people oblivious to the actual information desert we increasingly inhabit.

Why is that? Advertising provided the vast majority of revenues for journalism in the twentieth century and made doing news media lucrative. Advertisers needed to help pay for journalism to attract readers/viewers to news media who would then see their ads. That was the deal. Advertisers supported the news because they had no other choice if they wished to achieve their commercial goals; they had no intrinsic attachment to the idea of a free press.

The rise of advertising as the primary basis of support prompted the development of professional journalism, in part to protect the content of the news from direct commercial influence: advertising generally was regarded as a necessary evil for the subsidization of journalism. Professional journalism, in effect, was an effort to address the obvious tension between journalism as a necessary democratic institution and journalism as a commercial vehicle intended to maximize profits.

But those debates and concerns are now passé. In the new era of smart or targeted digital advertising, advertisers far less frequently place ads on specific websites and hope to appeal to whoever might visit them. Instead, they purchase target audiences directly and place ads through Internet ad networks that locate the desired targets wherever they are online. *Advertisers no longer need to support journalism or content creation at all.* This is probably why Rupert Murdoch, the greatest corporate media visionary of our times, abandoned his iPad/smartphone news venture, *The Daily*, in 2012; it is definitely why the *Guardian*, one of the most visited and venerated news websites in the world, concedes that it has no idea how it will be able to support its operations when and if it is forced to rely upon Internet revenues.

Advertising gave the illusion that journalism is a naturally, even supremely commercial endeavor. But when advertising disappears, journalism's true nature comes into focus: it is a public good, something society requires but that the market cannot provide in sufficient quality or quantity. Like other public goods, if society wants it, it will require public policy and public spending. There is no other way. The marriage of capitalism and journalism is over. If the United States is to have democratic journalism, it will require massive public investments.

This begs the question: How did the United States have a press system that was the envy of the world in the nineteenth century prior to the advent of mass advertising? It did so by having massive postal and printing subsidies for newspapers, which made the cost of production so low that there were many more newspapers per capita than anywhere else on Earth. In the first century of U.S. history, our politicians did not know the term "public good," but they treated the press in precisely that manner.

The great concern is that public money will lead to a government-controlled propaganda system like one finds in dictatorships and authoritarian regimes, or even in the more corrupt capitalist democracies like Italy. Sure, the United States had successful press subsidies in the nineteenth century, but that was then and this is now. In view of the entirely unaccountable national security apparatus that is embodied in the modern U.S. government, this is a legitimate and pressing concern. But the process to establish publicly supported journalism is part of the process of democratizing society. They go hand in hand.

This evidence suggests that the more democratic a nation is, the more it is able to subsidize journalism without having the resultant media be a puppet for the government. Every year *The Economist* magazine ranks all the nations of the world according to how democratic they are, using standard political science criteria. Every year the nations that top the list are invariably those nations that spend the very most per capita on public and community media. Freedom House, another organization that is decidedly unsympathetic to socialism, annually ranks all the nations of the world in terms of how free their press systems are. Government censorship is the threat that Freedom House is most concerned about. Every year the same nations that rank atop the *Economist's* list rule Freedom House's list of the freest and best press systems, places like Norway, Sweden, and Germany. The research shows this: in democratic nations, journalism subsidies tend to make the press more diverse and dissident and critical of the government in power. Like education, it is a public good, and, as with education, the more resources that are devoted to it, the better it will be, everything else being equal.

Although the left leads the fight for publicly supported journalism, it is a very popular program across the population once it is in place and people see the results. After the national elections in September 2013, Norway got its most conservative government in generations, including a crew of neoliberal know-nothings not unlike the leaders of the Republican Party in the United States. One of their campaign planks was to end government funding for Norway's massive public broadcasting system, as well as its extensive newspaper subsidies, which allow Oslo to have numerous daily newspapers rather than the one or two that would exist if left to the market.

These newspaper subsidies are mostly given to newspapers with low advertising revenues. They provide, for example, around 30 percent of the revenue for the left-wing daily newspaper *Klassekampen* (Class Struggle), and make its thriving newsroom possible. To give some sense of *Klassekampen*'s impact: if a U.S. daily newspaper sold newspapers to the same portion of the population that *Klassekampen* does in Norway, the U.S. paper would have a circulation of over one million copies every day. That would make it the fourth-largest daily paper in the United States. Conservative and liberal newspapers are eligible for the same subsidies and get them.

When the new Norwegian government took its proposal to defund media to the parliament in November 2013, the matter was rejected emphatically. There was opposition to the proposal from Norwegians across the political spectrum. In Norway, the newspaper subsidies go to commercial concerns. I think that is a non-starter in the United States—the last thing needed is another dose of corporate welfare—and makes decreasing sense as capitalists abandon the field. The crucial goal should be to establish a nonprofit, noncommercial, competitive, uncensored, and independent press system, embracing digital technologies. It is where the debate and discussion need to go.

The basis for the best proposal I have seen was inspired by a 1955 essay by Milton Friedman, in which he argued that public education should be dismantled. This followed from his philosophy that the only legitimate jobs for government should be "enforcing contracts, preventing coercion, and keeping markets free." Friedman acknowledged, however, that paying for the costs of education was a legitimate government expense, because of what he termed "neighborhood effects." By this he meant that everyone benefitted from an educated citizenry, even those who did not have children, so it was worthwhile for them to pay taxes to achieve that end. Education provides "better social and political leadership" that benefits everyone. By this Friedman meant particularly K-12 education and liberal arts education—the stuff that commercial interests would have no incentive to invest in directly, but that make for a much better society.

But though Friedman embraced a government role for providing the funding for public education, he thought the idea of government-run schools opened the door to a tyranny that should be avoided. He proposed that the entirety of public school spending should be divided up and apportioned equally among all the school-age children, with a voucher for that sum to be given for each child to the child's parents. The parents could then shop around for the best private school where the voucher would cover tuition. These private schools would be operated by nonprofit and for-profit institutions in competition with one another. Friedman argued that this would give us the best of both worlds: sufficient public support along with market competition.[27]

In recent years Friedman's ideas have increasingly been deployed in education—they were purely hypothetical for many decades after publication—and as far as I can see, they have been disastrous if the goal is to create better education for the whole of the population. (If the goal is to make investors rich by sucking on the public teat, that is another matter.) The problem is that education does not work well when it is conducted in accordance with a competitive, profit-driven model, something that someone like Friedman could never understand. But the evidence is overwhelming. No one has ever made money doing education, or at least good education. The upper classes invariably send their children to nonprofit schools with small class sizes, well-paid superior teachers, a minimum of standardized testing, and ample funding. If we were serious about great public education, we would do everything possible to extend that model to the balance of the population. We would also accept that the number-one barrier to success in school is poverty, and regard the elimination of childhood poverty as mandatory. Hence the nations with the best education systems in the world, like Finland, tend to follow cooperative lines like American upper-class schools and have little childhood poverty.[28]

But as inappropriate as Friedman's ideas may be when they are applied to education, they work really well when applied to journalism. There his notion of "neighborhood effects" applies in spades. Everyone benefits if there is an informed citizenry and institutions that monitor people in power, and the world becomes dystopian without that. And, as is the case in education, it is now self-evident that commercial interests no longer find journalism a profitable undertaking. The state must enter the field big-time.

This is where Friedman's idea about vouchers is brilliant: we get public funding without government control. Dean Baker has developed the idea (which John Nichols and I have embellished) of letting every American over the age of eighteen direct up to $200 of government money annually to any nonprofit medium of his or her choice. The only conditions would be that the recipient be a recognized nonprofit, that the recipient do no commercial advertising, and that whatever is produced by the subsidy be posted online immediately, made available at no charge, and enter the public domain. It would not be protected by copyright. This would amount to a $30 billion public investment with no government control over who gets the money. This would promote all sorts of competition as well, as entities would be competing for the monies. Commercial media would be ineligible for subsidies, but they could use the content, and anyone could start a medium, commercial or noncommercial, without needing anyone else's permission.

There are probably many other ways we could support a great free press system (and a great culture) in the digital era. It is high time to start that discussion. It is a necessary part, even a cornerstone, of the movement to democratize the United States. I have demonstrated how each of these reforms can appeal to people across the political spectrum, as they are rooted in fairness and a commitment to democracy. But make no mistake: these three reforms alone would radically reshape the nation and put the United States well on the way toward a post-capitalist democracy. We have no time to lose, and, given the brick wall of politics in Washington, we have nothing to lose. To quote a great saying from France in May 1968, "Be Realistic, Demand the Impossible."

Notes

1. America, I Do Mind Dying

1. Paul Krugman, "Secular Stagnation, Coalmines, Bubbles, and Larry Summers," *New York Times*, November 16, 2013, http://krugman.blogs.nytimes.com/2013/11/16/secular-stagnation-coalmines-bubbles-and-larry-summers/.

2. Thomas Piketty, *Capital in the Twenty-First Century*, trans. Arthur Goldhammer (Cambridge: Belknap Press of Harvard University Press, 2014). Originally published in France in 2013.

3. Bill Moyers interview with Paul Krugman, *Moyers and Company*, Public Broadcasting System, April 20, 2014.

4. Martin Gilens and Benjamin I. Page, "Testing Theories of American Politics: Elites, Interest Groups, and Average Citizens," *Perspectives on Politics* (Fall 2014).

5. Darryl Fears, "U.N. Climate Panel: Governments must do more in face of dire global-warming threats," *Washington Post*, April 13, 2014.

6. G. William Domhoff, *Who Rules America: Challenges to Corporate and Class Dominance* (New York: McGraw Hill, 2014), 207.

7. Daphne T. Greenwood, "The Decision to Contract Out: Understanding the Full Economic and Social Impacts," paper published by the Colorado Center for Policy Studies, University of Colorado, Colorado Springs, March 2014.

8. See Erik Brynjolfsson and Andrew McAfee, *The Second Machine Age: Work, Progress, and Prosperity in a Time of Brilliant Technologies* (New York: W. W. Norton, 2014).

9. I discuss Lincoln's view of the relationship of labor and capital in *Digital Disconnect*, chap. 2.

10. This point is developed in Ralph Nader, *Unstoppable: The Emerging Left-Right Alliance to Dismantle the Corporate State* (New York: Nation Books, 2014).

11. This episode and tradition are covered in Andrew J. Bacevich, *Breach of Trust: How Americans Failed Their Soldiers and Their Country* (New York: Metropolitan Books, 2013), chap. 9.

12. The Editors, "War Profiteering," *The Nation*, May 12, 2003, http://www.thenation.com/article/war-profiteering#.

13. Aaron Cantú, "Inside the Private Prison Industry's Alarming Spread across America," AlterNet, April 9, 2014, http://www.alternet.org/civil-liberties/inside-private-prison-industrys-alarming-spread-across-america.

14. Diane Ravitch, *Reign of Error: The Hoax of the Privatization Movement and the Danger to America's Public Schools* (New York: Alfred A. Knopf, 2013).

2. After the Nader Campaign: The Future of U.S. Left Electoral?

The original version of this article was published as "The Nader Campaign and the Future of U.S. Left Electoral Politics," *Monthly Review* 52/9 (February 2001): 1–22.

3. A New New Deal under Obama

This essay originally appeared as John Bellamy Foster and Robert W. McChesney, "A New New Deal under Obama?" *Monthly Review* 60/n9 (February 2009): 1–11. The piece was finished on December 21, 2008, before Obama assumed office.

1. The question of a "new New Deal" in the face of the deepening stagnation of U.S. capitalism is not a new one. See Harry Magdoff and Paul M. Sweezy, "A New New Deal?," *Monthly Review* 33/9 (February 1982): 1–10. On the 2008 economic crisis see John Bellamy Foster and Fred Magdoff, *The Great Financial Crisis* (New York: Monthly Review Press, 2008).

2. Associated Press, "Obama Team Weighs Up to $850 Billion Economic Jolt," December 18, 2008.

3. Alvin H. Hansen, *Fiscal Policy and Business Cycles* (New York: W.W. Norton, 1941), 85–87.

4. David Milton, *The Politics of Labor: From the Great Depression to the New Deal* (New York: Monthly Review Press, 1982).

5. Harry Magdoff and Paul M. Sweezy, "The Responsibility of the Left," *Monthly Review* 34/7 (December 1982): 6–9; Nick Taylor, *American-Made* (New York: Bantam, 2008); "FDR's New Deal Blueprint for Obama," CBS News, December 14, 2008, http://www.cbsnews.com.

6. Allan H. Meltzer, *A History of the Federal Reserve*, vol. 1 (Chicago: University of Chicago Press, 2003), 521; Dean L. May, *From New Deal to New Economics* (New York: Garland, 1981), 91–113, 122; Hansen, *Fiscal Policy and Business Cycles*, 88. Partly in response to the recession of 1937, Social Security was put on a "pay as you go" basis.

7. May, *From New Deal to New Economics*, 147–48; John Kenneth Galbraith, *Money: Whence It Came, Where It Went* (Boston: Houghton Mifflin, 1995), 232–36; Richard V. Gilbert, George H. Hildebrand, Jr., Arthur W. Stuart, Maxine Y. Sweezy, Paul M. Sweezy, Lorie Tarshis, and John D. Wilson, *An Economic Program for American Democracy* (New York: Vanguard Press, 1938). There were other authors of *An Economic Program for American Democracy* who were not able to sign it for various reasons, such as government jobs, including Alan Sweezy and Emile Despres. "Interview of Paul M. Sweezy," *The Coming of Keynesianism to America*, ed. David C. Collander and Harry Landreth (Brookfield, VT: Edward Elgar, 1996), 81.

8. John Kenneth Galbraith, *American Capitalism* (Boston: Houghton Mifflin, 1952), 69.

9. Paul A. Baran and Paul M. Sweezy, *Monopoly Capital* (New York: Monthly Review Press, 1966), 151–61. Quotation is from page 161 and is their emphasis.

10. Ibid., 164.

11. These two categories of government spending are referred to as exhaustive and non-exhaustive expenditures. On this see Francis M. Bator, *A Question of Government Spending* (New York: Collier Books, 1960), 17–46. On the construction of OECD accounts see François Lequiller and Derek Blades, *Understanding National Accounts* (Paris: Organisation for Economic Co-operation and Development, 2006).

12. See John Bellamy Foster, Hannah Holleman, and Robert W. McChesney, "The U.S. Imperial Triangle and Military Spending," *Monthly Review* 60/5 (October 2008): 9–13; Bureau of Economic Analysis, National Income and Product Accounts, Table 3.9.5.

13. "A Fighter Jet's Fate Poses a Quandary for Obama," *New York Times*, December 10, 2008.

14. C. Wright Mills, *The Causes of World War Three* (New York: Simon and Schuster, 1958), 85.

15. It should be pointed out that the other G-7 countries (and Sweden) referred to here face analogous problems, starting out at higher levels of government spending as a percentage of GDP. They too are caught in the stagnation trap and could use increases in government spending to lift their economies, but face powerful class forces at the top of the society that limit the magnitude and direction of such spending.

16. See Harry Magdoff and Paul M. Sweezy, "The Coming Crisis and the Responsibility of the Left," *Monthly Review* 39/2 (June 1987): 5.

4. THE WISCONSIN UPRISING

This article originally appeared as "The Wisconsin Uprising," *Monthly Review* 63/n.9 (February 2012): 46–53.

1. On this see Al Sandine, *The Taming of the American Crowd* (New York: Monthly Review Press, 2009).

2.   This point is developed in Jacob S. Hacker and Paul Pierson, *Winner-Take-All Politics* (New York: Simon and Schuster, 2010).

3.   John Nichols, "AFL's Trumka on Pols Selling Out Workers: 'I've Had a Snootful of This S**t!,'" *The Nation* Blogs, June 8, 2011, http://thenation.com.

4.   See John Maynard Keynes, *Essays in Persuasion* (New York: Harcourt, Brace, 1932), 372; John Bellamy Foster, "The End of Rational Capitalism," *Monthly Review* 56/10 (March 2005): 1–13.

5.   Alexander Cockburn, "The Waste Land," *CounterPunch*, September 10–11, 2011, http://counterpunch.org.

6.   Mike Davis, "How Obama Became the Curator of the Bush Legacy," *TomDispatch.com*, September 13, 2011, http://tomdispatch.com.

5. This Isn't What Democracy Looks Like

This article originally appeared as "This Isn't What Democracy Looks Like," *Monthly Review* 64/n6 (November 2012): 1–28. It was originally completed weeks before the 2012 election.

1.   Actual U.S. military expenditures (including all categories) are now over a trillion dollars but the acknowledged military spending associated with the Department of Defense is much less. For a full accounting for 2007 see John Bellamy Foster, Hannah Holleman, and Robert W. McChesney, "The U.S. Imperial Triangle and Military Spending," *Monthly Review* 60/5 (October 2008): 1–19.

2.   Aristotle, *Politics*, trans. Benjamin Jowett (Stilwell, KS: Digireads, 2005), 60. Aristotle was of course no friend of democracy but a supporter of an aristocratic constitution. Moreover, even the supporters of the *demos* in ancient Greece had in mind only male citizens, excluding women and slaves. See Ellen Meiksins Wood and Neal Wood, *Class Ideology and Ancient Political Theory* (New York: Oxford University Press, 1978).

3.   Journalists like Ken Silverstein, David Cay Johnston, and Robert G. Kaiser have each written devastating accounts of Washington's corruption at the hands of corporate lobbyists and moneyed interests. See Ken Silverstein, *Washington on $10 Million a Day* (Monroe, ME: Common Courage Press, 1998); David Cay Johnston, *Free Lunch* (New York: Penguin, 2007); Robert G. Kaiser, *So Damn Much Money* (New York: Knopf, 2009).

4.   Lawrence Lessig, *Republic, Lost* (New York: Twelve, 2011), 99, 123.

5.   Robert Weissman, "The Role of Federally-Funded University Research in the Patent System," testimony before the Committee on the Judiciary, U.S. Senate, October 24, 2007, http://essentialaction.org; Dean Baker, "The Levers of Power," *CounterPunch*, February 8, 2011, http://counterpunch.org.

6.   See John Bellamy Foster and Robert W. McChesney, "The Internet's Unholy Marriage to Capitalism," *Monthly Review* 62/10 (March 2011): 1–30.

7. See "Fossil Fuel Subsidies in the U.S.," http://priceofoil.org, as well as the work of Public Citizen at http://citizen.org.

8. Simon Johnson, "The Bill Daley Problem," *Huffington Post*, January 9, 2011, http://huffingtonpost.com.

9. Simon Johnson, "The Quiet Coup," *The Atlantic*, May 2009, http://theatlantic.com.

10. See Matt Taibbi, *Griftopia* (New York: Spiegel & Grau, 2010).

11. Lessig, *Republic, Lost*, 99, 123.

12. Ryan Grim, "Dick Durbin: Banks 'Frankly Own the Place,'" *Huffington Post*, May 30, 2009, http://huffingtonpost.com.

13. Glenn Greenwald, *With Liberty and Justice for Some* (New York: Metropolitan Books, 2011), chap. 3.

14. David Brooks, "Pundit under Protest," *New York Times*, June 13, 2011, http://nytimes.com.

15. See Larry M. Bartels, *Unequal Democracy* (New York: Russell Sage Foundation, 2008); Martin Gilens, "Inequality and Democratic Responsiveness," *Public Opinion Quarterly* 69/5 (2005): 778–96. There is a superb discussion of this in Jacob S. Hacker and Paul Pierson, *Winner-Take-All Politics* (New York: Simon and Schuster, 2010), chap. 4.

16. See, for example, Charles Simic, "A Country without Libraries," *New York Review of Books* blog, May 18, 2011, http://nybooks.com/blogs.

17. Joseph E. Stiglitz, "Of the 1%, by the 1%, for the 1%," *Vanity Fair*, May 2011, http://vanityfair.com.

18. E. J. Dionne, "American Needs a Better Ruling Class," syndicated column, April 17, 2011, http://heraldnews.com.

19. "Is the U.S. Becoming a Third World Country?," *Map Scroll*, April 15, 2009, http://mapscroll.blogspot.com.

20. Paul Krugman, "The Lesser Depression," *New York Times*, July 21, 2011, http://nytimes.com.

21. Timothy Noah, "The One Percent Bounce Back," *New Republic*, March 4, 2012, http://tnr.com.

22. Stiglitz, "Of the 1%, by the 1%, for the 1%."

23. Hacker and Pierson, *Winner-Take-All Politics*.

24. Chuck Collins, et al., "Unnecessary Austerity, Unnecessary Shutdown," Institute for Policy Studies, April 7, 2011, http://ips-dc.org.

25. Warren Buffett, "Stop Coddling the Super-Rich," *New York Times*, August 14, 2011, http://nytimes.com.

26. Bruce Western and Jake Rosenfeld, "Unions, Norms, and the Rise in U.S. Wage Inequality," *American Sociological Review* 76/4 (2011): 513–37.

27. Richard Wilkinson and Kate Pickett, *The Spirit Level* (New York: Bloomsbury Press, 2009).

28. George McGovern, *An American Journey* (New York: Random House, 1974).

29. Lost to history, for example, has been the very impressive burgeoning media reform movement of the 1970s. See Pamela Draves, ed., *Citi-*

zens Media Directory (Washington, D.C.: National Citizens Committee for Broadcasting, 1977).

30. See John Bellamy Foster and Robert W. McChesney, "A New New
Deal under Obama?" *Monthly Review* 60/9 (February 2009): 1–11.

31. See Judith Stein, *Pivotal Decade* (New Haven: Yale University Press,
2010); John Bellamy Foster, Robert W. McChesney, and R. Jamil
Jonna, "The Global Reserve Army of Labor and the New Imperialism," *Monthly Review* 63/6 (November 2011): 1–31.

32. John Bellamy Foster and Robert W. McChesney, *The Endless Crisis*
(New York: Monthly Review Press, 2012).

33. Robert Reich, "Why Washington Isn't Doing Squat about Jobs and
Wages," June 4, 2011, http://robertreich.org.

34. Lawrence R. Mishel et al., *The State of Working America 2012* (Ithaca,
NY: Cornell University Press, 2012), http://stateofworkingamerica.
org, 436.

35. John Bellamy Foster and Fred Magdoff, *The Great Financial Crisis*
(New York: Monthly Review Press, 2009).

36. For an excellent example of creative policy thinking see the June 27,
2011, special issue of *The Nation*, "Reimagining Capitalism," edited
by William Greider. It includes a dozen or so articles with concrete
proposals that are all outside the range of legitimate debate.

37. On Kalecki's relation to the Keynesian revolution see Joan Robinson, *Contributions to Modern Economics* (Oxford: Basil Blackwell, 1978), 53–60.

38. Michal Kalecki, *Selected Essays on the Dynamics of the Capitalist Economy* (Cambridge: Cambridge University Press, 1970), 139.

39. Paul Krugman, *End This Depression Now!* (New York: W. W. Norton,
2012), 94–95.

40. See John Bellamy Foster and Hannah Holleman, "The Financial
Power Elite," *Monthly Review* 62/1 (May 2010): 1–19.

41. See Foster and McChesney, *The Endless Crisis*, chap. 5.

42. Richard A. Oppel Jr., "Private Prisons Found to Offer Little in Savings," *New York Times*, May 18, 2011, http://nytimes.com.

43. Christopher Shays and Michael Thibault, "Reducing Waste in War-
time Contracts," *Washington Post*, August 28, 2011, http://washing-
tonpost.com.

44. John Gravois, "More Bureaucrats, Please," *Washington Monthly*,
March–April 2011, http://washingtonmonthly.com.

45. Lessig, *Republic, Lost*.

46. See Thomas Frank, *The Wrecking Crew* (New York: Metropolitan
Books, 2008).

47. Al Gore wrote an essay in 2011 making this point: "Climate of
Denial," *Rolling Stone*, July 7, 2011, http://rollingstone.com. See also
Naomi Klein, "Capitalism vs. the Climate," *The Nation*, November
28, 2011, 11–21.

48. John Maynard Keynes, *A Tract on Monetary Reform* (London: Mac-
millan, 1923), 80. Keynes justified his focus in this work on the short

run rather than the long run in economics.

49. Foster, Holleman, and McChesney, "The U.S. Imperial Triangle and Military Spending."

50. Nick Turse and Tom Engelhardt, "All Bases Covered," *Antiwar.com*, January 10, 2011, http://original.antiwar.com.

51. Andrew Bacevich, "Why Military Spending Is Untouchable," *CounterPunch*, January 27, 2011, http://counterpunch.org. For an analysis of the common (and largely unregulated) practice of retired generals moving to defense firms for extremely lucrative careers, thus guaranteeing the maintenance of the military budget among other things, see Bryan Bender, "From the Pentagon to the Private Sector," *Boston Globe*, December 26, 2010, http://articles.boston.com.

52. In Oliver Stone's 2009 documentary, *South of the Border*, former Argentine president Nelson Kirchner recounts a conversation with then-president George W. Bush in which Bush angrily rejected any government spending on infrastructure or social spending programs to expand the economy. Bush shared with Kirchner the secret of macroeconomics in the United States: "The best way to revitalize the economy is war. The United States has grown stronger because of war. All the economic growth of the United States has been encouraged by the various wars."

53. Quote from the 2009 film about Ellsberg, *The Most Dangerous Man in America*, directed by Judith Ehrlich and Rick Goldsmith.

54. Greenwald, *With Liberty and Justice for Some*.

55. Hannah Holleman et al., "The Penal State in an Age of Crisis," *Monthly Review* 61/2 (June 2009): 1–17.

56. Jimmy Carter, "Call Off the Global Drug War," *New York Times*, June 16, 2011, http://nytimes.com.

57. Michelle Alexander, *The New Jim Crow* (New York: New Press, 2010).

58. Kevin Phillips, *The Politics of Rich and Poor* (New York: Random House, 1990); William Greider, *Who Will Tell the People?* (New York: Simon and Schuster, 1992).

59. The classic text is Alex Carey, *Taking the Risk Out of Democracy* (Urbana: University of Illinois Press, 1996).

60. Michael Crozier, Samuel P. Huntington, and Joji Watanuki, *The Crisis of Democracy* (New York: New York University Press, 1975), 114.

61. Glenn W. Smith, "Republican Operative: 'I Don't Want Everyone to Vote,'" *FireDogLake*, October 12, 2008, http://firedoglake.com.

62. Interview with Lawrence Lessig, *Media Matters*, WILL-AM, November 20, 2011, http://tunein.com.

63. Lessig, *Republic, Lost*, 97; Mark Green, *Selling Out* (New York: Regan Books, 2002), 130.

64. John Kenneth Galbraith, *The Culture of Contentment* (Boston: Houghton Mifflin, 1992), 10.

65. Walter Dean Burnham, "The Appearance and Disappearance of the American Voter," in Thomas Ferguson and Joel Rogers, eds., *The Political Economy* (Armonk, NY: M. E. Sharpe, 1984), 112–37.

66. See Hacker and Pierson, *Winner-Take-All Politics*.

67. Sources: U.S. Census Bureau, "Reported Voting and Registration of Family Members, by Age and Family Income," various years; National Election Pool, Edison Media Research, and Mitofsky International, "National Election Pool General Election Exit Polls, 2004 [computer file]," ICPSR version (Ann Arbor, MI: Inter-University Consortium for Political and Social Research [distributor], 2005); ibid., "National Election Pool General Election Exit Polls, 2008 [computer file]," ICPSR version (ICPSR, 2010); Voter News Service, "Voter News Service General Election Exit Polls, 1996 [computer file]," ICPSR06989-v2 (ICPSR, 1997); ibid., "Voter News Service General Election Exit Polls, 2000 [computer file]," ICPSR06989-v2 (ICPSR, 2004). To determine number and proportion of additional votes in each election year assuming 80 percent turnout, I used the following procedure. First, a calculation was made of the difference between the voter turnout rate and 80 percent; then this was multiplied by the total voting-age population for the given group. For example, in 1996 the voting-age population reporting a family income of $15,000 or less was approximately 39.322 million. In that year, turnout for this same group was 49 percent, so 39.322 was multiplied by .31 (the difference between 80 and 49 percent), resulting in an additional 12.181 million votes. Exit polls, also stratified by income group (and in the same nominal dollars), determined how these additional votes would have been apportioned. In 1996, 53 percent of voters in this income group reported voting for a Democrat for president and 36 percent reported voting Republican. Therefore, in this particular year, Democrats would have received an additional 6.47 million votes and Republicans would have received an additional 4.394 million.

68. This story is told by Frances Fox Piven and Richard A. Cloward in their outstanding book *Why Americans Still Don't Vote* (Boston: Beacon Press, 2000), 150–51.

69. Matthew A. Crenson and Benjamin Ginsberg, *Downsizing Democracy* (Baltimore: Johns Hopkins University Press, 2002), 49.

70. See Lorraine C. Minnite, *The Myth of Voter Fraud* (Ithaca, NY: Cornell University Press, 2010).

71. E. J. Dionne, Jr., "How States Are Rigging the 2012 Election," *Washington Post*, June 19, 2011, http://washingtonpost.com.

72. Michael Cooper, "New State Rules Raising Hurdles at Voting Booth," *New York Times*, October 2, 2011, http://nytimes.com; Wendy Weiser and Lawrence Norden, "Voting Law Changes in 2012," Brennan Center for Justice, October 2011, http://brennancenter.org.

73. Cited in Ari Berman, "The GOP War on Voting," *Rolling Stone*, August 30, 2011, http://rollingstone.com.

6. The U.S. Imperial Triangle and Military Spending

This article originally appeared as John Bellamy Foster, Hannah Holleman, and Robert W. McChesney, "The U.S. Imperial Triangle and Military Spending," *Monthly Review* 60/5 (October 2008): 1–19.

1.   Office of Management and Budget, *Budget for Fiscal Year 2009*, Historical Tables, Table 3.2; Stockholm International Peace Research Institute, *SIPRI Yearbook 2008: Summary,* http://yearbook2008.sipri.org/files/SIPRIYB08summary.pdf, 10–11; SIPRI, Military Expenditure Database (United States), http://milexdata.sipri.org/result.php4. SIPRI data on U.S. military expenditures (drawn on here for estimates of increases in real military spending and for international comparison) are only marginally (about 5 percent) higher than the acknowledged national defense figures contained in the Office of Management and Budget Historical Tables, and are clearly based on these. Whereas the Office of Management and Budget lists $552.6 billion in total national defense for the United States spending in 2007, SIPRI provides a figure of $578.3 billion. It should be noted that SIPRI data, athough based on the same or similar nominal figures as the acknowledged U.S. national defense spending, registers a higher rate of increase in U.S. military expenditures than "reported in official U.S. data because of the method of conversion into constant dollars. SIPRI uses the consumer price index (CPI) for price conversion for all countries, and the U.S. official figures are converted using military-specific deflators. Thus the SIPRI data show the trend in the purchasing power of the military budget had it instead been spent on typical consumer goods and services, and the U.S. official data show the trend in its purchasing power for military goods and services. The nominal change is the same for the two series." *SIPRI Yearbook* 2007, 275.

2.   Michal Kalecki, *The Last Phase in the Transformation of Capitalism* (New York: Monthly Review Press, 1972), 96.

3.   Eric Hobsbawm, *On Empire: America, War, and Global Supremacy* (New York: Pantheon, 2008), 57–59.

4.   C. Wright Mills, *The Power Elite* (New York: Oxford University Press, 1956), 198. It should be noted that Hobsbawm is not alone in promoting what can be called the "cabal theory." See a discussion of this in John Bellamy Foster, *Naked Imperialism* (New York: Monthly Review Press, 2006), 13, 18, 107–8, 117–20.

5.   "WPB Aide Urges U.S. to Keep War Setup," *New York Times*, January 20, 1944; Charles E. Wilson, "For the Common Defense," *Army Ordnance* 26/143 (March–April 1944): 285–88; Fred J. Cook, "Juggernaut: The Warfare State," special issue, *The Nation*, October 28, 1961, 285; Jonathan Feldman, *Universities in the Business of Repression* (Boston: South End Press, 1989), 149–50. Charles E. Wilson did not literally use the term "permanent war economy," widely attributed to his January 19, 1944, speech. Rather, he spoke of a "program of

industrial preparedness" for war that would be "permanent and continuing." On the end of the Second World War and military spending see Robert L. Heilbroner, *The Making of Economic Society* (Englewood Cliffs, NJ: Prentice-Hall, 1980), 160.

6. Joan Robinson, *Contributions to Modern Economics* (Oxford: Basil Blackwell, 1978), 8–9. For an account of the role of military Keynesianism in successive U.S. administrations see Lynn Turgeon, *Bastard Keynesianism* (Westport, CT: Greenwood Press, 1996).

7. Kalecki, *Last Phase*, 75–83, 95–97. Kalecki's analysis of military spending derived originally from his analysis of the importance of armament expenditures in Nazi Germany's economy and then he extended the basic argument to the role military spending was to play in post–Second World War capitalist economies.

8. Ibid.; Cook, "Juggernaut," 292.

9. Kalecki, *Last Phase*, 97; Harry Magdoff, *The Age of Imperialism* (New York: Monthly Review Press, 1969), 185.

10. These five reasons, presented in essentially this order, were provided by Baran and Sweezy to account for the growth of militarism in their classic chapter on "Militarism and Imperialism" in *Monopoly Capital* (New York: Monthly Review Press, 1966), 178–217. It is worth noting that their argument was geared primarily to military spending *for empire* and only turned to its *macroeconomic benefits* in absorbing surplus and staving off long-run stagnation at the end. The same structure to the argument on military spending (empire first, economy second) can be seen in Harry Magdoff, *Imperialism: From the Colonial Age to the Present* (New York: Monthly Review Press, 1978), 198–212. Hence critics such as Larry Griffin, Joel Devine, and Michael Wallace, who later attempted empirically to test the *Monopoly Capital* argument, which they characterized as a "'naïve' model . . . which suggests that the degree to which national output is absorbed by military spending should be dependent on aggregate economic conditions such as unemployment," were clearly attacking a "naïve model" of their own devising. Ironically, after rejecting this naïve model, these same authors ended up concluding that in the face of declining monopoly profits the U.S. state intervenes to absorb surplus through increases in military expenditures—a view much closer to Baran and Sweezy's own argument, but lacking its emphasis on empire over macroeconomics. See Larry J. Griffin, Joel A. Devine, and Michael Wallace, "Monopoly Capital, Organized Labor, and Military Expenditures in the United States, 1949–1976," *American Journal of Sociology* 88 (1982): supplement, S113–S153.

11. Baran and Sweezy, *Monopoly Capital*, 159, 161, 177, 208–11. Baran and Sweezy's contention more than four decades ago that civilian government purchases had about reached their outer limit as a percentage of GDP by 1939 was borne out in subsequent developments. In 1939 civilian government purchases were 13 percent of GDP; from 1960 to

the present they have averaged 14 percent of GDP (and were also 14 percent in 2006). *Economic Report of the President, 2008*, 224, 250.

12. The foregoing quotes from Slichter, Luce, *U.S. News and World Report*, Lawrence, and Harris are all taken from Cook, "Juggernaut," 285, 300–301. See also Fred H. Cook, *The Warfare State* (New York: Collier Books, 1962); Baran and Sweezy, *Monopoly Capital*, 207–13.13. U.S. National Security Council, NSC-68, April 1950, "Section D: The Remaining Course of Action," James M. Cypher, "The Basic Economics of 'Rearming America,'" *Monthly Review* 33/6 (November 1981): 12–13; Noam Chomsky, "The Cold War and the Superpowers," *Monthly Review* 33/6 (November 1981): 4–5.

14. Charles Erwin Wilson, quoted in Cook, "Juggernaut," 277, 299.

15. Eisenhower, quoted in ibid., 276–79.

16. Baran and Sweezy, *Monopoly Capital*, 205.

17. The classic argument on how nuclear weapons were continually *used* by the United States as *direct threats* to achieve its ends was made by Daniel Ellsberg, "Call to Mutiny," in E. P. Thompson and Dan Smith, eds., *Protest and Survive* (New York: Monthly Review Press, 1981), i–xxviii.

18. Robert Kaplan, *Imperial Grunts* (New York: Random House, 2005), 3.

19. Jurgen Brauer, "United States Military Expenditure," in *Arms, War, and Terrorism in the Global Economy Today*, ed. Wolfram Elsner (Hamburg: LIT Verlag, 2007), 61–66.

20. The design format of this table was adapted from Cypher, "Basic Economics of 'Rearming America.'"

21. Benjamin A. Mandel and Mary L. Roy, "Federal Budget Estimates for Fiscal Year 2007," *Survey of Current Business* (Bureau of Economic Analysis), March 2006, 13.

22. Jurgen Brauer, "Data, Models, Coefficients: The Case of United States Military Expenditure," *Conflict Management and Peace Science* 24 (2007), 58; see also Brauer, "United States Military Expenditure," 67.

23. Stockholm International Peace Research Institute, *SIPRI Yearbook 2003* (Oxford: Oxford University Press, 2003), 365; Brauer, "United States Military Expenditure," 66; and "Data, Models, Coefficients," 56. I have not included Homeland Security in these figures, in line with SIPRI and NATO's exclusion of civil defense programs.

24. *SIPRI Yearbook 2008: Summary,* 10–11.

25. James Cypher, "From Military Keynesianism to Global Neoliberal Militarism," *Monthly Review* 59/2 (June 2007): 45–48; Chalmers Johnson, "Why the U.S. Has Really Gone Broke," *Le Monde Diplomatique*, February 2008.

26. The complete set of data is not provided in this article, but follows the above method throughout.

27. For this general argument see Foster, *Naked Imperialism*, esp. 107–20.

28. Ibid., 55–66; Chalmers Johnson, *The Sorrows of Empire* (New York: Henry Holt, 2004), 151–85.

29. The military resurgence after periods of relative decline arose in both cases at the tail end of Democratic administrations: Carter in the late 1970s and Clinton in the late 1990s, and gathered momentum in the Republican administrations that followed: Reagan in the 1980s and George W. Bush at the beginning of the 2000s.

30. Robert W. McChesney, *The Political Economy of Media* (New York: Monthly Review Press, 2008), 105, 108.

31. Norman Soloman, "The Military-Industrial-Media Complex," *Extra*, July–August 2005, http://www.fair.org/index.php?page=2627.

32. Baran and Sweezy, *Monopoly Capital*, 213–17.

33. See John Bellamy Foster and Robert W. McChesney, "Preface," in Foster and McChesney, eds., *Pox Americana: Exposing the American Empire* (New York: Monthly Review Press, 2004), 7–10; McChesney, *Political Economy of Media*, 491–500.

7. The Penal State in an Age of Crisis

This article originally appeared as Hannah Holleman, Robert W. McChesney, John Bellamy Foster, and R. Jamil Jonna, "The Penal State in an Age of Crisis," *Monthly Review* 61/2 (June 2009): 1–17.

1. I have taken the term "penal state" from Loïc Wacquant, "Ordering Insecurity: Social Polarization and the Punitive Upsurge," *Radical Philosophy Review* 11/1 (2008): 9–27. Unlike Wacquant, however, my object here is not to present an all-encompassing theory of the penal state as representing a stage in the development of the state as a whole. Rather, I use the term in this article in a more limited way as a parallel concept to that of the welfare state. Thus "penal state spending," as I employ it, is conceptually equivalent to "public safety spending" and is to be juxtaposed to "public welfare spending."

2. John Bellamy Foster and Robert W. McChesney, "A New New Deal under Obama?" *Monthly Review* 60/9 (February 2009): 1–11.

3. In 1934 and 1975 temporary peaks in civilian government spending as a percentage of GDP of around 15 percent resulted from the fact that private production and consumption as percentages of GDP contracted faster than the civilian government share. This was followed in both cases by a reversion to the mean in the share of civilian government spending. With civilian government spending as a percentage of GDP in 2008 at 15 percent a similar dynamic may well be at work.

4. John Bellamy Foster, Hannah Holleman, and Robert W. McChesney, "The U.S. Imperial Triangle and Military Spending," *Monthly Review* 60/5 (October 2008): 1–19.

5. Roy Walmsley, International Centre for Prison Studies, "World Prison Population List (8th ed.)," January 2009. For a historical view on incarceration in the United States since its founding, see John Bellamy Foster, Harry Magdoff, and Robert W. McChesney, "Prisons and

Executions—the U.S. Model," *Monthly Review* 53/3 (July–August 2001): 1–18.

6. Bureau of Justice Statistics, "Prisoners in 2007," Appendix, Tables 8 and 10 (version revised February 12, 2009).

7. Michael K. Fauntroy, "Toward Reform of Criminal Justice," *Washington Times*, April 28, 2009.

8. Bureau of Justice Statistics, "Prisoners in 2007," Appendix, Tables 11 and 12 (version revised February 12, 2009).

9. Interview with David Simon, *Bill Moyers Journal*, PBS, April 17, 2009.

10. Quoted in Christopher Hayes, "Webb's Prison Crusade," *The Nation*, May 4, 2009.

11. Quoted in ibid.

12. For a chart on imprisonment and inequality of various countries, see "Imprisonment: In Brief," Equality Trust, http://equalitytrust.org.uk.

13. Bruce Western, Meredith Kleykamp, and Jake Rosenfeld, "Did Falling Wages and Employment Increase U.S. Imprisonment?" *Social Forces* 84/4 (2006): 2306.

14. On the jobless rate, see "Notes from the Editors," *Monthly Review* 60/11 (April 2009).

15. Loïc Wacquant in Glenn C. Loury, *Race, Incarceration, and American Values* (Cambridge, MA: MIT Press, 2008), 60.

16. Loury, *Race, Incarceration, and American Values*, 11: Gerald Shargel, "No Mercy," *Slate.com*, June 14, 2004.

17. Karl Marx and Frederick Engels, *Collected Works*, vol. 16 (New York: International Publishers, 1975), 489.

18. James Q. Wilson, *Thinking about Crime* (New York: Basic Books, 1975), 172.

19. Bureau of Justice Assistance, "Emerging Issues on Privatized Prisons," February 2001.

20. Vicky Pelaez, "The Prison Industry in the United States: Big Business or a New Form of Slavery?" Global Research, March 10, 2008.

21. Quoted in Howard Zinn, *A People's History of the United States* (New York: HarperCollins, 2003), 515.

22. Bureau of Justice Statistics, "Recidivism of Prisoners Released in 1994," June 2002.

23. Legal Action Center, "After Prison: Roadblocks to Reentry," 2004.

24. Senator Jim Webb, "Why We Must Fix Our Prisons," *Parade.com*, March 29, 2009.

25. "A Nation of Jailbirds," *Economist*, April 2, 2009.

26. On the horrendous conditions in U.S. prisons, see John J. Gibbons and Nicholas de B. Katzenbach, co-chairs, *Confronting Confinement: A Report of the Commission on Safety and Abuse in America's Prisons* (New York: Vera Institute of Justice, 2006); Michael Santos, *Inside: Life Behind Bars in America* (New York: St. Martin's Press, 2006).

27. "A Nation of Jailbirds," *Economist*, April 2, 2009.

28. Becky Pettit and Bruce Western, "Mass Imprisonment and the Life Course: Race and Class Inequality in U.S. Incarceration," *American Sociological Review* 69 (2004): 151–69, 164.

29. U.S. Bureau of Justice Statistics, Prisoners in 1978 and Prisoners in 2007; José Luis Morín, "Latinas/os and U.S. Prisons," *Latino Studies* 6/1 (2008): 11–34.

30. David V. Baker, "American Indian Executions in Historical Context," *Criminal Justice Studies* 20/4 (2007): 351.

31. Amnesty International, "Migrants Languish in Detention in US," March 26, 2009.

32. Pamela S. Karlan in Loury, *Race, Incarceration, and American Values*, 48–49; "A Nation of Jailbirds," *Economist*, April 2, 2009; "Felony Disenfranchisement," Sentencing Project, http://sentencingproject.org.

8. The State of Media and Media Reform

This interview was conducted by Megan Boler and took place over the telephone on February 23, 2007. Boler is based in Toronto, which explains the references to "in the U.S.A." in the interview. This chapter originally appeared as "The State of the Media: An Interview with Robert McChesney," in Megan Boler, ed., *Digital Media and Democracy: Tactics in Hard Times* (Cambridge, MA: MIT Press, 2008), 53–70. Thanks again to Megan Boler and to Pamela Quick at MIT Press for their permission to reproduce it here.

9. Walter Lippmann and the Crisis of Journalism

This article was originally published in Robert W. McChesney and Victor Pickard, eds., *Will the Last Reporter Please Turn Out the Lights?* (New York: New Press, 2011).

1. Robert W. McChesney and John Nichols, *The Death and Life of American Journalism: The Media Revolution that Will Begin the World Again* (New York: Nation Books, 2010).

2. Michael Schudson, "The 'Lippmann-Dewey Debate' and the Invention of Walter Lippmann as Anti-Democrat, 1986–1996," *International Journal of Communication* 2 (2008): 1031–42.

3. Walter Lippmann and Charles Merz, "A Test of the News: An Examination of the News Reports in the *New York Times* on Aspects of the Russian Revolution of Special Importance to Americans, March 1917–March 1920," supplement to *The New Republic*, August 4, 1920; Lippmann, *Liberty and the News* (1920; reprint, Princeton: Princeton University Press, 2008).

4. Lippmann and Merz, "A Test of the News," 1.

5. Lippmann, *Liberty and the News*, 29.

6. Lippmann and Merz, "A Test of the News," 41.

7. Ibid., 3.

8.   Lippmann, *Liberty and the News*, 37.

9.   Ibid., 2. My emphasis.

10. Ibid., 28.

11. Lippmann and Merz, "A Test of the News," 3.

12. Ibid., 4.

13. Lippmann, *Liberty and the News*, 5–6.

14. Ibid., 8.

15. Ibid., 45.

16. Upton Sinclair, *The Brass Check* (1919; repr., Urbana: University of Illinois Press, 2003).

17. Walter Lippmann, *Public Opinion* (New York: Harcourt, Brace, 1922), 335–36, 361.

18. Lippmann, *Liberty and the News*, xxv.

19. McChesney and Nichols, *The Death and Life of American Journalism*, 176.

20. Lippmann, *Liberty and the News*, 45.

21. Lippmann and Merz, "A Test of the News," 41.

22. Lippmann, *Liberty and the News*, 60, 59.

23. Ibid., 46, 47.

24. Ibid., 9.

25. Ibid., 60.

26. Ibid., 41.

27. Lippmann and Merz, "A Test of the News," 42.

28. Lippmann, *Liberty and the News*, 60.

29. Lippmann and Merz, "A Test of the News," 41.

30. Lippmann, *Liberty and the News*, 34, 38, 39, 57.

31. Ibid., 32, 59.

32. Ibid., 39.

10. THE PERSONAL IS POLITICAL: MY CAREER IN PUBLIC RADIO

I was commissioned in 2013 to write this piece by Toby Miller for a forthcoming book he is editing for Routledge with the working title of *The Routledge Companion to Global Popular Culture*. I thank Toby for giving me the idea for the piece and allowing me to run it here first.

1.   Robert W. McChesney, *Digital Disconnect: How Capitalism Is Turning the Internet against Democracy* (New York: New Press, 2013).

2.   Edward S. Herman and Noam Chomsky, *Manufacturing Consent: The Political Economy of the Mass Media* (New York: Pantheon, 1988).

3.   Jeff Cohen, conversation with author, 2005.

4.   John Nichols and Robert W. McChesney, *Dollarocracy: How the Money and Media Election Complex Is Destroying America* (New York: Nation Books, 2013).

5.   Jacob S. Hacker and Paul Pierson, *Winner-Take-All Politics: How Washington Made the Rich Richer—and Turned Its Back on the Middle Class* (New York: Simon and Schuster, 2010).

11. THE CULTURAL APPARATUS OF MONOPOLY CAPITAL

This article originally appeared as John Bellamy Foster and Robert W. McChesney, "The Cultural Apparatus of Monopoly Capital: An Introduction," *Monthly Review* 65/3 (July–August 2013): 1–33.

1. See Robert W. McChesney, *Digital Disconnect: How Capitalism Is Turning the Internet against Democracy* (New York: New Press, 2013).

2. For a longer discussion of the origins and development of the political economy of communication, see Robert W. McChesney, *Communication Revolution: Critical Junctures and the Future of Media* (New York: New Press, 2007).

3. The critique tended to be more that *Monthly Review* underplayed the importance of media and communication than that it was wrong about these matters. On the rare occasions that *MR* covered the political economy of communication, it was sympathetic, and characterized the study as a necessary and logical part of monopoly capital. See the assessment of Herbert Schiller's work in Douglas Dowd, "Monopoly Capitalism and Mind Management," *Monthly Review* 26/11 (November 1974): 32–36.

4. Paul A. Baran and Paul M. Sweezy, *Monopoly Capital* (New York: Monthly Review Press, 1966); Dallas Smythe, "Communications: Blindspot of Western Marxism," *Canadian Journal of Political and Social Theory* 1/3 (Fall 1977): 1–27.

5. See Dan Schiller, *How to Think about Information* (Urbana: University of Illinois Press, 2006), chap. 1.

6. See Robert W. McChesney, "What Ever Happened to Cultural Studies?," in *American Cultural Studies,* ed. Catherine A. Warren and Mary Douglas Vavrus (Urbana: University of Illinois Press, 2002), 76–92.

7. Baran and Sweezy, *Monopoly Capital*, 112–41. Many of the implications of Baran and Sweezy's analysis of the sales effort with respect to the development of modern marketing were developed in Michael Dawson, *The Consumer Trap* (Urbana: University of Illinois Press, 2005).

8. See Paul A. Baran and Paul M. Sweezy, "Theses on Advertising," *Science and Society* 28/1 (Winter 1964): 20–30.

9. The Labour Party, *Report of a Commission of Enquiry into Advertising* (London: Labour Party, 1966), 33–40, 201, 204. Baran and Sweezy's testimony was solicited through the influence of Nicholas Kaldor, who was a member of the Advertising Commission but was forced to resign in 1964 when he was appointed special advisor to the Chancellor of the Exchequer. Kaldor's work on advertising, which was closely related to that of Baran and Sweezy, was heavily quoted in the final report.

10. *The Scientific-Industrial Revolution* (New York: Model, Roland, and Stone, 1957), 7. To support himself on top of his professional salary and to obtain funds for research, Paul Baran occasionally wrote reports for the Wall Street firm of Model, Roland and Stone. He was

commissioned to do a report on technology but was pressed for time, so he asked Sweezy to do it for him. The resulting report was issued by the firm with no author indicated, but Sweezy considered it one of his best pieces of writing. The original copy is in the Sweezy archives at Harvard University. Harry Braverman made use of Sweezy's argument on the scientific-industrial revolution in this pamphlet to construct much of his own argument on the scientific-technological revolution. See Braverman, *Labor and Monopoly Capital* (New York: Monthly Review Press, 1999), 115.

11. See John Bellamy Foster, "A Missing Chapter of Monopoly Capital: Introduction to Baran and Sweezy's 'Some Theoretical Complications,'" *Monthly Review* 64/3 (July–August 2012): 3–17. The original draft of the culture and mental health chapter, "The Quality of Monopoly Capitalist Society II," was found along with related papers in a file in the Sweezy papers at Harvard University. The final draft with Sweezy's edits is located in the Baran Papers, Monthly Review Foundation.

12. Another "missing chapter," on the theoretical issues arising from their model was located at the same time and published in *Monthly Review*. See Paul A. Baran and Paul M. Sweezy, "Some Theoretical Implications," *Monthly Review* 64/3 (July–August 2012): 24–59.

13. As Sweezy wrote in the preface to *Monopoly Capital*: "Whatever was drafted by one of us [for the book] was criticized at length by the other, and in most cases redrafted and recriticized more than once. Everything now in the book had been through this process before Baran's death. Apart from putting together the entire manuscript into finished form, the only thing I have done has been to leave out material that would have been two additional chapters. This material was in rough draft at the time of his death, but in each case one or the other of us had raised important questions which still remained to be discussed and resolved. Since neither chapter was essential to the theme of the essay as a whole, the best solution seemed to be to omit them altogether. I reached this conclusion the more easily since even without these chapters the book turned out to be longer than I had expected or we had originally intended." Paul M. Sweezy, Preface, in Baran and Sweezy, *Monopoly Capital*, ix. From the first, Sweezy had been concerned that the "cultural mess," given that it was left to the end of the manuscript, not be given short shrift as a result (Sweezy to Baran, July 23, 1957, Baran Papers, Monthly Review Foundation). Baran had indicated that "if anything," he would "tend to accentuate its importance" (Baran to Sweezy, July 29, 1957, Baran Papers, Monthly Review Foundation).

14. E. P. Thompson, "The Segregation of Dissent," in Thompson, *Writing by Candlelight* (London: Merlin Press, 1980), 8.

15. On Baran as the political economist of the Frankfurt School, see M. C. Howard and J. E. King, *A History of Marxian Economics*, vol. 2

(Princeton: Princeton University Press, 1992), 114–15. Pollock himself, of course, was the main economist associated with the school, but Baran's work would far eclipse his. Sweezy was less directly influenced by the Frankfurt School, but he early took on many of the propositions on history and dialectics of Georg Lukács and Karl Korsch.

16. Peter Marcuse recalls: "I had only met Baran once, during the war, when my father was with the OSS [Office of Strategic Services].... I was maybe 12 at the time. Baran had come over to our house to talk to my father, and they stayed up a long time. I asked my father later why Baran had come, and he told me Baran wanted to talk about whether capitalism was ultimately bad for the capitalists as well as the workers, and I gather they agreed it was. My father was working on *Eros and Civilization* at the time (on the side, not at OSS!), and I assume that was the context. They really respected each other." Peter Marcuse to John Bellamy Foster, personal communication, July 4, 2012. Baran referred to Adorno's work not only in the missing chapter on culture that he drafted for *Monthly Review*, but also in *The Political Economy of Growth*. His close attention to Adorno's and Horkheimer's work was shown in his correspondence with Marcuse, e.g., Paul A. Baran to Herbert Marcuse, July 10, 1962, Baran Papers, Monthly Review Foundation. Erich Fromm is also discussed in Baran's letters.

17. In focusing on culture as a general way of viewing literary, artistic, and intellectual work, Baran and Sweezy were, in Williams's terms, using the concept in "one of its predominant twentieth-century senses," and the one most related to questions of power. They differentiated this from more capacious anthropological uses of the term to refer to a definite way of life. See Raymond Williams, *What I Came to Say* (London: Hutchinson Radius, 1989), 199.

18. Paul A. Baran (writing under the pseudonym Historicus), "Better Smaller but Better," *Monthly Review* 2/3 (July 1950): 85–86.

19. Early outline of "Monopoly Capital," ca. 1957, Baran Papers, Monthly Review Foundation.

20. The notion of the "apparatus" as representing the material conditions of art can already be seen in Hegel's philosophy of art, where he refers to the "apparatus of its [art's] merely material nature." G. W. F. Hegel, *Introduction to Hegel's Philosophy of Fine Art* (London: Kegan Paul, Trench, 1886), 72.

21. Rowitha Mueller, *Bertolt Brecht and the Theory of the Media* (Lincoln: University of Nebraska Press, 1989), 15–16; Bertolt Brecht, *Brecht on Theatre* (New York: Hill and Wang, 1964), 34. The word *culture* in parentheses follows the Mueller quote, despite that current editing conventions would have required it to be placed in square brackets, as it is not to be found in Brecht's statement. According to Mueller, "the term apparatus" in Brecht is "a broad category" that includes "every aspect of the means of cultural production, from the actual technological equipment to promotion agencies, as well as the class that is in

possession of the means of production." Mueller, *Bertolt Brecht*, 15.

22. Brecht, *Brecht on Theatre*, 34–35.

23. Ibid., 23, 48.

24. Paul A. Baran, *The Longer View* (New York: Monthly Review Press, 1969), 32; Mueller, *Bertolt Brecht and the Theory of the Media*, 24; Astrid Oesmann, *Staging History: Brecht's Social Concepts of Ideology* (Albany: State University of New York Press, 2005), 107.

25. Walter Benjamin, *Understanding Brecht* (London: New Left Books, 1971), 87, 102. It should be noted that Benjamin's key essays on Brecht, including "The Artist as Producer," were not published until 1966 and were not available to Baran when he drafted the chapter on culture for *Monopoly Capital*, though he would have been familiar enough with these ideas through his knowledge of Brecht's work and the Frankfurt School discussions of the early 1930s.

26. Brecht, *Brecht on Theatre*, 47–52.

27. Axel Honneth, *The Critique of Power* (Cambridge, MA: MIT Press, 1991), 23–26.

28. Erich Fromm, *The Crisis of Psychoanalysis* (Greenwich, CT: Fawcett Publications, 1970), 158–60; Eike Gebhardt, "Introduction to a Critique of Methodology," in *The Essential Frankfurt School Reader*, ed. Andrew Arato and Eike Gebhardt (New York: Urizen Books, 1978), 387–388. The concept of "cultural apparatus" was not specifically defined in Fromm's essay, but he was later to use the category mainly in the Brechtian sense. See Erich Fromm, *The Sane Society* (New York: Rinehart, 1955), 163. It is noteworthy that Baran and Sweezy thought Fromm's early work (no doubt including his 1932 essay) was so important that they considered translating it for Monthly Review Press. See "Notes on Planned Translations from the German," n.d., ca. 1957, Baran Papers, Monthly Review Foundation.

29. Max Horkheimer, "Authority and the Family," in Horkheimer, *Critical Theory: Selected Essays* (New York: Continuum, 2002), 59–60, 67–68.

30. Herbert Marcuse, "33 Theses," in Marcuse, *Collected Papers*, vol. 1 (London: Routledge, 1998), 221. On Marcuse's use of the concept of cultural apparatus, see his *Eros and Civilization* (New York: Vintage Books, 1955). Earlier, in his 1941 article "Some Social Implications of Modern Technology," Marcuse had presented what he called "the technical apparatus of industry, transportation, and communication" as the crucial, if partial, mediating factor of modern mass alienation. He stated that "the term 'apparatus' denotes the institutions, devices and organizations of industry in their prevailing social setting." There was, he said, "no personal escape from the apparatus." Yet a social escape was perhaps conceivable, requiring a struggle over the cultural apparatus in particular. Herbert Marcuse, "Some Social Implications of Modern Technology," in Arato and Gebhardt, *The Essential Frankfurt School Reader*, 138, 143, 180.

31. Honneth, *The Critique of Power*, 23–26.

32. Ibid., 18.

33. Erich Fromm, *The Revision of Psychoanalysis* (Boulder, CO: Westview Press, 1992), 56.

34. Fromm, *The Sane Society*, 163; Baran to Sweezy, November 28, 1956, Baran Papers, Monthly Review Foundation.

35. Stanley Aronowitz, *Taking It Big: C. Wright Mills and the Making of Political Intellectuals* (New York: Columbia University Press, 2012), 241–42.

36. C. Wright Mills, *The Politics of Truth* (Oxford: Oxford University Press, 2008), 204, 263.

37. Ibid., 217–18, 221.

38. Ibid., 213.

39. E. P. Thompson quoted in Daniel Geary, *Radical Ambition: C. Wright Mills, the Left, and American Social Thought* (Berkeley: University of California Press, 2009), 196.

40. E. P. Thompson, "The New Left," *The New Reasoner* 9 (Summer 1959): 1–17, http://marxists.org. Thompson's submission to the Pilkington Committee was listed in the report as connected to the publication *New University* and as having dealt with "Minority interests and broadcasting," presumably referring to the issue of political minorities. Such issues were taken up in the Pilkington Report in sections on "Party Political Broadcasting" and "The News." Thompson's 1961 piece "The Segregation of Dissent," written for *New University* and addressing "minority causes" and "minority journals," fits this description. The New Left Review Ltd. also submitted a memorandum to the Pilkington Committee (published in *New Left Review* prior to the release of the Pilkington Report). Thompson apparently saw the New Left Review Ltd.'s submission as overly culturalist and reformist, focusing on issues of popular culture more than media control and making too many concessions with respect to the latter. United Kingdom, *Report of the Committee on Broadcasting, 1960* (London: HMSO, 1962), 92–101, 320, 327; "Which Frame of Mind? . . . Evidence to the Pilkington Committee on the Future of Broadcasting and Television," *New Left Review* 7 (1961): 30–48; Thompson, "The Segregation of Dissent"; Michael Kenny, *The First New Left* (London: Lawrence and Wishart, 1995), 103–8.

41. Raymond Williams, *Communications*, 3rd ed. (London: Penguin, 1976), 180–89.

42. Raymond Williams, *The Long Revolution* (London: Chatto and Windus, 1961), 338–39.

43. E. P. Thompson, "The Long Revolution—II," *New Left Review* 10 (July–August 1961): 34–39.

44. E. P. Thompson, *The Making of the English Working Class* (New York: Vintage, 1963). For Thompson the English working class of the nineteenth century developed a "resistance movement" to the acquisitive society that was not just backward-looking but truly radical in its con-

ception, and though it ultimately lost out in the struggle, partly through its inability to gain control of the means of production, including the means of intellectual production, and thus of the wellsprings of social and cultural existence, it nonetheless remained a "heroic culture." Thompson, *The Making of the English Working Class*, 832.

45. Uncited quotations from Baran and Sweezy in this introduction are to Paul Baran and Paul M. Sweezy, "The Quality of Monopoly Capitalist Society: Culture and Communications," *Monthly Review* 65/3 (July–August 2013): 43–64.

46. Baran and Sweezy's use of the term "cultural industry" in the introduction to their piece no doubt reflected the influence of Frankfurt School cultural theorist Theodor Adorno. See T. W. Adorno, "Television and the Patterns of Mass Culture," in *Mass Culture,* ed. Bernard Rosenberg and David Manning White (Glencoe, IL: The Free Press, 1960), 484. This essay by Adorno is cited in Baran and Sweezy's chapter. Baran, a close reader of Horkheimer and Adorno, as indicated in his correspondence with Marcuse, was also undoubtedly familiar with the chapter in *The Dialectic of Enlightenment* on "The Culture Industry: Enlightenment as Mass Deception." See Max Horkheimer and Theodor Adorno, *The Dialectic of Enlightenment* (New York: Continuum, 1972), 120–67.

47. I thank John J. Simon, who spent his career in book publishing and knew Baran, Sweezy, and Huberman well in this period, for making this point.

48. Huberman testimony in Leo Huberman and Paul M. Sweezy, "A Challenge to the Book Burners," *Monthly Review* 4/4 (August 1953): 161.

49. On the active struggles over the cultural apparatus in the 1930s, including in the realm of publication, and how this faded in the 1950s and after, see Michael Denning, *The Cultural Front: The Laboring of American Culture in the Twentieth Century* (London: Verso, 1997).

50. Sweezy had suggested in his letter to Baran on December 5, 1962, to include a general discussion of books for the elite and elite culture in the chapter. Baran replied on December 7, 1962, that the point of the discussion of culture and communication was to focus on the cultural "state of the people," which is why books marketed to the elite were excluded from the draft. However, he indicated that he intended to add something on this (Baran Papers, Monthly Review Foundation).

51. Mickey Spillane, *The Mike Hammer Collection*, vol. 2 (New York: New American Library, 2001), 132; Roland Végső, *The Naked Communist: Cold War Modernism and the Politics of Popular Culture* (New York: Fordham University Press, 2013), 160–169; Christopher La Farge, "Mickey Spillane and His Bloody Hammer," in Rosenberg and White, *Mass Culture*, 176–185; Frances Stoner Saunders, *The Cultural Cold War* (New York: New Press, 1999); and Bryan Palmer, *Cultures of Darkness* (New York: Monthly Review Press, 2000), 373–74.

52. Eric Hobsbawm, *Fractured Times: Culture and Society in the Twentieth Century* (London: Little, Brown, 2013), 262–63. Baran and Hobsbawm, who were good friends, had co-authored a critique of Walt Rostow's *Stages of Economic Growth*. See Baran, *The Longer View*, 52–67.

53. Leo Huberman and Paul M. Sweezy, "Behind the FCC Scandal," *Monthly Review* 9/12 (April 1958): 401–11.

54. Sweezy, in his early comments on the original draft of this chapter, questioned the emphasis on the three great television networks as representing a "tight oligopoly" that controlled the industry. As he wrote in a letter to Baran on December 5, 1962: "This whole paragraph stressing the great power of the networks seems out of focus in light of the statement on the next page that they are merely processors and agents. The latter is, in my view, a more accurate assessment of their role" (Baran Papers, Monthly Review Foundation). By the time he prepared the later draft of the chapter in late 1964, however, Sweezy had clearly come around to Baran's view.

55. Leo Huberman and Paul M. Sweezy, "The TV Scandals," *Monthly Review* 11/8 (December 1959): 280.

56. Ibid., 281. My emphasis.

57. Brecht, *Brecht on Theatre*, 48–49. The influence of Brecht on Baran's thought was particularly evident as he was wont to quote him from memory. Baran to Sweezy, February 20, 1962, Baran Papers, Monthly Review Foundation. Nick Baran dimly recalls hearing Brecht's *Dreigroschen Oper* (*Threepenny Opera*) on his father's record player when he was a child. Nicholas Baran to John Bellamy Foster, personal communication, April 24, 2013. It is not surprising, then, that the entire approach to the cultural apparatus in the Baran and Sweezy chapter on culture can be seen (particularly in the discussion of book publishing) as having a Brechtian emphasis, focusing on the relation of the artist to the apparatus and seeing the latter as an object of struggle.

58. United Kingdom, *Report of the Committee on Broadcasting* (Pilkington Report); Jeffrey Milland, "The Pilkington Report: The Triumph of Paternalism?," in *Narrating Media History*, ed. Michael Bailey (London: Routledge, 2009), 95–107.

59. Baran and Sweezy, "The Quality of Monopoly Capitalist Society."

60. Franz Kafka, *The Trial* (New York: Modern Library, 1964), 276. Kafka is mentioned in Baran's correspondence. See, for example, the excerpt from Baran to Sweezy, July 4, 1963, in Paul M. Sweezy and Leo Huberman, eds., *Paul Alexander Baran (1910–1964): A Collective Portrait* (New York: Monthly Review Press, 1965), 61. In 1938 Benjamin wrote on Brecht and Kafka: "The decisive thesis of all of these plays [by Brecht] emerges clearly for the reader. . . . It can be summed up by a sentence from Kafka's prophetic novel *The Trial*: 'The lie is made into a universal system.'" Walter Benjamin, *Selected Writings* (Cambridge, MA: Harvard University Press, 2002), 332.

61. Baran and Sweezy, "The Quality of Monopoly Capitalist Society."

62. In "If Labour Wins," *Monthly Review* 15/6 (October 1963): 328, Miliband explained that no "deep structural changes" would result.

63. Ralph Miliband, "Review of C. Wright Mills, *Power, People and Politics*," *British Journal of Sociology* 15/1 (1964): 79.

64. Herbert Marcuse, *One-Dimensional Man* (Boston: Beacon Press, 1964), xvii.

65. Ibid., 66–71, 257.

66. These pessimistic conclusions were strongly criticized in Fromm's unpublished critique of Marcuse. See Fromm, *The Revision of Psychoanalysis*, 125–29.

67. Marcuse, *One-Dimensional Man*, 71. Marcuse drew on Baran and Sweezy's analysis of monopoly capitalism in his later work. See, for example, Herbert Marcuse, *Counter-Revolution and Revolt* (Boston: Beacon Press, 1972), 5.

68. A year before, on October 7, 1962, Baran had written to Marcuse: "Oo, oh! Where did your manuscript get stuck? I am lusting after it like a thirsty man for water and I don't know how I can get hold of it. Send it to me, I beg you, even if it has not yet attained a condition of absolute perfection and even if you are still caught up in the process of 'purification.' It will be sent back to you as quickly as possible and I will be infinitely indebted to you in gratitude." This was followed by a discussion of new work by Horkheimer and Adorno. Baran to Marcuse, October 7, 1962, Baran Papers, Monthly Review Foundation; original in German, translated by Joseph Fracchia. Marcuse replied a week later, referring to "massive difficulties getting it published. At present there are three copies with different presses." Marcuse to Baran, October 27, 1962, ibid. I would like to thank Joseph Fracchia for his translations from the Baran–Marcuse correspondence.

69. Baran to Sweezy, October 10, 1963. On Marcuse's view of Baran, see Herbert Marcuse, "Tribute to Baran," in Sweezy and Huberman, *Paul A. Baran*, 114–15.

70. Raymond Williams, "Class and Voting in Britain," *Monthly Review* 11/9 (January 1960): 333.

71. Paul M. Sweezy, "Paul Alexander Baran: A Personal Memoir," in Sweezy and Huberman, *Paul A. Baran*, 48.

72. Baran and Sweezy, *Monopoly Capital*, 339, 363.

73. Ibid., 366.

74. Raymond Williams, *Britain in the Sixties: Communications* (Harmondsworth: Penguin, 1962); Williams, *The Long Revolution*, 366.

75. Labour Party, *Report of a Commission of Enquiry into Advertising* (London: Labour Party, 1966), 33–40, 201, 204; Raymond Williams, *Communications* (New York: Barnes and Noble, 1967), 155–56. Baran and Sweezy provided written testimony to the Labour Party's Advertising Commission, and Williams was listed as a submitter of oral evidence.

76. Williams, *Communications*, 156. The Pilkington Report indicated that Williams's memorandum to the Committee on Broadcasting had addressed the following topics: "BBC and ITA: Existing Services: Licence Fee: Third television programme: Regional broadcasting: Local sound broadcasting: ITA to collect advertising revenue direct: Broadcasting and Television Council: Educational Broadcasting: Consumer Research programmes." *Report of the Committee on Broadcasting* (Pilkington Committee), 329. Since Williams's memorandum to the Pilkington Committee was completed at the same time he was working on *The Existing Alternatives in Communications* and on his book *Communications,* his Pilkington Committee memorandum likely reflected similar concerns (as suggested by the Committee on Broadcasting's listing of its contents). Williams also referred to the Labour Party's Advertising Commission Report (to which he and Baran and Sweezy had given testimony) in the second edition of his book; however, the report was released while the book was in press, so he was only able to add a footnote indicating that "its majority recommendations amount to a useful short-term programme of action and ought, in my view, to be firmly supported." Williams, *Communications*, 156.

77. Williams, *Communications*, 17–19.

78. Ibid., 129–30, 166–73.

79. Ibid., 156–58. The long-run response to the Pilkington Report and the decline of the BBC-centered system are described in Nicholas Garnham, *Capitalism and Communication* (London: Sage, 1990), 128–32.

80. Jürgen Habermas, *The Structural Transformation of the Public Sphere* (Cambridge, MA: MIT Press, 1989), 249–50.

81. Nicholas Garnham, *Structures of Television*, rev. ed. (London: British Film Institute, 1980), 14. First published in 1973.

82. Williams, *Communications*, 3rd ed. (Harmondsworth: Penguin, 1976), 184.

83. Ibid., 186–87.

84. Garnham, *Structures of Television*, 9.

85. Williams, *Communications*, 3rd ed., 183.

86. "Ecuador's President Attacks US over Press Freedom Critique," Real News Network, May 21 2013, http://therealnews.com/t2/index.php?option=com_content&task=view&id=31&Itemid=74&jumival=10225.

12. A Sharp Left Turn for the Media Reform Movement

An earlier version of this article originally appeared as "Sharp Left Turn for the Media Reform Movement: Toward a Post-Capitalist Democracy," *Monthly Review* 65/9 (February 2014): 1–14.

1. Robert W. McChesney and John Nichols, *Our Media, Not Theirs: The Democratic Struggle against Corporate Media* (New York: Seven Stories Press, 2002).

2. Robert W. McChesney, *The Problem of the Media* (New York: Monthly Review Press, 2004).

3. I develop this theme, and much of what else appears in this chapter, in my book *Digital Disconnect: How Capitalism Is Turning the Internet against Democracy* (New York: New Press, 2013). Citations and sources for all of the points made in my three proposals can be found there.

4. John Nichols and Robert W. McChesney, *Dollarocracy: How the Money and Media Election Complex Is Destroying America* (New York: Nation Books, 2013).

5. In 2012, two major studies were published along these lines: Martin Gilens, *Affluence and Influence: Economic Inequality and Political Power in America* (Princeton: Princeton University Press, 2012); and Kay Lehman Schlozman, Sidney Verba, and Henry E. Brady, *The Unheavenly Chorus: Unequal Political Voice and the Broken Promise of American Democracy* (Princeton: Princeton University Press, 2012). See also Larry M. Bartels, *Unequal Democracy* (New York: Russell Sage Foundation, 2008); Martin Gilens, "Inequality and Democratic Responsiveness," *Public Opinion Quarterly* 69/5 (2005): 778–96; and Jacob S. Hacker and Paul Pierson, *Winner-Take-All Politics: How Washington Made the Rich Richer—and Turned Its Back on the Middle Class* (New York: Simon and Schuster, 2010).

6. Alberto Riva, "Jimmy Carter: U.S. 'Has No Functioning Democracy,'" Salon.com, July 18, 2013, http://salon.com.

7. "U.S. Commerce–Stock Market Capitalization of the 50 Largest American Companies" (table), April 30, 2014, http://iweblists.com.

8. Ryan Grim, "Dick Durbin: Banks 'Frankly Own the Place,'" *Huffington Post*, May 30, 2009, http://huffingtonpost.com.

9. "Labour Pains: Workers' Share of National Income," *Economist*, November 2, 2013, 77–78.

10. John Bellamy Foster and Robert W. McChesney, *The Endless Crisis: How Monopoly-Finance Capital Produces Stagnation and Upheaval from the USA to China* (New York: Monthly Review Press, 2012).

11. Sasha Abramsky, *The American Way of Poverty: How the Other Half Still Lives* (New York: Nation Books, 2013).

12. Naomi Klein, "How Science Is Telling Us All to Revolt," *New Statesman*, October 29, 2013, http://newstatesman.com.

13. Robert Scheer, "What the Pope Got Right about Capitalism," *Nation*, December 3, 2013, http://thenation.com.

14. John Nichols, "A Socialist Wins in Seattle," *Nation*, December 16, 2013, http://thenation.com.

15. This point is explained in Tim Wu, *The Master Switch: The Rise and Fall of Information Empires* (New York: Alfred A. Knopf, 2010).

16. Brendan Greeley and Scott Moritz, "Bananas: How T-Mobile Plans to Survive by Blowing Up One of the Most Profitable Business Models Around," *Bloomberg Business Week*, November 4–10, 2013, 66.

17. U.S. Government Accountability Office, "Telecommunications: Federal Broadband Deployment Programs and Small Business," Washington, D.C., February 2014, http://www.gao.gov/assets/670/660734.pdf.

18. Susan Crawford, "The Wire Next Time," *New York Times*, April 27, 2014.

19. Eric Schonfeld, "Vint Cerf Wonders If We Need to Nationalize the Internet," *TechCrunch*, June 25, 2008, http://techcrunch.com.

20. Conversation with Sue Gardner, executive director of the Wikimedia Foundation, San Francisco, California, October 22, 2013.

21. Professor Andrew McAfee, cited in David Streitfeld, "Amazon Delivers Some Pie in the Sky," *New York Times*, December 2, 2013.

22. Milton Friedman, *Capitalism and Freedom* (Chicago: University of Chicago Press, 1962).

23. Franklin D. Roosevelt, "Appendix A: Message from the President of the United States Transmitting Recommendations Relative to the Strengthening and Enforcement of Anti-trust Laws," *American Economic Review* 32/2, pt. 2, Supplement, Papers Relating to the Temporary National Economic Committee (June 1942): 119–28.

24. Henry C. Simons, *Economic Policy for a Free Society* (Chicago: University of Chicago Press, 1948).

25. Andre Schiffrin, *Words and Money* (London: Verso, 2011).

26. The material in this section is drawn from *Digital Disconnect*, as well as Robert W. McChesney and John Nichols, *The Death and Life of American Journalism: The Media Revolution that Will Begin the World Again* (New York: Nation Books, 2010).

27. Milton Friedman, "The Role of Government in Education," in *Economics and the Public Interest*, ed. Robert A. Solo (New Brunswick, NJ: Rutgers University Press, 1955), 123–44.

28. For the best arguments and evidence on this matter, see Diane Ravitch, *Reign of Error: The Hoax of the Privatization Movement and the Danger to America's Public Schools* (New York: Alfred A. Knopf, 2013).

Index